WHY TORTURE DOESN'T WORK

Why Torture Doesn't Work

The Neuroscience of Interrogation

Shane O'Mara

 Harvard University Press

Cambridge, Massachusetts
London, England
2015

First Printing

Library of Congress Cataloging-in-Publication Data

O'Mara, S. M. (Shane M.)

Why torture doesn't work : the neuroscience of interrogation / Shane O'Mara.

pages cm

ISBN 978-0-674-74390-8 (cloth : alk. paper)   1. Psychic trauma.

2. Psychological abuse.   3. Torture.   I. Title.

RC552.T7O43 2015

616.85'21—dc23   2015015973

To Maura *and* Radhika,

who have enriched my life beyond anything I could have imagined; and to my parents Mary and Rory, and my parents-in-law, Maureen and Peter, and to all of the many members of my family, and extended family

Contents

One did not know what happened inside the Ministry of Love, but it was possible to guess: tortures, drugs, delicate instruments that registered your nervous reactions, gradual wearing-down by sleeplessness and solitude and persistent questioning.

—George Orwell, *1984*

Introduction

This book has had a very particular origin. One Saturday morning in April 2009, I was sitting at home reading the *Irish Times* newspaper—specifically an article by the journalist Peter Murtagh regarding the recent release of what quickly became known as the "Torture Memos." I was greatly disturbed by what he recounted. Reading his article, and subsequently reading the memos themselves, led me to think about the logic, nature, and purpose of torture as an information extraction methodology and the effects torture might have on the brains of the tortured. This in turn led me to write some papers focused on what we know about the effects of imposition of severe stressors on neuropsychiatric and neuropsychological function in the context of torture. Limited in scale and scope as these papers were, they did not contain good news for the proponents of torture as a methodology for information extraction from the memory systems of the unwilling. The information available in the biomedical literature (and in particular the neuroscientific, experimental psychological, and physiological literatures) was actually devastating to the case made by the authors of the Torture Memos (and other protorture proponents). There was much more information available than a few research papers could hold, and there were many more issues to be dealt with too—hence, a book. Here, I take this much larger evidence base and apply it to the case made for the torture and coercion described in the Torture Memos. The larger evidence base is even more devastating to the theories presented therein.

I take a moral stand against torture, but here I do not seek to add to the considerable and sophisticated philosophical, ethical, and legal literature on torture. The analysis presented lies outside this debate, arguing that even if there were good moral grounds to torture people, it would be unwise to do so for practical reasons (dangerous ground to tread, I am fully aware). In other words, adopting a phrase from Carla Clark, I argue that torture is as ineffective as it is abhorrent. The case against torture in this book is made in consequentialist and instrumentalist terms—as these are the terms generally employed by torture's proponents. Remember, legal and philosophical arguments have been and are made on instrumentalist and consequentialist grounds in favor of torture (*there's a bomb; lives must be saved; do something, quick, and* NOW!). The protorture and procoercion case is almost always made with an ad hoc mixture of anecdote, cherry-picked stories, and entirely counterfactual scenarios that the authors usually find convincing—like the ticking time scenario. The pro-torture and procoercion arguments are not made on the basis of a systematic examination of the evidence base. Even now, despite all the revelations we now have, no such evidence-based case for torture has been made with the breadth, depth, and vigor required for the protorture case to have any remote semblance of credibility even on its own terms. The empirical reality is this: the intelligence obtained through torture is so paltry, the signal-to-noise ratio so low, that proponents of torturing detainees are left with an indefensible case when the protorture case is examined on the terms in which they make the case for torture, especially when considered against other, effective, noncoercive methods. And it seems to me that there is no greater or stronger case to be made against a practice or a theory (for that is what is advanced in the Torture Memos—a theory of the relationship between coercion, stress, and the induced recall of particular item and episodic information from memory) that it fails completely on its own terms. It fails in the intelligence outcomes sought but lost, the pathologies of psychological function it causes, the corruption of good investigative and humane interrogative practice it induces, the corrosion of institutions and democracies it causes, the lives it ruins. In short, torture, when analyzed in instrumentalist terms, fails as an interrogative methodology and fails for reasons that are grounded in what we know about what happens within the brain as the result of the imposition of the chronic, severe, and extreme stressor states used in torture.

It also seems to me, having read many of these protorture cases, that at least some authors are motivated by a barely uttered desire to engage in torture (or, rather, to have to torture conducted on their behalf by Orwell's "rough men") for retributive or punitive reasons. Attempting to dress the protorture case as an attempt at information extraction from the brains of the unwilling serves only to confuse the case they make. Here, naively perhaps, I have taken the theories and arguments employed by the Torture Memos at their word: that the techniques described were devised and employed solely in the sincere belief that they were demonstrably empirically necessary to ensure that prisoners revealed the contents of their long-term memory systems. That torture might be used for other purposes—for retribution or punishment, to instill or provoke terror, to generate predetermined intelligence to bolster particular political intentions, to secure confessions for legal convictions, or whatever—is deliberately placed outside the scope of the analysis presented here.

The brain is the organ responsible for generating and regulating the expression of our thoughts, emotions, and behaviors. These are, of course, manifold—extending from generating consciousness to the control of your diurnal rhythms, to your capacity to read this book while breathing and maintaining posture and gastric transit, to numerous other functions. A central function of the brain is generating and sustaining normal cognitive and emotional function and doing so within a fairly narrowly circumscribed range in order to allow us to behave adaptively. The imposition of severe and sustained stressors greatly impairs the capacity of the brain to appropriately regulate the expression of thoughts, emotions, and behaviors. Neuropsychiatric conditions such as posttraumatic stress disorder, certain psychoses, generalized anxiety disorder, and major depressive disorder are therefore likely outcomes of having been subjected to torture. In what has become known as the Bybee memo (drafted by John Yoo but signed by Assistant Attorney General Jay Bybee in August 2002), for a procedure to rise to the level of torture, the following criterion is disingenuously advanced: "Physical pain amounting to torture must be equivalent to intensity to the pain accompanying serious physical injury, such as organ failure, impairment of bodily function, or even death." The case will be advanced and elaborated here that imposing the severe stressors used during torture where they result in neuropsychiatric disorders actually does constitute impairment of bodily function and organ failure—because the brain is not able to carry out its normal autoregulatory functions as a result of having been pushed to great extremes during the experience of torture. Thus, coercive practices resulting in these outcomes are an egregious violation of the standards laid down in the memos—even on their own terms. I examine these theories and arguments on their own terms, using what we know about the brain as the lens to focus the discussion and evidence. One word of warning here: it is important to emphasize a key philosophical prior. Donald Hebb, one of the giants of psychology and neuroscience, famously wrote in 1949 that "modern psychology takes completely for granted that behavior and neural function are perfectly correlated, that one is caused by the other." It will be important for the reader to attempt to adopt the perspective of a neuroscientist: to set aside Cartesian ghosts and deep distinctions between the mental and physical that are occasionally used by nonneuroscientists or nonpsychologists. An entirely naturalistic framework is adopted in the analysis presented here.

I hope this book may stimulate colleagues in neuroscience, psychology, and psychiatry to become more deeply involved in these public policy issues. We now know a great deal about brain and behavior, and an honest appraisal of what we know would have avoided the grotesque cul-de-sac that interrogation practices were driven into over these past years by scientifically uninformed amateurs who were, as we shall see, making it up as they were going along. Honorable exceptions apart, I have been surprised by the relative silence of neuroscientists, psychologists, and psychiatrists who conduct research work on stress and stressors or the brain systems supporting memory or who work on related clinical psychiatric conditions regarding the use of the techniques described in the Torture Memos. There are great opportunities to educate, inform, and generate new knowledge available, if researchers take the opportunity to conduct their work in meaningfully cross-disciplinary ways. There is no shortage of people with an opinion on torture in the media, however, and especially ones who, starting from their own fanciful imaginings, can spin a gossamer-light justification for coercion and torment. On the other hand, there is a profound shortage of people who have studied carefully the evidence on torture: what it is, what it does, and what it has been used for. Literature on the subject is plentiful; minimally, Darius Rejali's astonishing, scholarly, and profoundly affecting book *Torture and Democracy* should be studied carefully by all who wish to have an opinion on this terrible topic. The strange, abstracted, Vulcan-like musings provided by certain lawyers, policymakers and public commentators would be even more risible and ridiculous if they were not taken seriously by so many. There is here, for a forensically minded cognitive psychologist, a dramatic case study in cultural cognition, motivated reasoning, and confirmation bias present in their writings and public perorations. (Kahan and Kahnemann have separately investigated these phenomena at length, and their works make important reading in this context.) Torture in movies and television presents us with a similar problem: what we see is what the screenwriters, cinematographers, and directors imagine. The nauseating reality of torture as it has been practiced through the ages, and the purposes for which it has been practiced, is missing. The usual purpose of torture by state actors has not been the extraction of intentionally withheld information in the long-term memory systems of the noncompliant and unwilling. Instead, its purposes have been manifold: the extraction of confessions under duress, the subsequent validation of a suborned legal process by the predeterminedly guilty ("they confessed!"), the spreading of terror, the acquisition and maintenance of power, the denial of epistemic beliefs, and many more purposes besides. A visit to the torture museums dotted around Europe should be sufficient to convince one of this, if a reading of the relevant historical and political literature does not. In the end, this book is a call for evidence-based reasoning—not legitimation of intellectually vapid and fanciful scenarios. We must do as scientists do: discard even our dearly held or oft-repeated theories when the evidence demonstrably finds them wanting.

1

Torture in Modern Times

Worried politician:	I know that these guys know something that they don't want us to know.
Evidence-based investigator:	How do you know?
Worried politician:	I just know. Now how do I squeeze it out of them? You know, within the law?
A lawyer:	I know a way . . .

This book is focused on a terrible reality: the use and persistence of torture and, in particular, its disastrous effects on the brains of its victims. Torture has been with us for all of recorded history. Until recently, though, we thought that liberal democracies were leaving it behind. The "war on terror" and the subsequent release by U.S. president Barack Obama of the so-called Torture Memos in 2009 have made it clear that torture is still very much with us. These memos fueled a major international controversy on the use of torture as a tactic or method in the war against terrorism. The controversy was fueled further by a variety of leaks, memoirs, newspaper and Internet accounts and blogs, books, and major reports by, among others, the International Committee of the Red Cross, the Constitution Project, and the Senate Intelligence Committee. Here, I examine the contemporary use of torture specifically as a method for extracting information from captives. I examine the effect that torture has on the fabric of the brain and on the retrieval of memories that are its supposed focus—after all, if torture is the attempt to force information from the unwilling, *it is the attempt to force information retrieval from the memory systems of the brains of the unwilling.* A fundamental argument presented here is that the motivation for the use of torture to force information from the memories of the unwilling comes from culturally shared, introspectively derived, and empirically ungrounded psychological and neurobiological beliefs that are fundamentally and demonstrably untrue. This logic for the use of torture—that torture can (and should) be used to motivate captives to reveal information intentionally withheld under normal interrogation—is examined in depth here. Such information is, by definition, stored in the memory systems of the brains of captives. One argument presented at length here is that the effects of torture are, contrary to the beliefs of its proponents, quite the reverse of those intended. Torture is a profound and extreme stressor that causes widespread and enduring alterations to the very fabric of the brain—including in the connections between brain cells (synapses) on which memory depends. Unsurprisingly, therefore, torture also causes many psychopathological changes in the person who is tortured; more surprisingly, it is likely to cause not dissimilar changes in the torturer.

This book is quite deliberately not about the long and difficult fight to extirpate torture as a legally, politically, and culturally sanctioned practice. The international legal position on torture is clear, precise, and nonnegotiable in its definition and in its implications. Torture is immoral and illegal, and signatories to the United Nations Conventions must not engage in, condone, commission, or facilitate torture. Instead, I develop two related issues: why laypeople, policy-makers, and others believe the imposition of "severe pain or suffering, whether physical or mental, . . . intentionally inflicted on a person" (torture) is a reasonable interrogatory technique, and what we know about the effects of the imposition of such "severe pain or suffering, whether physical or mental," on the brain systems supporting memory, mood, and other functions. This book is written from the perspective of an experimental neuroscientist and discusses torture in the light of what we know about its effects on the brain. I offer one caveat at the outset: torture itself is not a neuroscience concept per se. Instead, I use the concepts of stress, stressors, pain, anxiety, and the like as these are reasonably well defined and map reasonably well onto the methods used in torture and what are sometimes tendentiously and casuistically called "enhanced interrogation techniques."

There is a vast legal, political, historical, moral, and ethical literature on torture. The analysis presented here differs from many others in an important respect: it is consequentialist and addresses the utilitarian use of and arguments for torture directly on their own terms. The analyses presented here are therefore not a priori deontological (I note that the moral and philosophical arguments for and against torture tend to fall into this category of analysis). I agree with the moral, ethical, and legal case against torture, but I believe it is important not simply to focus on the prior rights and wrongs of its use: it is vital to analyze the logic, methods, and outcomes of this logic of the uses of torture on its own terms. This last point is critical: defenders of torture as a method of extracting information assume that torture works or at least that torture can work, or that torture can be made to work (and, one presumes, "work better" than the nontorture alternatives). Thinking through the evidence base relevant to these assumptions is much more challenging, and it requires that we focus on the logic presented for the use of torture to forcibly access detainees' long-term memories, as well as on the actual consequences of torture on the integrated neuropsychological functioning of the person who is subjected to it (and, less obviously, on the person who imposes the torture).

Torture by Democracies in Modern Times

Despite the United Nations Convention against Torture (1984), torture still occurs, practiced by a wide variety of state and criminal actors for sadistic, instrumental, and other reasons. It is more pervasive in autocratic countries, but many countries under stress have resorted to torture, including democracies. Arguably, the most extensive campaign of torture conducted in modern times by a Western democracy was that conducted in Algeria by France, during the course of the Franco-Algerian war. Many thousands were subjected to torture, especially in the Casbah, using beatings, electrocution, near-drowning, and stress positions. French actions were hardly unique. During the 1970s, for example, elements of the United Kingdom Military and Security Services resorted to the use of the so-called Five Techniques (starvation/sparse diet; sleep deprivation; hooding; exposure to a continuous white noise; stress positions) in the campaign against the Irish Republican Army (IRA) in Northern Ireland. Ian Cobain, in his history of torture in the modern United Kingdom, also notes that "the Five Techniques were always supported by a sixth, unspoken technique: anyone who refused to maintain the stress position would be severely beaten" (2012, 130). And what was the explicit purpose of the Five Techniques? An investigation concluded that "the Five Techniques applied together were designed to put severe mental and physical stress, causing severe suffering, on a person in order to obtain information from him" (ibid., 160; see also Shallice 1972 for an early psychological perspective on the Five Techniques).There are many other such examples of democracies under stress resorting to torture as a shortcut alternative to normal investigative practice (see Rejali 2007). Such outbreaks in the use of torture have been the subject of many detailed accounts by journalists, historians, legal scholars, and even sometimes the torturers themselves. This book is not the place to rehearse this history; as stated, the masterwork in this area is Darius Rejali's

Torture and Democracy (2007), which makes the case that democracies have never entirely given up torture and have indeed pioneered certain methods to avoid public scrutiny, methods that leave no physical marks (so-called white torture). Alberto Gonzales, the former U. S. Attorney General, remarked in a 2015 interview: "When I think about torture it's broken bones, electric shocks to genitalia. It's pulling your teeth out with pliers. It's cutting off a limb. That's torture. Is waterboarding at the same level? I'd say probably not." Gonzales is making the all-too-common mistake of consulting the contents of his consciousness to define torture—not statute law, not international treaties, not medical authorities, not the scholarly literature. This leaves us with a problem: when we think of torture, our thinking is deeply colored by images of medieval cruelty: the rending of flesh, the breaking of bones, and pain made visible through scar and scream. We do not think of techniques that leave no visible record of their presence, techniques that manipulate the metabolic and psychopathological extremes of body, brain, and behavior, and which are, by any reasonable standard, torture.

Torture is all too common worldwide, and as mentioned, other democracies have resorted to torture techniques during times of great national stress, when perceived others or out-group members were subjected to extremes during interrogation sessions. The murderous attack by al-Qaeda on September 11, 2001, had many enduring consequences, not least on the United States' treatment and interrogation of prisoners. A covert and overt war was launched against al-Qaeda (and the Taliban). When prisoners were captured, U.S. military and intelligence officials naturally wanted information from them about their networks and any potential or further threats that may exist. How could officials ensure that the prisoners were revealing all they knew during interrogation? Pressure built to make the interrogations tougher. Speculation spread that interrogations were being conducted in new ways (for the United States). Vice President Dick Cheney reinforced the speculation when he revealed that the United States might resort to the "dark side"; he was to describe (in an interview in October, 2006) the decision to employ the waterboard as a "no-brainer." Similarly, President George W. Bush, in a public acknowledgment that new interrogation procedures had been devised for use on captives, stated, "These procedures were designed to be safe, to comply with our laws, our Constitution, and our treaty obligations. . . . I can say the procedures were tough, and they were safe, and lawful, and necessary" (press conference, September 6, 2006).

A substantial debate took place within the U.S. government about how to conduct interrogations to ensure that captives provided all the information contained in their memories to the greatest extent possible. And so the notion of so-called enhanced interrogation techniques (EITs—a euphemism for coercive interrogation techniques or torture) was born. EITs were notionally designed to ensure compliance with the questioning of the interrogator and, as a result, to facilitate the release of intentionally withheld information from the memories of captives. Jane Mayer, in her pioneering book *The Dark Side,* explains the thinking thus: "Scientific research on the efficacy of torture is extremely limited because of the moral and legal impediments to experimentation. Before endorsing physical and psychological abuse, *the Bush Administration did no empirical study.* The policy seems to have been based on some combination of political preference and intuitive belief about human nature. Yet from the start, top White House officials were utterly convinced that coercion was foolproof. John Yoo, in an informal aside at a book signing in Washington, said unabashedly, 'It works—we know it does. The CIA says it does and the Vice President says it does' " (2008, 119; emphasis added). This is a striking and remarkably credulous assertion from someone who is qualified as a lawyer, working in an evidence-based profession. A declassified report from the Office of the Inspector General (2004) reviewed the internal evidence for the efficacy of these techniques, describing them as a "subjective process" which is "not without some concern" (p. 85); that there were "limited data on which to assess their individual effectiveness" (p. 89). The evidence on the actual efficacy runs to a scant five pages in a more than 250 page report (including supporting appendices). We now know from the report of the Senate Select Committee on Intelligence (the Torture Report) that an "informal operational assessment" of the program determined that it would not be possible to assess the effectiveness of the CIA's enhanced interrogation techniques without violating "Federal Policy for the Protection of Human Subjects" regarding human experimentation (SSCI 2014, Findings and Conclusions, Point 16, p. 13). So an empirical study was impossible under law, because the legal standards that must be met to safeguard human participants in empirical research would be breached by such a study—because the human participants could not be safeguarded! The Senate report also confirms that the CIA conducted no "significant research to identify effective interrogation practices, such as conferring with experienced U.S. military or law enforcement interrogators, or with the intelligence, military, or law enforcement services of other countries with experience in counter-terrorism and the interrogation of terrorist suspects. Nor are there CIA records referencing any review of the CIA's past use of coercive interrogation techniques and associated lessons learned" (SSCI 2014, 20).

The empirically and ethically unmoored supportive line of thinking for torture was put bluntly and starkly by Rick Santorum, the former U.S. senator and seeker of the Republican Party's nomination for the U.S. presidential election of 2012. Santorum, in a comment regarding Senator John McCain's repudiation of torture, stated, "He doesn't understand how enhanced interrogation works. I mean, you break somebody, and after they've broken they become cooperative" (Summers 2011). (And he said this of someone who had been tortured in Vietnam for five years.) Other nomination-seeking candidates supported his remarks. Statements of this type can be multiplied manifold. The Constitution Project reported, "Jose Rodriguez, head of the CIA's counterterrorism center from 2002 to 2005, has said, 'this program was not about hurting anybody. This program was about instilling a sense of hopelessness and despair on the terrorist,' and hopelessness led detainees to 'compliance'" (2013, 206). Another example: "The CIA, he said, 'put him in that position to get him to talk. They took it that pain equals cooperation'" (Mayer 2008, 256). Similar assertions are dotted through the Torture Memos themselves. You do not need to go far to find people in the popular media arguing similarly. Charles Krauthammer of the *Washington Post* and a Fox News contributor argued in 2005 that "it would be a gross dereliction of duty for any government not to keep Khalid Sheikh Mohammed isolated, disoriented, alone, despairing, cold and sleepless, in some godforsaken hidden location." Ironically, Krauthammer is a qualified psychiatrist; were he to actually apply his professional knowledge of psychiatric management, he would, perhaps, come to the view of this book. His argument seems driven more by a desire to punish than to tap into Khalid Sheikh Mohammed's knowledge in a reliable way. There are or have been many others willing to argue along similar grounds (such as the noted legal scholar Alan Dershowitz, 2002): some have renounced their earlier thinking; others have not.

The underlying (psychological) logic of these assumptions is that through a process of "breaking someone" the person will subsequently become compliant and that this, in turn, will loosen his or her tongue. We return to this type of thinking again and again throughout this book. It is not at all clear what "breaking someone" means. Thus, to try to understand what is meant, we need to ask some questions about what will actually be done to the person. Does, for example, coercively enforcing an extended period of sleep deprivation enhance compliance or increase the motivation of the suspect to comply with the instructions of the questioner? The answer (logically) is yes, no, or maybe, depending on the circumstances and the personal characteristics of the sleep-deprived individual. A second necessary question, though, is just as important—does sleep deprivation interact in a positive, negative, or neutral way with the brain systems supporting memory, cognition, and mood? The hope of the interrogator who uses such coercive techniques has to be that the effects will be at worst neutral and at best positive on these brain systems. It should be clear that, when put in these terms, this hope is not obviously the case. In other words, do these techniques actually enhance the outcomes of the interrogation? And how would we ever know that they, in fact, do? The situation becomes even more complicated when you consider what evidence counts as true and false. There is an important distinction between false-positive and false-negative, true-positive and true-negative discovery rates when conducting biomedical and other forms of research. The key bias in thinking about evidence is to focus solely on what are retrospectively thought to be true-positive signals and to disregard the likelihood of false-positive and false-negative discovery rates. In other words, those who are invested in coercion will cherry-pick the data in order to suit the needs of a predetermined narrative which suggests that torture worked and will work again in the future. The signal-to-noise issue arises again and again when considering how to understand what the outcomes of torture are. The Senate Torture Report says, "the interrogation team later deemed the use of the CIA's enhanced interrogation techniques a success, not because it resulted in critical threat information, but because it provided further evidence that Abu Zubaydah had not been withholding the aforementioned information from the interrogators" (SSCI 2014, 37). Here, a lack of information provided under coercion is used to prove a negative (something that logicians contend is impossible). If a captive reveals nothing despite the enhanced interrogation techniques, then he must actually know nothing. Of course, the alternative conclusion is that the coercive techniques militate against his revealing anything under coercion: as the old saw has it, absence of evidence is not evidence of absence.

Finally, let us examine the frequent use of the phrase "to break someone" as the object of torture. This is a most remarkable phrase—it rolls off the tongue, it is easy to state, and it sounds like it might actually mean something. But what does "breaking someone" actually mean? In medieval times, it referred to victims being tied to a wheel and their limbs systematically being broken with a hammer. A description of the torture from the time describes how a convict was beaten into "a sort of huge screaming puppet writhing in rivulets of blood, a puppet with four tentacles, like a sea monster, of raw, slimy and shapeless flesh mixed up with splinters of smashed bones" (Merback 1999, 160–161, citing a witness testimony from Hamburg in 1607 where a person was broken, braided, and died on the wheel). People who blithely say that someone should be broken during torture in order to ensure compliance can hardly be aware of the origin of the phrase "to break someone." They must mean something else—but what do they mean? Does "breaking someone" mean fracturing a person's personality and integrated psychological function through the imposition of severe, chronic, and psychiatrically injurious trauma—as might be found in a war veteran suffering posttraumatic stress after the strain of extended, life-threatening combat? And how will "breaking someone" affect the person's brain systems supporting cognition, memory, and mood? And how will it affect the person's recall for prior episodes, facts, or events or future planned actions? These are among the kinds of questions that we will attempt to grapple with in this book.

Torture as an Interrogative Device in the Torture Memos

In 2009, the president of the United States of America, Barack Obama, released a series of legal memos providing great detail regarding the interrogatory techniques applied to certain captives in U.S. custody in Guantanamo Bay. (I use the collected edition of these memos edited by David Cole [2009] throughout this book, but they are widely available for download.) These memos were written by various agents of the U.S. government to provide both legal interpretation and legal cover for the enhanced interrogations conducted on certain terrorist suspects. The memos have been widely discussed in the popular press, radio, television, and blogs and have been the subject of extensive comment in court cases (and correspondingly have been discussed in fine detail in formal legal and other proceedings). There has been a widespread debate, for example, on whether the authors of these memos failed in their duty of care in the interpretation and implementation of the appropriate laws, conventions, treaties, and national and international obligations when devising standards for interrogations were concerned, and this debate is not yet settled. At the time of writing, there is also a major controversy regarding the release in December 2014 of the executive summary (as well as supporting documents and some dissenting opinions) of a 6,000-page report regarding torture by the CIA, produced by the Senate Intelligence Committee led by Senator Diane Feinstein. The report suggests that the CIA went further than the memos allowed and that no useful intelligence was gathered as a result of the use of torture and coercion. These conclusions have been contested by some people, and the public interest would be best served by the immediate release of the entire unredacted report. I discuss in Chapter 7 how it may be possible using other legal means to ensure that the evidence of what has been done in the name of the state is revealed in a public forum.

The enhanced interrogation techniques discussed in the memos are as follows:

- *Attention grasp:* "Grasping the individual with both hands . . . on each side of the collar opening, in a controlled and quick motion. In the same motion . . . the individual is drawn toward the interrogator."

- *Facial hold:* "To hold the head immobile. One open palm is placed on either side of the individual's face."

- *Facial slap:* "The interrogator slaps the individual's face with fingers slightly spread. The hand makes contact with the area directly between the tip of the individual's chin and the bottom of the corresponding earlobe . . . to induce shock, surprise, and/or humiliation."

- *Walling:* "The individual is placed with his heels touching the wall. The interrogator pulls the individual forward and then quickly and firmly pushes the individual into the wall. It is the individual's shoulder blades that hit the wall. . . . The head and neck are supported with a rolled hood or towel . . . to help prevent whiplash. . . . The false wall is . . . constructed to create a loud sound when the individual hits it [to induce] further shock and surprise."

- *Wall standing:* "Used to induce muscle fatigue. The individual stands four to five feet from a wall, with his feet spread approximately to shoulder width. . . . His fingers support all of his body weight. The individual is not permitted to move or reposition his hands or feet."

- *Stress positions:* "Sitting on the floor with legs extended straight out in front of him with his arms raised above his head"; "kneeling on the floor while leaning back at a 45-degree angle."

- *Cramped confinement:* Placing the individual in a small box in darkness for up to two hours, in a larger box for up to eighteen hours.

- *Sleep deprivation:* "To reduce the individual's ability to think on his feet and, through the discomfort associated with lack of sleep [to a maximum of eleven days], to motivate him to co-operate." Sleep deprivation was induced by shackling captives in either standing or horizontal positions for prolonged periods, so that sleep was impossible. Furthermore, prisoners were required to void or relieve themselves into diapers during the generally standard period of sleep deprivation of seventy-two hours, although one detainee was subjected to 180 hours of sleep deprivation (Constitution Project 2013, 214).

- *Insect placed in a confinement box:* "You (the CIA interrogator) would like to place Zubaydah [suspected al-Qaeda terrorist] in a cramped confinement box with an insect. . . . He appears to have a fear of insects."

- *Waterboarding:* "The individual is bound securely on an inclined bench. . . . The individual's feet are generally elevated. A cloth is placed over the forehead and eyes. Water is . . . applied to the cloth in a controlled manner. . . . Air now is slightly restricted for 20 to 40 seconds due to . . . the cloth, . . . increas[ing] . . . carbon dioxide level[s] in the individual's blood. This increase in the carbon dioxide level stimulates increased efforts to breathe. This effort plus the cloth produces the perception of 'suffocation and incipient panic,' i.e., the perception of drowning."

Additional techniques were also disclosed by the report of the Constitution's Project's Task Force on Detainee Treatment. One captive, for example, "was interrogated for approximately 20 hours a day for seven weeks; given strip searches, including in the presence of female interrogators; forced to wear women's underwear; forcibly injected with large quantities of IV fluid and forced to urinate on himself; led around on a leash; made to bark like a dog; and subjected to cold temperatures" (2013, 39). A final technique described in the Senate Intelligence Committee report is the use of rectal infusion or rectal feeding on at least one prisoner: a lunch "of hummus, pasta with sauce, nuts, and raisins was 'pureed' and rectally infused" (SSCI 2014, 100, 115). Another prisoner (Khalid Sheikh Mohammed) was subjected to "rectal rehydration without a determination of medical need" (ibid., 82).

That these techniques would be listed and discussed in these bold terms is quite remarkable. That they should surface in documents as serious discussion points about how to secure information from prisoners in a twenty-first-century democracy is even more remarkable. The techniques proposed are not pragmatically justified by the underlying experimental cognitive psychology of memory. They are listed in a way that never questions the underlying thinking that generated them in the first place. Little by way of moral or ethical argument is provided. The techniques themselves lack any symmetry, as they are solely aversive and coercive in nature. No techniques are presented that build on any innately rewarding processes—for example, our innate need for affiliation or meaningful social bonding and rapport. There is also a presumption that techniques violating the norms underpinning the normal social contract will facilitate recall. There is a relevant and important biomedical research literature that describes the likely consequences of the use of each of these techniques. A dispassionate review of the relevant literature, focused on the evidence base and deliberately testing the underpinning theoretical assumptions, needs to be at the heart of decision making. Such a dispassionate review, however, undermines the intuitive assumptions about the effects of torture on motivating recall and retrieval of information from memory.

Folk or Commonsense Explanations

Nonscientists offer explanations of phenomena in the natural world or in the social world that are often based on intuitive or introspective notions or thoughts largely untempered or unmoderated by scientific theory or empirical observation. Some commonsense explanations are so deeply embedded that it can be extremely dangerous to challenge or even qualify them. In physics, for example, generations of educated people assumed that the sun traveled around the earth, with the earth fixed and stationary in space, as an explanation of our experience of night and day. To challenge ideas like these can be unsettling and even dangerous. Galileo, for example, was famously brought before the Inquisition for suggesting an alternative explanation for the succession of night and day: the idea that the earth moved and rotated in space and that the sun was stationary (the heliocentric hypothesis). He was shown the *strumenti di tortura* to induce him to abjure his heretical ideas.

Folk or naive explanations based on intuitions and ill-explained rationalizations are no less common in thinking about psychology and human behavior. These explanations of why we and others do the things that we do revolve around ideas such as desires, wishes, needs, personal responsibilities, motivations, and the exercise of volition or free will. "Why did you drink the water just now?" "I drank it because I am thirsty. I sweated a lot, I needed some water, therefore I drank." It should be obvious, if you think about this for a moment, that explanations like this are not explanations—at best, they are a kind of a label. This kind of explanation is even more unhelpful when we try to put two different types of explanation to rationalize something together. "Why did you deprive the prisoner of water?" "I deprived the prisoner of water so that he would become thirsty, and because he has become thirsty, he is more likely to tell me what I want to know, in order to get access to water." There is a certain logic to an explanation like this, and it feels in certain ways compelling. Maintaining hydration is an absolute prerequisite to all known forms of life. It should not come as a surprise, however, that the explanation of why we actually drink when we are thirsty is much more complex than the lay explanation. Drinking involves a complex set of changes in the organs of the body, the detection of these changes by the brain, and then the engagement of brain circuits that involve fluid seeking and subsequent fluid consumption. Physiologists typically distinguish between thirst that arises from osmotic changes and thirst that arises from hypovolemic changes. Osmoti-cally driven thirst arises because of the change in the concentration of small electrolytes (solutions of charged particles such as dissolved salt) in bodily fluids. Hypovolemic thirst arises because of fluid loss that occurs during the course of normal metabolic activity, including from perspiration from heating and exercise and from the normal transit of food through the gut. By weight, the body of a seventy-kilogram male will be approximately 70 percent water. Driving this concentration down will result in a very strong desire to replace that fluid, whereas driving it up will result in fluid excretion. I have used the word *desire* here deliberately. *Desire* is actually a mask for a whole series of changes that occur in the periphery and in the brain. The detail of the changes need not concern us here, just the fact that a series of changes in the kidneys, gut, and other peripheral organs results in signals passing to the hypothalamic centers of the brain, which then entrain other brain areas in a series of goal-oriented consummatory and motor acts that result in liquid consumption and thirst reduction. The key point here is that the *experience* of thirst in consciousness—which we take to be primary because of its overwhelming imposition into our conscious awareness—is actually at the end of the causal chain leading us to drink. It is not at the start—and this is why we confuse cause and effect so easily in mental life.

There are many other widely accepted—but false—beliefs re-garding psychological and brain function. They are false not only because there is no evidence to support them but also because they conflict with what we actually know about how the brain works. Some of these beliefs we will put to the test in this book. Others we can note in passing here. You do not only use 10 percent of your brain (this myth is one that will not die—but to the victims of brain damage, it is clearly and obviously wrong). Ordinary people brought in off the street will electrocute someone to the point of death be-cause a scientist provides the necessary justification; and they are not psychopaths. Most psychopaths are not homicidal maniacs. Yes, other people can get you to see what is not there, even when it is obvious that one line *is* longer than another. Schizophrenics do not have split personalities. Split personality is at best a very rare condition, if it truly exists at all, whereas schizophrenia is surprisingly common—about 1 percent of the population suffer from it in varying degrees. Human memory is actually pretty poor and unreliable, and memories do change through time. Recall in the presence of a group leads to memory distortions, and you may not be aware of these distortions. Flashbulb memories, despite their seeming vividness, are no more reliable than any other form of memory. Repression of memories after trauma is actually uncommon and has proven difficult to demonstrate reliably. Persistence and intrusiveness of traumatic memories is the usual case—hence the prevalence of posttraumatic stress disorder.

False beliefs about the world can and do have real-world consequences. Why would people run the real risk of their children suffering brain damage or death from measles, mumps, or rubella by not vaccinating them, rather than the nonrisk of autism from vaccinations? And why are irrational, evidence-free beliefs so persistent? This is because evidence-based reasoning is not easy for many people. Consulting the contents of consciousness via introspection is easier than consulting the empirical evidence. Adopting evidence-based stances can be costly with regard to one's position in one's social group, where a premium may be placed on the maintenance of in-group cohesion, even when it is contrary to the available evidence. However, for public policy, we must and should consult the evidence base, not our own personal prejudice base.

What Types of Evidence Are Admissible? What Types of Evidence Should We Consider?

The availability of the Torture Memos and related documentation presents a rarely afforded opportunity. The logic and arguments for why the various enhanced interrogation techniques would be effective in facilitating the release of intentionally withheld memories are presented at great length. The memos and related documents are valuable, for they allow us to examine the beliefs of the authors in some detail to test these beliefs against the evidence base and current theory, so we can assess whether they are valid. As we proceed, the key thing is to think of an evidence base as falling along some form of continuum, which extends from anecdotes, through some form of systematic description, through some form of systematic observation, to correlations, and finally to causal and mechanistic analyses. Anecdotes are not evidence and are not relevant to evidence-based discussions.

The work of science over the centuries has been to devise standards of evidence and methods of collecting data that allow us to test our ideas, theories, and hypotheses about how the world works in a systematic and reliable way. Science proceeds by systematically interrogating the world, providing evidence that we can use to make judgments about the truth, or otherwise, of the statements or claims that we make about the nature of the world. Science proceeds in a fashion that is quite different from the methods that are applied to evidence in the course of a legal process. As is well known, legal standards of proof revolve around the concepts of reasonable doubt in criminal trials and the balance of probabilities in civil trials. However, in both of these cases, the adjudication of evidence is about an event that has occurred in the past. In effect, a balance sheet is created describing scenarios, and these scenarios are used by the jury or by the judiciary, along with a variety of procedural, legal, and other rules, to determine the guilt or innocence, the culpability or otherwise of a person on trial. This kind of decision-making process is not at all close to the way evidence is considered in science. Evidence in science goes through different processes before it is accepted as part of the canon of science. Science is incremental, is underpinned by probing and substantive open debate, and is driven by two important processes. The first is peer review of experimental data; the second is independent replication of experimental data. Peer review means that when new data are submitted for publication, the article is sent out to independent review by the journal to which it is submitted. The quality of the article is adjudicated on by two, three, four, or more independent scientists coming to a view on the quality of the article: the procedures within the article, how well they have been described; the quality of the data analysis and the extent to which the article, as submitted, moves us beyond the current state of the art; and the extent to which the article reinforces and replicates what is already known. This process is fallible, occasionally has been subject to fraud, and is one that causes the working scientist no end of anxiety. Fraud can happen, and the peer-review process is itself imperfect. This is where the other vital component of the scientific process intervenes: the independent replication of the originally reported finding through tens or hundreds of laboratories. Science is successful because it is an open, data-driven process, which seeks to define and understand underlying causal mechanisms.

Kinds of Evidence: Standards for Decision Making

Understanding causality is a profoundly difficult problem: did event A, because it preceded event B, cause event B, or was it merely correlated with event B? To answer questions like this, we must conduct empirical, and preferably experimental, studies. We must attempt to understand the deep structures present, because attempting causal inference from what are observational data is a fraught undertaking. Understanding causality provides a route to underlying mechanisms and thus the opportunity to provide a deep theoretical understanding of the phenomenon at hand. Here, a deep theoretical understanding refers to the idea that with a good theory, the details are predictable, outcomes of experiments can be stated a priori with a high probability that the predicted outcomes will obtain, hypotheses are well founded, and the hard-won knowledge we have obtained is part of the larger body of science.

Understanding causality is also a prime concern of the counter-terrorism effort and of the interrogation program conducted by the CIA. In the aftermath of the release of the Senate Intelligence Committee report on torture by the CIA, the director of the CIA, John Brennan, made an extraordinary set of remarks regarding the efficacy of the CIA's own torture program: "Our reviews indicate that the detention and interrogation program produced useful intelligence that helped the United States thwart attack plans, capture terrorists and save lives. But let me be clear. We have not concluded that it was the use of EITs within that program that allowed us to obtain useful information from detainees subjected to them. The cause-and-effect relationship between the use of EITs and useful information subsequently provided by the detainee is, in my view, unknowable" (Hosenball 2014, quoting John Brennan, press conference, December 11, 2014). These remarks can be interpreted in multiple ways, but the emphasis on causality is important here. At the core of the protorture argument is the belief that torture is causally efficacious at ensuring the tortured person's compliance with the verbal demands of the interrogator so that the person reveals what he or she knows. There is an assumption that there is some underlying mechanism driving truth-telling forward from the actual or threatened experience of coercion, torment, and torture. Despite the opacity of Brennan's words (which seem phrased to provide cover to past beliefs and behaviors and—even more appallingly—to leave the door open for torture as a interrogative tool in the future), they indicate that there is not a unidirectional causal relationship between torture and reliable and veridical information obtained from the memories of the tortured. Brennan goes further to seemingly occlude matters by saying, "There was very valuable intelligence obtained from individuals who had been, at some point, subjected to EITs." Again, multiple interpretations are possible here, but a simple reading

is that the use of torture was essentially uncorrelated with information obtained from the tortured. Behind these remarks, though, there
does seem to be a degree of understanding that untutored, uninformed thinking and action has led the CIA badly astray. Brennan,
in strong contradistinction to the proponents of torture in the popular
media, displays an important subtlety and nuance of thinking through
these quotations. The repeated use of the word "unknowable" is a
surprising epistemological evaluation of the quality of the intelligence
obtained in his response to the Senate committee's findings. Presumably, Brennan has chosen to use this word in this context because it
is about as strong a word of repudiation as is possible for him, given
his position, to use. However, there is another way of proceeding here.
Philip Zelikow suggests we compare the evidence on intelligence
successes during the coercive-technique era and after this time. He
states that when the evidence is analyzed, there "is no evident correlation between intelligence success and the availability of extreme
interrogation methods" (2012, 43; although he reminds us that other
variables were important too).

Standards for Empirical Evidence

At the core of the protorture position lies the core theory that the
imposition of extremities of stress will drive the truth-telling process forward in a veridical fashion. Determining the relationship
between an intervention and an outcome is difficult, but it can be
done. In drug trials, for example, the gold standard for admitting a
drug (an intervention) into the panoply of biomedical treatments is
a multicenter, randomized, double-blind, placebo-controlled, large-
scale clinical trial. This is a very demanding level of evidence. *Multicenter* means that data are collected from multiple centers applying
similar standards and protocols to data collection; *randomized* means
that participants in the trial are placed in a treatment group or a placebo group or a no-treatment group on a randomized basis—perhaps

by a random-number generator. *Double-blind* treatment means that the subjects themselves are blind to the treatment they are receiving; they do not know whether they are receiving a placebo or a pill with an active ingredient, and physicians administering the drug are blind to whether they are administering a placebo or a pill with an active ingredient. *Large-scale* means that many volunteers are used in the experimental trial—so that thousands of data points are collected to aid decision making. Finally, *clinical* simply means that subjects are recruited through a clinic and are given a full biomedical assessment prior to induction into the trial in order to ensure that they are appropriate subjects for it. Standards like these raise the bar very high indeed for the type of evidence that can be admitted or used for a drug trial, a process that is entirely correct and appropriate. It should never be the case that a drug would be administered on the basis of a physician or two believing on the basis of a hunch that such-and-such a treatment is the appropriate way to proceed to treat some medical condition. This standard has evolved over the past fifty to a hundred years; it has been a hard-fought standard to achieve and is one that needs enforcement by the relevant regulatory authorities (such as the Food and Drug Administration [FDA] of the United States). Where patient treatment is concerned, any treatment standard that falls below this evidential bar will almost certainly be unacceptable. However, there was no attempt to use this form of evidence-based thinking in the decision-making process that resulted in the decision to employ coercive and torture techniques as the basis for prisoner interrogations.

A different type of scientific evidence derives from formal and systematic experiment. This is where variables of interest are directly compared, controlled, and measured; two or three conditions are compared, and their treatment is varied in some systematic and controlled way. Ideally, we should also make a prediction about likely outcomes on the basis of prior theory and evidence and test these predictions from the collected data using statistical procedures. An example of an experiment in psychology might begin with giving participants some complex material to learn. For example, we might give them some prose to read; we might give them a book on which they are going to be questioned at some later point in time; we might give them a series of faces and ask them to learn names that go with those faces. We will ask them to recall this material at some later time, having performed some intervention. (I ignore here how we will test statistically the differing outcomes.) We can easily conduct an experiment of the following type. We can select volunteers—say a group of young participants in their twenties—and we can pretest them to ensure that they all have more or less similar IQs and levels of education. We then randomly assign them to one of a few different treatment groups. Group A, which we will refer to as the control group, are given the material to read and then simply go about their daily business for some period of time. We test them subsequently on some measure of recall. Group B might stand semiclothed in the cold for 120 minutes (in a climactic chamber) in the time between their learning and the testing. Group C might be given a warm drink and some form of social interaction in between. We then ask the following question: what do we predict will be the outcome when we come back to each of those subjects and examine subsequent recall for the material we have given them to learn? The purpose of the control group, group A, is to set a baseline for the level of recall we would expect to see in the absence of any determined, distinct, and systematically applied intervention. Now, with regard to what happens to recall in group B—the group that is made to stand in the cold for 120 minutes—and group C, whom we have met for a nice conversation and a warm drink, what do we expect? Do we expect that the cold group will have greater or lesser levels of recall compared to the social interaction group, or do we expect that the control group will have the greatest level of recall? Remember, in an experiment of this type, compliance and motivation are not issues. The participants are all volunteers, so we would expect across all participants that their willingness to recall material voluntarily should (on average) be approximately the same. Group B's condition mimics (in part) the temperature manipulation sometimes imposed during torture. Group C's condition mimics rapport building sometimes used in interrogation. There is an evidence base that can be brought to bear on these questions, as there are studies in the literature that address such questions. If we were to take an alternative—for example, if we were to subject our volunteers repetitively to a severe stressor (such as waterboarding) between their learning and testing—what do we expect? Do we expect that recall will be enhanced, or do we expect that recall will be in some way diminished? What do we predict will be the effect on the brain systems that support learning and memory? Will the brain systems supporting recall be enhanced, or will their function be diminished? We can ask questions like this across a whole range of other variables. What will be the effect of exposure to very loud noises? Or of interrupting sleep for very long periods of time? Or of the manipulation of diet? There is a relevant literature that allows us to explore the consequences of manipulations of this type on the brain systems supporting memory, mood, and intention.

Cargo Cult Science, Coercive Interrogation, and Torture

The Torture Memos and other sources provide many instances when the language of science is appropriated to apparently underscore the idea that the techniques were well founded in the various sciences of physiology, neuroscience, and psychology. *Cargo cult science* is a phrase given to us by the late U.S. physicist Richard Feynman that refers to the use of the language and even behaviors that bear some resemblance to science but critically without the scientific method and the intellectual commitments that follow from the adoption of the scientific method. The use of coercive interrogations has regrettably resulted in the occasional appropriation of the language of science to bolster the case for their use. The FBI interrogator Ali Soufan says (in his book *The Black Banners*) that a contractor psychologist, identified by the Constitution Project as James Mitchell, replied, "This is science," when challenged by Soufan on the use of nudity and sleep deprivation as interrogation tools (2011, 373). This of course is an attempt to prevent and blunt discussion by invoking a greater authority. However, as we shall see, the science converges on the finding that substantial sleep deprivation actually results in terrible cognitive deficits, including memory loss. In other evidence, U.S. Senator Carl Levin provides a transcript of a discussion in which "Mr. Fredman, the senior CIA lawyer, . . . described for the group the so-called 'wet towel' technique, which we know as waterboarding. Mr. Fredman said 'it can feel like you're drowning. The lymphatic system will react as if you're suffocating, but your body will not cease to function' " (Kiel 2008). It will come as a very considerable surprise to physiologists and anatomists that this ductless secretory organ system (distributed principally in the armpits, groin, and trunk), usually thought of as having immune and fluid-recovery functions, has a respiratory function—the detection of hypoxia and asphyxiation. This is quite a revision of its actual function. In reality, of course, here you have nothing more than the unedifying and indecorous spectacle of a lawyer reaching into his limited personal grab bag of physiological knowledge to adorn a sentence with the language of science in making his case to an apparently similarly credulous group of listeners.

Waterboarding is cited in the Torture Memos as causing elevations in the blood's carbon dioxide levels (although this is not given the formal technical term of hypercapnia). The sources of this information are not provided, but some degree of physiological knowledge underwrites this section of the memo, although the technical terminology of respiratory physiology (for example, Hering-Breuer reflexes, chemosensing, gas exchange, ventilator rate and pattern, pneumotaxic and apneustic centers) is not employed. Remarkably, however, no data are cited on the effects of hypercapnia or indeed hypoxia (decreased blood oxygen) on brain function. Nor are data cited on the effects of carbon dioxide narcosis—a state of deep stupor or unconsciousness that might result from acute and repeated waterboarding. Instead, we find a different worry expressed about the waterboard: that of the possibility of "hyponatremia (i.e., reduced concentration of sodium in the blood) if the detainee drinks the water" (Cole 2009, 169). There is a trivial problem and a more serious problem here. The trivial is straightforward: ingestion of liquid into the stomach (except if it is forced) is very difficult when the head is below the level of the gut (try it). More seriously, hyponatremia (water intoxication) results from the ingestion of hugely excessive quantities of water (some estimates suggest in excess of eight liters per day; Valtin 2002). The quantities of water to be used during waterboarding, as described in the memos, even at their most extreme and assuming maximal ingestion of the water, would never reach these levels. Thus, we have a peculiar situation where an essentially nonexistent medical risk of waterboarding (hyponatremia) is considered at great length, but the actual risk of waterboarding (dry- and wet-drowning, choking, and the like) are left unconsidered. Thus, the appearance of considering a medical risk of waterboarding has been provided, but the actual medical risks are not considered or discussed: a grim example of a bad-faith analysis camouflaged as its opposite. Similar considerations apply to aspiration of food through vomiting, which is also considered—the risk here is real but is obviated by feeding captives only liquid food. The other method of actually eliminating risk—by not employing the waterboard—is left unconsidered.

We find other odd locutions elsewhere in the Torture Memos, such as the following statement: "You describe that in an initial confrontational incident, Zubaydah showed signs of sympathetic nervous system arousal, which you think was possibly fear" (Cole 2009, 115). No data are provided to substantiate the assertion that indeed there was sympathetic drive present, which could only be reliably measured by appropriate physiological monitoring and challenge. I doubt that any attempt was made to measure synaptic drive in the preganglionic sympathetic fibers terminating in the adrenal medulla, for example. The assertion that the state described corresponded to an inferred psychological state of fear is oddly phrased, as if a curious zoological specimen were being observed by a person unused to the experience of human emotions. Again, we are seeing a decorative use of scientific language, this time in the service of distancing the observer from the reality of the psychological states that the captive was likely to have been experiencing. As a final example, the Torture Memos consider sleep deprivation in a variety of places, and phrases from the neuropsychological literature appear (for example, impaired cognitive performance; visual hallucinations; visual-spatial motor tasks and short-term memory tests; hallucinations; psychotic symptoms; paranoid ideas). That sleep deprivation causes psychopathological disorders is acknowledged (although the evidence is at best presented in a partial fashion in the memos), but at no point is the thought developed to its logical conclusion—that sleep deprivation might actually work contrary to its desired outcome. Such arguments are concocted to give the appearance of having considered the evidence and found in favor of the use of coercion and torture, when the reality is different. The policy is decided, and then the evidence is retrofitted to ensure that it coheres with the policy decision. Legal scholars have come to a similar conclusion regarding the legal arguments used to buttress the memos (for example, Cole 2009; Sands 2008). Cole comments, for example, that "because the questions were so difficult, however, one would expect a good-faith analysis to reach a nuanced conclusion, perhaps approving some measures while definitely prohibiting others. Yet on every question, no matter how much the law had to be stretched, the OLC lawyers reached the same result—the CIA could do whatever it had proposed to do" (2009, 4).

Exploring the Counterfactuals Regarding the Efficacy of Torture

This book examines why laypeople, policy makers and others believe that torture might be efficacious. It argues that laypeople make fallacious arguments based on uninformed intuitions about the cognitive neurobiological functions of the brain systems supporting intention, motivation, stress, mood, and memory. Further, these arguments are made unsupported by the evidence base. A key position advanced here is that torture has more or less exactly opposing effects to those intended; it negatively affects the brain systems concerned with intention, motivation, stress, mood, and memory. Now, what of the counterfactual? Suppose that the evidence base was different and that the imposition of extreme stressor states as occur during torture did not have negative effects on the brain systems concerned with memory, intention, motivation, mood, and stress. What should our attitude toward torture be then? There are at least three possible answers. First, torture is illegal and immoral and therefore should not occur anyway, and those who engage in it or facilitate it should be prosecuted to the fullest extent of the law. Second, the counterfactual as posed suffers from a problem of symmetry, as it is represented as the polar opposite to the position that torture does not work. However, as any logician knows, the possible universe of counterfactuals for this and indeed any other family of problems is infinite, bounded only by our capacity to imagine them. If we consider the implications of any possible counterfactual, we are bound to consider more counterfactuals than those that spring naturally to mind. Suppose some humans enjoyed being tortured? This is not impossible—at least within limits. Some psychiatric patients engage in self-injurious behavior and in self-mutilation. Some people seek extremes of experience through masochistic behaviors. Others surf the edges of death through autoasphyxiation and similar practices. Suppose torture enhanced motivated retrieval of information but simultaneously made retrieval impossible. Suppose torture enhanced retrieval but impaired interoception (perception of one's own bodily states). Suppose torture enhanced neurocognitive function generally. The point here is not to trivialize torture but to show that the consideration of a counterfactual does not actually prevent investigation of the world as it is. Finally, the position of the scientist is to try to describe the world as it is, not as it might be under some other set of circumstances that do not obtain.

This book argues that lay intuitions and assumptions regarding memory, motivation, and stress are very unhelpful as a guide to designing interrogation regimes. The fundamental argument is one that is deeply counterintuitive to anyone who relies on his or her own introspection about how to proceed with interrogation. Furthermore, the book argues that these intuitions are based on what people see on television or film or a narrow range of personal experience. It appears to be the case, for example, that one popular television series, *24*, profoundly influenced interrogation practice, which, if true, would be depressing and disturbing. Philippe Sands recounts in *Torture Team* how interrogators in Guantanamo used *24* for inspiration for interrogation methodology. The Constitution Project goes even further:

> The show was familiar to many at Guantánamo in 2002. "We saw it on cable," Lieutenant Colonel Diane Beaver recalled. "People had already seen the first series. It was hugely popular. . . . [Jack Bauer] gave people lots of ideas." Retired FBI interrogator Joe Navarro told Task Force staff: "Keep in mind there are 17,000 different police departments across the country so there's quite some variance, but the average law enforcement

officer in the United States in their career receives between eight and fifteen hours of [suspect] interview training. What fills in the rest? People use words and techniques from popular culture and what's trendy." (2013, 258)

And indeed torture features as a tongue-loosening device in a re-markable array of movies and television series. A quick shortlist would include *24*, *Dexter*, *Buffy the Vampire Slayer* (and the spin-off *Angel*), *Romanzo Criminale*, *The Shield*, *Game of Thrones*, *Waking the Dead*, *Criminal Minds*, *The Walking Dead*, *The Wire*, *Wire in the Blood* (in an especially gruesome episode, involving a Shankill Butcher–style living dismemberment), *Homeland*, *Spooks*, *Law & Order: Special Victims Unit*, and so many others. There was even a French television documentary—*Le Jeu de la Mort* (The Game of Death)—that required contestants to apparently administer 460-volt electric shocks to punish contestants who did not correctly an-swer questions; clips are available online. Similarly, many movies feature torture as a plot staple (for example, *Casino*, *Casino Royale*, *Payback*, *Zero Dark Thirty*, to name just a few; it even features in children's movies, such as *Wreck-It Ralph* and *The Incredibles*). Tor-ture in the popular media is represented almost exclusively as the preserve of those who need information that is locked in the head of someone else and for whom an assault on the bodily and psycho-logical integrity of another person in the service of acquiring such information is a necessity (and perhaps of little or no consequence to the torturers). It is little wonder, therefore, that fed on such a diet, certain among our leaders think that such tactics are reasonable and appropriate and that they might surmise that these tactics might work to loosen the tongues of suspects in custody. However, there is a profound error in thinking present here. Torture may be genu-inely effective in getting people to do things they do not want to do, such as signing false confessions, in order to provide the evidence required for a show trial. Donald Rayfield's remarkable book *Stalin and His Hangmen* (2004) is replete with such examples, as is history more generally (I have already noted the signal example of Galileo). The error here lies in thinking that this means torture may therefore be useful for extracting real information. Napoleon knew otherwise: "The barbarous custom of having men beaten who are suspected of having important secrets to reveal must be abolished. It has always been recognized that this way of interrogating men, by putting them to torture, produces nothing worthwhile. The poor wretches say anything that comes into their mind and what they think the interrogator wishes to know" (Bonaparte 1798, 128). The important corollary here is that the use of torture to ensure that a corrupted legal process is ostensibly served or to ensure that an epistemic position be abjured is rarely if ever represented in the popular media. There are few popular cinema or television treatments of the Soviet show trials or of the Inquisition or of the methods used to obtain confessions in these circumstances. Similarly, the use of torture as the punishment for guilt—especially in the forms of torture represented in the torture museums dotted around Europe—does not feature in popular media. That these historically more accurate and frequent uses of torture are absent from the screen is a testament to how an absence of evidence drives thinking, policy, and behavior too. We will now take a brain's-eye view of torture, the better to illustrate what we know of the brain and of the uselessness of our lay intuitions and feelings as a guide to action. We will start this journey by focusing first on how the brain's circuits and microcircuits support memory and executive functions.

2

How the Brain Supports Memory and Executive Functions

Interrogator: I want to know what he knows. How good is his memory? Can't we just get him to play the tape in his head and tell us what's on it?

Psychologist: What did you eat for dinner on the fifth of November last year? Where did you eat? Who did you eat it with? What clothes were they wearing? What did you talk about? What music was playing? What time did you eat at—exactly? What did you drink?

Interrogator: Are you serious? How do you expect me to remember details like those?

Psychologist: Why don't you just play the tape in your head and tell us?

An interrogation, an interview, a debriefing session, a chat, a conversation: all of these potential modes of interaction rely at their heart on socially embedded, psychological, and brain-system mediated uses of language and memory. Humans, as E. J. Masicampo and Roy Baumeister argue (2013), use language and memory for socially adaptive and transactive purposes. We are exquisitely sensitive to the utterances of others, and they in turn to ours. Words, verbal utterances, elicited or voluntary statements should therefore be treated as easily contaminated trace evidence and not necessarily as reliable evidence, because the purpose of memory and language—why it evolved—is to serve our survival in a social world. Memory and language did not evolve for truth-telling or information-recording purposes per se but rather to serve our social and survival needs. This implies a very different view of these intrinsic human functions than might be understood by most people. In this light, we should expect memory to be relatively fluid and modifiable in the light of social demands and current circumstances.

At the heart of a standard interrogation is a question-and-answer process. The questions, whether oblique or direct, are used to elicit information from the long-term memory of the subject. These verbal statements may then be used as the basis for further action—to generate findings that might be used to help proceed in an investigation, to provide evidence for a legal process, to build up a picture of the activity of the individual and his or her group. This latter activity might be of the group and its leaders, ideology, internal tensions, or whatever. These verbal protocols (as they are referred to in experimental psychology) therefore form the basis for understanding what it is the subject knows. However, interrogation itself happens in a social context: it occurs between two or more people, with one person leading the process and the other following. Power relations during interrogations are asymmetric, and in addition to the explicit information retrieval, there are inevitably implicit and explicit social interactions and transactions overshadowing the interrogation as well. Here we will concentrate on the memory-related aspects of the process; we will turn to the interrogation itself in the final chapter.

How should we interpret these protocols: are these verbal utterances a faithful representation of the knowledge requested from the subject's long-term memory? There are at least three possibilities:

1. These protocols do in fact provide an accurate representation of the contents of the subject's memory. This is not the same as what he or she has experienced—what you can remember and what you have experienced are not the same thing.

2. These protocols provide only what the subject wants you to know—not necessarily lies but not necessarily an accurate representation of what he or she has experienced.

3. These protocols provide some accurate and inaccurate information and should be treated with care—and really treated not as an accurate video-camera-like representation of past events but as a fragile and trace or gist-like representation of past events.

How the verbal protocols are to be recorded, coded, and interpreted is a separate and very significant problem, which we will not consider here. What we will consider next is what we know of the science of learning and memory and in particular what we know of the fragility of human memory.

Formally, learning is a change in an organism's behavior resulting from some prior experience, that is, from the interaction between the organism and the environment. Memory is the ability to recognize or to recall a previous experience, and a memory trace is a representation of that previous experience. We learn to respond to our given names, for example, before we acquire expressive language, and we retain this information perhaps one hundred years later, unless we have suffered some form of serious brain insult. This is an astonishing feat of memory, given the range of experience and change (development, education, maturation, senescence) that a brain undergoes over such an extended time period. Learning and memory have been investigated systematically and experimentally for well over a century now, and a descriptive terminology and set of methodologies for probing learning and memory have evolved over that time. At a psychological level, a distinction is generally drawn between short-term (or working) memories and long-term memories. Short-term memories are memories held in mind for short periods of time. A classic example is recalling a telephone number for the couple of seconds it takes to dial that number. Long-term memories are of much greater duration—for facts or events going back over periods from hours to days to weeks or even decades. Working memory is often regarded as having a substantial overlap with short-term memory. An example of working memory is when you are given a digit string, and you are subsequently asked to reverse the order of that digit string—to recall the numbers in the reverse order to which they were called out to you. Try this: repeat the following sequence of numbers backward 3, 5, 3, 7, 1, 7, 1, 6, 2, 6. Most people can recall perhaps seven or eight numbers in the forward sequence. Recalling the sequence backward (in reverse order) is a different matter. It is effortful, takes time, and without adopting special strategies, is more or less impervious to practice. This number sequence is easy to chunk—353; 717; 1; 626—it consists of three number palindromes (353; 717; 626); and international and area dial codes. Thus, working memory allows you to keep the memory in mind for a period of time and allows you to do something with it during that period of time. Sometimes certain components of working memory and long-term memory are also regarded as sharing common mechanisms, because items deliberately rehearsed in working memory can end up in long-term memory.

We can probe memory in a variety of ways. One way has been hinted at already: to store in mind and then recall items of information after a short period of time. A classic method is to ask people to learn material of some description (word lists, prose, or other types of material) and then at some point to probe the recall of that material. We might ask people to inspect faces and learn names that go with those faces (a simple form of associative memory—face-name pair learning—essential for everyday life). We might ask them to remember complex visual-spatial patterns and to recall and attempt to reproduce those patterns. We might ask them to learn the layout of a virtual maze that they navigate in three dimensions on a computer. We could then introduce some manipulation, such as a stressor, as discussed in Chapter 1, and examine the effect this has on subsequent recall. There are many ways of probing memory, limited only by experimental ingenuity. When we probe for the memory itself, there are important procedural distinctions drawn between cued recall, free recall, forced choice memory, and recognition memory. In cued recall, we might provide part of the original stimulus and ask the participant to provide the remainder of the stimulus (e.g., the first two numbers of the telephone number to be recalled). In free recall, participants are prompted to recall the previously learned information, and they can do so in any order. In forced choice recall, they might have to recall that word list in the exact order in which it was presented; whereas, in a recognition task, they may be given a larger word list with a mixture of words that seem previously unseen and asked to choose the words that they had seen previously. The person is prompted to report on the contents of his or her memory about a specific topic, an event, or material, at some time later than the time at which the event may have occurred. Thus, inferences can then be drawn about what the person knows, and his or her statements can be compared over time for their internal consistency and external validity (assuming there are other forms of evidence that can be used to test or corroborate the statements made by the person).

Cutting across all of these different types of memory is a distinction between explicit memories (sometimes called declarative memories) and implicit memories (sometimes referred to as procedural memories). The key characteristic of an explicit memory or a declarative memory is that it is verbally accessible to consciousness and is something that can be spoken about. Examples are the ability to answer questions like *Where was I? What was I doing? What did I have for breakfast? Can I solve problems in differential calculus?* and *Can I ride a bicycle?* Being able to ride a bicycle and knowing that you can ride a bicycle provides an interesting dissociation between these two different types of memory. The knowledge that you can *do* something is different from the knowledge of *how to do* that something. Learning to ride a bicycle is a good example of how this may be so. Learning to ride a bicycle is something that occurs slowly and incrementally. It occurs with practice through time, and it is something that is exceedingly difficult to describe to somebody else how to do. Telling people who have never cycled but who would like to do so that they need to center their mass in dynamic equilibrium with the environment while maintaining a relatively upright position approximately parallel with the earth's gravitational vertical and then applying forces of so many Newtons to the pedals underneath their feet will only get you so far. To learn how to actually ride a bicycle, especially without stabilizers, you need to actually climb on board and start cycling. And ask children how they do it, and you will get a reply like "I just did"—which does not help very much. Complex motor acts of this type are encoded by and are supported by brain systems that operate in parallel to, but are independent of, the brain systems that support declarative memories (that is, memories of the type *Where was I? What was I doing? What was I thinking? How was I feeling?*). Declarative memories can, across a wide range of circumstances, be extremely malleable; that is to say that there can be a difference between people's memories of what they say they were doing and what they were actually doing. People's memories of how they say they were feeling and how they were actually feeling can be at dramatic variance with each other, as we will see from studies of individuals' flashbulb memories about the events of September 11, 2001. By contrast, procedural memories are less plastic and are more stimulus and context specific. A phone number can be recalled across a wide range of contexts. The procedural skills used to ride a bicycle do not transfer easily to learning to play a piano or to swinging a golf club accurately.

There continues to be considerable confusion among lay members of the public about the nature of memory, from the terminology used to describe memory to what people believe human memory to be like. Sometimes, the phrase *short-term memories* is used by members of the public to refer to episodic memories extending back over a period of weeks to months. Usually, in cognitive neuroscience we would take the view that the temporal extent of short-term memory is from seconds to minutes at most. *Recency memory* would usually be the phrase applied to memories that are from the temporally close past (quite exactly where the dividing line should be placed has not been settled theoretically or empirically). Minimally, it usually extends over several sleep cycles; the most recent memories placed in long-term memory are the ones that are in fact the most labile and most subject to loss or interference. This is because they have not been elaborated through the semantic networks of memory particularly well and have not been the subject of extensive retrieval practice. Members of the public also have beliefs about memory that are simply untrue. The psychologists Daniel Simons and Christopher Chabris have conducted a large-scale representative survey of the U.S. public. Large fractions of the public believe contentions that are not accepted by expert opinion, and substantial numbers of respondents agreed with propositions that conflict with expert consensus, including the belief that amnesia results in the inability to remember one's own identity (83 percent agreement); an especially problematic and incorrect belief—that memory works like a video camera—is accepted by 63 percent of the population, with 48 percent of respondents believing that human memory is permanent and 55 percent believing that it can be enhanced by hypnosis. As we will see, the malleability, lability, and impermanence of memory is much more the rule. In fact, one of the preeminent researchers of human memory and of false memories, Elizabeth Loftus, in a TED talk provides a useful metaphor for human memory, that it "is constructed and reconstructed. It's more like a Wikipedia page—you can go change it, but so can other people" (2013; see also May 2013). In other words, the evolved purpose of memory is to serve the adaptive needs of present and future behavior. It is not, contrary to our native metacognitive intuitions, to provide a faithful record of our past experiences.

Stories from a Patient

Amnesia is the loss of the ability to recall certain types of previously experienced information. We have learned much about memory from studying carefully selected patients with circumscribed lesions of the brain. Patient H.M. is both the most famous and the most tested patient in the history of neuropsychology. His real name was Henry Molaison; he was born in 1926 and he died in 2008. At the age of nine, he suffered a traffic accident that led to him having constant and profoundly disabling epileptic fits. His epilepsy did not respond to drug treatment. In 1953, he underwent neurosurgery for his epilepsy, focused on his temporal lobes. These are the lobes of the brain at the sides of the head, adjacent to and below the temples. The operation was described as a "frankly experimental operation" by his surgeon, William Scoville (see Corkin 2013 for the fullest account available). The recordings of the electrical activity in H.M.'s brain (the EEG) showed that the severest focus of his epilepsy was in two particular structures in the temporal lobes (the hippocampal formation and the amygdala); these structures were surgically excised. The happy consequence of this surgery was that his epileptic seizures were reduced dramatically in frequency and severity. The unexpected consequence was that he suffered a severe and intractable amnesia that did not resolve over the remainder of his life.

H.M.'s amnesia revealed much about the structure of human memory and indeed about the brain structures supporting memory. His amnesia did not affect his recall of his early life and of events prior to the surgery (so-called remote memories). However, he lost the ability to retain information about personally experienced events that occurred after his surgery (anterograde amnesia). So, for example, he would quickly forget people he had met moments previously; he could not recall what he had eaten at a previous meal; he was unable to learn or retain new information about the facts and events of his everyday life. Other types of memory appeared to be unaffected in H.M. His short-term memory appeared normal. If he was given a telephone number to recall and then asked subsequently to verbalize it, he could do this easily. Distract him though, and the memory of the telephone number disappeared. He could learn motor skills, for example, so he became very proficient at mirror drawing: he was able to draw images quickly and easily that were reversed using a mirror box, he but retained no knowledge of the fact that he could do so. His IQ also remained unchanged, and it appeared to be in the normal range.

The study of H.M. introduced certain crucial ideas into the literature: first, that the hippocampal formation plays a crucial role in certain types of memory; second, that differing brain regions may be associated with differing types of memory; and third, that memory itself is not unitary. Memory has differing components with differing temporal extents, and these depend on activity in differing brain regions. H.M. was conscious of the fact that he had a deficit in memory, so he was not anosagnosic. In other words, he was aware that he had a neuropsychological deficit—that he had an amnesia. In one of his interviews, he said somewhat poignantly, "Every day is alone in itself, whatever enjoyment I've had, and whatever sorrow I've had. . . . [It is] like waking from a dream" (Milner, Corkin, and Teuber 1968, 217).

In summary, we can think of the brain as supporting a number of different types of memory that normally work seamlessly and easily together. First, there is a system concerned with short-term or working memories, which processes information over a period of seconds to perhaps minutes; second, there is a parallel brain system concerned with procedural learning—things like being able to play the piano, being able to ride a bicycle, how to write with a pen, how to type—memories that are by and large difficult to verbalize but are learned through practice; finally, there is a brain system concerned with supporting the recall of information about personally experienced events, the things that you experience during the course of everyday life. These systems interact with each other, and they also operate in parallel. It is clear, for example, that information in short-term memory may need at some point to get into long-term memory. It is clear that it is useful to know that you know how to do something, even if you are unable to articulate the basis on which you can do it, like being able to ride a bicycle.

How Do Memories Become Consolidated in the Brain?

We have just focused on the brain structures that are required for particular types of memory. We next need to address how memories are encoded by brain cells. There have been a series of suggestions about how memories can be laid down (or consolidated) in the brain. Alexander Bain, a British utilitarian philosopher, suggested (in 1855) that "for every active memory, every exercise of bodily aptitude, every habit, recollection, train of ideas, there is a specific grouping or coordination of sensations and movements by virtue of specific growths in the cell junctions" (p. 90). This idea influenced thinking over the coming 150 years very profoundly. The theory that connections between brain cells form the basis for memories was given its strongest impetus by the Spanish neuroanatomist Santiago Ramon y Cajal, who introduced the neuron doctrine (see Shepherd 1991 for a historical account). This is the hypothesis that the functional units of the brain were individual brain cells and that the key point of interaction between brain cells was the synapse (a denotation we owe to the neurophysiologist Charles Sherrington; see Burke 2007 for a historical account). D. O. Hebb gave us a theory by which the memory trace (engram) may be written into the brain. This was in his famous neurophysiological postulate. He suggested "that we should assume. . . . that the persistence or repetition of a reverberatory activity (or trace) tends to induce lasting cellular changes that add to its stability" (1949, 62). In other words, some form of reverberatory activity in a group of brain cells might cooperate with structural changes in the brain. These structural changes consolidate a memory in an enduring form over the long term. This idea gave rise to what is now known as Hebb's rule. This is a simply stated rule: "When an axon of a cell A is near enough to excite a cell B and repeatedly and persistently takes part in firing it, some growth process or metabolic change takes place in one or both cells so that A's efficiency as one of the cells firing B is increased" (Hebb 1949, 62). This rule has been reinterpreted in many ways. The most common one is that "cells that fire together wire together." The changes resulting from coactivity between brain cells is responsible for the laying down of memory traces in the brain. The Hebb rule is important because it suggests a specific hypothesis by which the brain encodes memories. It also suggests a means by which the hypothesis might be tested because it suggests that the functional unit underlying memory is the synapse. A different way of expressing this idea is that memory is woven into the very fabric of the brain. Disturb the fabric of the brain, through stress, injury, infection, or whatever, and you may disturb how memories encoded, consolidated, and retrieved by the brain.

The Frontal Lobes: Intention, Executive Function, Working Memory

The frontal lobes of the human brain have been the subject of investigation for at least 150 years. A very famous patient, Phineas Gage, came to light as a result of an accident during railway construction in the state of Vermont. Gage's story has been told many times now, but it has generated a wealth of hypotheses about the functions of the frontal lobes and has continued to do so right up to the present day. One day, Gage was blasting rock for a railway cutting. He had an accident with a tamping iron (a long metal rod of about one and a quarter inches in diameter and three feet seven inches in length), which was used to pack explosives into excavated fissures or holes in rock. This was a very dangerous occupation, as forcing the explosive into the rock would occasionally cause sparks and thus the explosive to ignite while the person holding the tamping iron was close by. This is exactly what happened to Gage; the tamping iron was blown from his hands, entered his cheek, passed through his eye, and emerged through the top of his skull, causing massive and extensive damage to his frontal lobes. Gage fell over unconscious and was lifted onto the back of a cart and left to die. Remarkably, he did not die and gradually recovered. But Gage's personality appeared to have changed quite dramatically. Case notes written up by his attending physician came to light, and Gage has become in death one of the most remarked on case studies in the history of neuropsychology. Dr. John Martyn Harlow noted that Gage was "no longer Gage" (1848, 392). Whereas before he had been a careful and attentive worker, he now was given to profanity and excessive drinking; he no longer paid attention to his family and became dissolute, rowdy, and difficult to deal with. He survived for about nine years postinjury—a remarkable period of time to survive at a time when neither antibiotics nor modern surgical techniques were available.

Subsequent case studies concluded that the original observations by Gage's physician pointed in an interesting direction. They have given rise to the modern idea that the seat of executive functions (that is, the functions of the brain that are concerned with intention, with planning, with impulse control, with delay of gratification, possibly even with volitional behavior) is largely localized to the frontal lobes. Patients who suffer damage to the frontal lobes are referred to as suffering from the dysexecutive syndrome (Baddeley and Wilson 1988). Patients suffering from this syndrome tend to be poor at delaying gratification for any particular desire they happen to have at any particular time. They have poor impulse control; they can be very aggressive and disinhibited and can be somewhat unpleasant people to be around. They also suffer from problems with short-term or working memory. Their working memory capacity tends to be reduced, particularly if there is damage to an area of the frontal lobes known as the dorso-lateral prefrontal cortex (DLPFC). They also have difficulty in intentionally accessing memories; in other words, their ability to recall specific items of information from their past can be compromised as the result of the damage that they have suffered. Indeed, brain-imaging studies that focus on activations during intentional memory-retrieval tasks disclose a network of activations involving the frontal lobes, the temporal lobes, and the hippocampal formation during the intentional recall of information from long-term memory.

Brain Networks Supporting Memory

The brain systems that regulate memory, intention, and stress have been identified and much probed over the past twenty or thirty years. Standard human episodic memory is supported by a network of brain areas including the hippocampal formation, the cortices of the temporal lobe, the anterior thalamic nuclei, and other structures such as the mammillary nuclei. Recalling previously learned information activates a variety of brain areas, especially prefrontal cortex and the hippocampus. Moreover, activity in prefrontal cortex is particularly associated with intentionally controlling access to, and retrieval of, memories. These brain areas are extensively interconnected with the frontal lobes and also send large outputs into the hypothalamic-pituitary-adrenal (HPA) axis. This means that there is a strong output from these brain areas focused on the brain and body systems concerned with regulating the response to stress. The HPA axis in turn sends both direct and indirect return inputs to the frontal lobes and the hippocampal formation. Each one of these brain systems is involved in regulating the other, so much so that it would be reasonable to refer to them as a *reciprocal triad of interconnected and coregulating* brain areas. The structural and functional integrity of the hippocampus and the prefrontal cortices, as well as regular sleep, are essential for normal memory function. When these brain areas function improperly, both memory and executive functions (intention, planning, and regulation of behavior) can be impaired (see, for example, Aggleton and colleagues 2010 and the references therein).

The Fallibility of Memory

Memory has a constructive and reconstructive quality. Formally, we can show that memory is fallible by means of forgetting curves, which plot the decay in recall for test items over time. We can show that people have a very poor memory for all sorts of events and that they even have a very poor memory for their own attitudes through time. Moreover, we can show that memory itself can vary according to the demands of the circumstances that are placed on memory; for example, when one is with a group and the group asserts that such-and-such a set of events happened, you modify your own recall to comply with the consensus memory of the group. Data of this type challenge profoundly any simple videotape model of memory. The implication here is again straightforward: the memories of interviewees need to be elicited with great care and subtlety in order to avoid contamination by the interviewer. Can we realistically assume that memories are stable and reliable? In short, we cannot and should not; we should understand and accept that memory is fallible and that memories are not necessarily stable or unstable. It is the case, though, that the failures of human memory, while numerous, can be understood.

Daniel Schacter of Harvard University has written a famous book titled *The Seven Sins of Memory* (2001; see also Schacter 1999). In this book, he isolates the pervasive problems with human memory, naming them as follows: transience, absent-mindedness, blocking, misattribution, suggestibility, bias, and persistence. His important and substantive point is to emphasize the frailty and fragility of memory (and, by implication, the boundedness of individual cognition). This list of seven sins can be classified into two groups. The first is the so-called sins of omission; these are transience, absent-mindedness, and blocking. The result here is a failure to recall something, for example, facts or events. The second category is the sins of commission: these are misattribution, susceptibility, bias, and persistence, when you have a memory of something and this memory is not correct, or there is some pathological quality to this memory. We will examine each of these sins in greater detail.

Transience refers simply to the fact that particular memories decay over time. The quality and quantity of a memory that we can access diminishes as time passes. *Blocking* occurs when one memory interferes with another. A common example of this is the tip-of-the-tongue phenomenon, in which something is almost accessible but for some reason your ability to find a particular word is just not quite there. *Misattribution* is a problem with source monitoring. This is when a memory that is correct is retrieved, but the source itself is misattributed. *Suggestibility* occurs when memories are distorted in some way by the provision of new information or leading questions, as, for example, when you are led to believe over the course of questioning that something is true that is not, because of the presence of new or misleading information in the question. Courtrooms usually have strict rules about the use of leading questions for this very reason. *Bias* in memory refers simply to the effects of emotion, age, mood, preparedness, and other variables on memory, either in the conditions under which the memory itself was initially acquired or during recall. Bias can occur at either of these stages. In a classic study on consistency, Gregory Markus (1986) tracked political attitudes of individuals through time (from 1973 to 1982) and looked at the extent to which individual attitudes shifted from liberal to conservative over that time. He then asked people to state how conservative they were on the previous occasion that their conservatism was measured and compared that with the results that they gave at the time. The results are striking: people remembered themselves as being more conservative nine years before than they actually were at that time. In other words, their recall of what they were like at some point in the past was modified in order that it be consistent with their present political attitudes. *Persistence* can be pathological; it occurs when intrusive and disturbing memories, for example, of trauma, persistently appear in consciousness. This is common in posttraumatic stress disorder, in which the sounds and images of the traumatic event are persistently intrusive for the sufferer.

Why do these phenomena occur? Memory is not a photographic record where the events that occur in one's life are passively logged and accessed easily without difficulty at any particular point in time. Instead, it appears that what people remember is the gist of a memory and not the full experience in its original and veridical form. There are all sorts of reasons why this might be the case, but the simplest reason is probably that this is the price that we pay for having a memory that serves us as well as it does in everyday life. Word-access failures, that is, our inability to remember particular words, happen with some frequency, but the average adult knows somewhere between 15,000 and 20,000 words and can access these words during conversation or reading with great facility, ease, and millisecond precision. Our memory is astonishingly good at acquiring a wide variety of skills and information across a wide variety of domains, but the consequence of this ease of acquisition is that memories of events and information can become distorted over time.

We will now discuss some examples of this fallibility because, in the context of our discussion, they are especially revealing, and they have a particular relevance, given the real-world events to which they refer. The first is an example of the variability through time of

President George W. Bush's memory for the events of 9/11: the public record of his recall changes through time. The second again uses the events of 9/11 to examine people's recall of what happened at that time, their recall of the specific events, including how they felt, to examine the malleability of memory over time. Finally, we will examine how others can influence our recall and what the neural basis for this kind of influence on our memory is.

Flashbulb Memories as an Example of the Inconsistency of Memory through Time

When I think of September 11, 2001, it has a clarity and quality that September 11, 2000, or indeed any other random September 11 does not have for me. This quality is sometimes referred to as a flashbulb memory, a memory that has a picture-like quality, a vividness and an emotional content. The story of that day is told and retold over time. Memories of this type assume an apparent resilience in one's own mind that they may actually not have when compared to records of what really happened. The events of this day therefore provide a suitable test bed against which to test changes, distortions, or omissions in memory through time. In other words, they will allow us, given the extensive public records that are available, to look for the presence of at least some of the seven deadly sins of memory. Quite a number of articles have appeared examining recall for the events of 9/11 and how recall of these events can become distorted over time. Daniel Greenberg of Duke University provides one such case study in the journal *Applied Cognitive Psychology*: the apparent false flashbulb memory of President George W. Bush for the events of that day. President Bush was interviewed on three occasions (December 4, 2001; December 20, 2001; and January 5, 2002), when he described what he was doing and what he felt during the events of 9/11. For memory 1 and memory 3 (December 4, 2001; and January 5, 2002), he recalls watching the events on TV; but we know this was not the case as he was sitting in a classroom in Florida at the time, and there was no footage available at that time of the events. In memory 2, December 20, 2001, he recalls his adviser Karl Rove bringing him the news. As Greenberg notes, conspiracy theories are not needed to explain these inconsistencies. In President Bush's case, given the all-pervasive nature of the coverage and the huge political stresses and strain he must have been under, the reconstructive aspect of his recollective memory had not finalized a complete narrative. As Greenberg puts it, "like so many others, he appears to be suffering from a near textbook case of false recall" (2004, 367).

The psychologists Jennifer Talarico and David Rubin of Duke University have examined the nature of flashbulb memories for 9/11. They asked fifty-four Duke University students to record their memories of the 9/11 attacks on September 12, 2001, that is, within twenty-four hours of the events occurring. They also asked the students to record their memories of a recent everyday event. The students completed an open-ended questionnaire with a variety of questions that probed what they were doing and where they were when they heard the news, and they also completed the Autobiographical Memory Questionnaire (AMQ). Talarico and Rubin then tested the participants one week, six weeks, or thirty-two weeks later. They found that the consistency and inconsistency for flashbulb memories and everyday memories was about the same. In other words, the frequency with which distortions and incorrect memories appeared was the same for everyday memories as it was for flashbulb memories over time. The key difference was that people had strong emotional feelings about the events of 9/11 that they did not have for everyday memories, and these feelings correlated very strongly with their own beliefs in the accuracy of recall *but not with the consistency* of their own memories. The authors summarized this finding in the pithy title to their article, "Confidence, Not Consistency, Characterises Flashbulb Memories," in which they conclude that "a flashbulb event reliably enhances memory characteristics such as vividness and confidence" (2003, 455). They leave us with an interesting question of why people are so confident for so long in the accuracy of their own flashbulb memories. We should as a consequence learn to tease apart the confidence or certainty that someone has in a memory from the content and accuracy of the memory. We can be both completely confident and completely wrong in our recall.

The issue of changes in the consistency of memory over time is addressed in a large-scale study by researchers who conducted a study of 3,000 people in seven U.S. cities. William Hirst and his colleagues (2009) examined memories one month, eleven months, and thirty-five months after 9/11, focusing on four particular issues:

1. The long-term retention of flashbulb and event memories.

2. The comparative retention of emotional reactions with the retention of other features of a flashbulb event.

3. Possible differences in the underlying processing associated with the formation and retention of flashbulb and event memories.

4. The factors shaping long-term retention, including the role of memory practices for the events of 9/11.

The methodology the researchers adopted consisted of longitudinally administered repeated surveys (available online at 911memory .nyu.edu). These surveys were repeated through time in order to compare the rate of forgetting a year after the events of September 11 with the rate of forgetting after three years. Hirst and his colleagues examined the relationship between forgetting and flashbulb memory and between forgetting and event memory. They found that the rate of forgetting of a flashbulb memory slows substantially after a year; in other words, the rate of forgetting slows from year 1 to year 3. They also found that the memories for the emotions specifically present at the time of the events were forgotten more quickly; they were not remembered as well as the specific features associated with the event. These studies and others like them are very important in revealing that even very publicly visible events that involve substantial images of trauma and death replayed regularly and consistently in the media, for which the images are very well available, still become, at the individual level, subject to distortion in recollection over time. Studies like these are useful because the conditions of encoding are more or less similar across individuals. Except for those who were directly present at the site of the events, people will experience the events through television, over the Internet, over the radio, and via newspapers and other media, so the conditions of learning are more or less similar across a great diversity of individuals. Because the events were a one-time occurrence but hugely significant, the content of the memory is controlled for across individuals. In turn, this means that the contents and context of the memory can be verified against the external contemporary record that is available. The recollections of the individuals themselves can be tested through time against both the public record and the record of what it was that they recalled at that particular time. The longitudinal aspect of studies like this is particularly valuable because it allows a within-subject comparison: in other words, the measurement of the change in the evolution of one's own memories through time. Studies like this point to the reality that memories do change through time; what we believe about our own memories and about what we have done at particular points in time can be inconsistent with what actually happened at that time. Given the preceding discussion, the utterances of detainees in response to standardized questioning through time would be very useful as a source of data for empirical investigation. It would be most useful and instructive if systematic analyses of these types were conducted on the repeatedly elicited verbal protocols collected from questioned detainees. In principle, it should be possible, assuming questioning occurs in a systematic and reliable fashion, to assess the changes through time and questioning of the elicited memories of interviewed detainees. Regrettably, such large-scale analyses are unavailable (or at least are unpublished in the peer-reviewed literatures).

Eyewitness Testimony

It is practically a truism in psychology that the testimony of eyewitnesses regarding personally witnessed events can be very variable and inaccurate. Elizabeth Loftus (of the University of Washington) has uncovered a whole variety of such phenomena (Loftus and Doyle 1997). For example, if you show participants a movie of a car crash, say, a blue car that drives through a junction and hits a red car, and you ask them at some time point later, "How fast was the black car going when it crashed into the yellow car?" a substantial number of people will remember the presence of a black car and a yellow car, despite the fact that they were originally exposed to a blue car and a red car. This is the misinformation effect, and it is a demonstration that eyewitness memory can be easily contaminated by postevent information supplied by leading questions or other sources. The type of question asked can profoundly affect people's memory function as well. If you prime people in different ways, using words such as *collided* or *crashed* or *speeded,* the average estimates of the speed at which the car was traveling will be considerably greater than if you use words like *moving* or other words to indicate that the car may have been traveling at a slower speed.

This particular topic is especially important to explore, as it bears directly on three very important questions: (a) What effect does stress have on the initial learning or acquisition of information? (b) What effect does stress have when it occurs in the interval between learning and subsequent recall? And (c) What effect does stress imposed at the time of recall have on information recalled? Answers to these questions speak to what can be reliably elicited from an interviewee during the course of an interview or interrogation. Extensive investigations have been conducted into these questions both in human participants and in relevant preclinical animal models of cognition and memory.

Charles Morgan of Yale University, whose work with combat soldiers we will explore at greater length later, has conducted extensive experiments examining the effects of intense stressors on a wide variety of psychiatric, hormonal, and other outcomes in military personnel. In one set of experiments, he has examined the eyewitness memories reported by combat veterans who are exposed to life-threatening events during simulated combat. Morgan and his colleagues have shown that their testimony can be very inconsistent and that it is subject to very substantial error. These soldiers were confined to a mock prisoner-of-war camp; they were placed in isolation and subjected to interrogation after forty-eight hours of sleep deprivation and food deprivation. The type of interrogation varied: the participants were either exposed to high-intensity interrogation first, with physical confrontations that were very real and substantial in nature, and then subjected to low-stress interrogations in which no physical confrontation was present; or they were exposed to the reverse conditions—they were engaged in low-stress interrogation first, followed by a high-stress interrogation that involved a real physical confrontation. Participants were then asked to identify their interrogators via either a lineup, a photo spread, or a sequential photo presentation. The researchers also measured psychological symptoms of dissociation using the Clinician-Administered Dissociative States Scale (CADSS). They examined the rate at which subjects across low-stress to high-stress conditions showed identifications of their interrogators that were either true positive, false positive, true negative (when they identified correctly that a foil—a person who had not interrogated them—did not, in fact, interrogate them); and false positive (when they misidentified somebody who had not interrogated them as having interrogated them). They found, across all conditions, a remarkable outcome. To quote the study,

"Contrary to the popular conception that most people would never forget the face of a clearly seen individual who had physically confronted them and threatened them for more than thirty minutes, a large number of subjects in this study were unable to correctly identify their perpetrator. These data provide robust evidence that eyewitness memory, for persons encountered during events that are personally relevant, highly stressful, and realistic in nature, may be subject to substantial error" (Morgan and colleagues 2004, 274). In fact, the data show that the greater the level of stress experienced, the worse the level of performance. For example, the true (positive) response rate in the high-stress condition was only between 30 and 49 percent, depending on whether a live lineup or a sequential photo presentation of the interrogators was used; whereas in the low-stress condition, the correct rates were as high as between 62 and 76 percent. Similarly, the false-positive rates, in the high-stress condition, were very high indeed, varying between 51 and 68 percent (depending on the presentation method); whereas, in the low-stress condition, they were only between 12 and 38 percent. Stress hormones were not measured in this particular study, so it is not possible to give an independent measure of the extent to which stress hormones were provoked by the conditions of the study. However, the participants were all experienced military personnel who might be expected, as a result of their training, to have developed some reserve or resilience where stress is concerned. Despite this, they still showed substantial errors in eyewitness identification. Morgan and colleagues conclude, "All professionals would do well to remember that a large number of healthy individuals may not be able to correctly identify suspects associated with highly stressful, compared to moderately stressful, events" (277). Interestingly, the confidence ratings of the soldiers were more or less the same across all categories, so despite the fact that the subjects made very substantial numbers of errors in the high-stress conditions, their confidence in their own judgment was more or less the same as their confidence in the low-stress condition. This suggests that one's level of confidence in one's own judgment of one's own memory can be separated from the accuracy of that memory, especially under conditions of stress. Interrogators would do well to remember that a high level of asserted or apparent confidence for a memory is not a good proxy for the accuracy of that judgment. There is a further key point to draw out here: the soldiers in the study were willing participants. In other words, compliance and motivational state were not issues that would affect performance. And yet performance is hugely and substantially degraded by these stressors. How degraded will performance be in someone who is subjected to the extreme stressor states imposed during torture?

Some degree of psychological or psychiatric distress is reasonable to expect in detainees. It would be useful also therefore to understand how recall is affected in a group suffering posttraumatic stress disorder (PTSD). Jianjian Qin and colleagues (2003) examined a group of psychiatric patients for their reactions to and memories of the September 11 attacks. They conducted a survey approximately one month and ten months after the attacks. They found that the PTSD groups were more negatively affected compared to a trauma control group—not a terribly surprising finding, as this is a vulnerable group. However, an interesting pattern occurred across time for the PTSD group. The initial autobiographical memories and event memories recalled were about the same for the PTSD group and the control group, but significant forgetting of event memory occurred in the PTSD group. At the same time, emotional aspects of the memory became inflated—that is, they were overexpressed and overemphasized. One possible problem with this study is that the return rates of the second survey at time point 2, three to four months later, were significantly down (by about 35 percent in controls and 50 percent in the PTSD group). The key point, however, is that this group, because of a preexisting psychopathology, experienced significant distortions in the content of their memory over time. We have previously mentioned the concept of "breaking someone," which means subjecting a person to sufficiently prolonged stressors that substantial, negative, and enduring changes in his or her personality and behavior occur. How is this different from a PTSD patient or indeed any other patient in extreme psychiatric distress? And is inducing such extreme psychiatric distress without effect on memory? We can only conclude otherwise.

These studies show that in normal, healthy, and motivated adults, there is a significant distortion in memory through time, even after what is a relatively short period of time, from a few months to a year or so. There are all sorts of reasons for this: individual human cognition is frail, and it is bounded; our states of attention, emotion, motivation, and so on vary through time. The memory systems of the brain perform at high levels already, as we must more or less effortlessly recall staggering amounts of information and rapidly integrate it with our ongoing behavior in order to function adaptively according to current and future contexts. Encoding of detailed autobiographical knowledge might fall into the nice-to-know category rather than the must-know category, depending on the needs of the moment, as far as the brain is concerned. There may also be transactive memory processes at work. In social organizations and in social dyads (e.g., married couples), it may be that there are specializations in recall. One person may remember certain types of information (for example, one partner might remember all the birthdays of children and nieces and nephews, whereas the other might remember the position of all the tools and sports kit). Celia Harris and colleagues (2014) show that under situations of free recall, joint recollection paradigms result in quantitatively and qualitatively richer memories when both parties are actively engaged in recall. The social exchanges and discussions resulted in a shared, cooperative memory search that was superior to recall conducted alone. Interrogations that attempt to piece together knowledge about the activity of a group thus should not be based on the premise that each member of the group will have very similar memories of all the important events that happen in the group. As we shall see in Chapter 7, extreme similarity of shared memories may actually be evidence for the rehearsal of a made-up cover story.

How the Presence of a Group Can Distort the Memories of an Individual

Just being a member of a group—even one just brought together for the purposes of conducting an experiment—can have a profound effect on what you remember. Groups play an important role in moderating the memories of individuals who are part of the group. The group consensus about what has happened powerfully affects the memory an individual has of what actually did happen. This is a remarkable claim, but it can be demonstrated experimentally. There are many cases of false recollection occurring as a result of social pressure and interpersonal influence. This is a process known as memory conformity. It happens because of social interaction, exposure to mass media, or even as a result of leading questions in a courtroom setting. Knowing that exposure to group judgments about the past can significantly distort memory, the neuroscientist Micah Edelson and his colleagues from Israel and England conducted a study focusing on the effect of social conformity on the stability of memory over time. They first distinguish between "private conformity," when the actual memory representation of the person becomes altered because of exposure to the group, and "outward conformity," when the individuals go along, on the surface, with the judgment of the group but privately maintain their own judgment as to what is the "correct" memory. The key point here is that differing types of conformity rely on differing processes in the brain, despite the two conditions being *behaviorally* identical. It is not possible from looking at or listening to somebody's responses to know whether the person actually believes what he or she is saying or if the person is merely saying what he or she is saying because the group is saying it too. But it should be possible, in principal, to isolate brain signatures that discriminate between these two different cases. We should expect to see distinct patterns of activations of certain circuits in the brain that support memory and social cognition corresponding to these two different conditions.

The researchers devised a clever four-part protocol to manipulate memories via social processes. At time point 1, participants came to the lab in groups of five and viewed a documentary. At time point 2, three days later, they completed a memory test, which provided a baseline for their memory of the documentary that they had viewed. At time point 3, four days later, they came back to the lab and lay in a brain imaging (MRI) scanner while answering the same questions as before. On this occasion, however, they were provided, on some trials, with the false answers of their companions to questions about the content of the documentary. They were shown the pictures of the people they had viewed the documentary with and were given their consensus answers (which were false) regarding incidents in the documentary. A battery of appropriate controls was conducted as well. Then, at time point 4, the subjects were brought back to answer the memory test again and told that the answers that their companions had given were chosen randomly. This manipulation makes the answers that their companions had given (more or less) uninformative. The data were very striking: behavioral memory errors were strikingly easy to induce. Participants conformed to the majority judgment (the *false* judgment) in 68 percent of trials. When they were told that the answers given by the majority were actually random answers and not correct answers, they reverted to their own previous correct answer in 60 percent of the trials. This means that they maintained an erroneous or incorrect memory as a result of this social conformity intervention in 40 percent of the trials. Despite being told that the answers that they had been provided were uninformative (because of the prior exposure to the answers of the group:

the four other companions they had viewed the film with), participants continued, at least 40 percent of the time, to falsely recall incorrect answers.

The brain told its own story, too, on the social intervention trials. A particular activation signature was found that predicted private conformity—the now-changed memory. The amygdala showed enhanced activation on these trials. Moreover, an analysis of the strength of connectivity between the hippocampal formation and the amygdala showed that the strength of the connectivity was increased between these structures. When these two conditions were present in the brain, it was possible to predict, at the group level, the long-lasting alterations to memory that resulted from the group intervention. The researchers' conclusions are very striking: "memory is highly susceptible to alteration due to social influence, creating both transient and persistent errors" (Edelson and colleagues 2011, 110). These finding suggest that "this may be a mechanism by which social influence produces long-lasting alterations in memory" (110), and they highlight the critical role of the amygdala in mediating this influence. A final point is worth considering, which Edelson and his colleagues emphasize particularly. Humans are social beings and are involved in social and group contexts where differing individuals have different experiences. The researchers suggest that "memory conformity may also serve an adaptive purpose because social learning is often more efficient and accurate than individual learning. For this reason humans may be predisposed to trust the judgment of the group, even when it stands in opposition to their own original beliefs. Such influences and their long-term effects, the neurological basis of which we describe here, may contribute to the extraordinary levels of persistent conformity seen in authoritarian cults and societies" (111). This finding suggests that memory conformity can emerge in such groups and is sufficiently powerful that it can override individual memory processes. Interrogation of individuals from such groups may therefore be particularly problematic. The storytelling essential to the coherence of such groups may obliterate crucial and telling individual differences in memory that are vital for understanding the fine-grained detail of individual and group roles. The mythmaking occurring in such groups—which binds them together and for which an accurate memory of what happened would be a hindrance—likely has its origins in this plastic process of memory. Data of this type present a particular implication for the interpretation of verbal protocols elicited from differing individuals from the one group: memories of transactive group processes are likely to be both fluid and inconsistent within and between individuals and also across time—without any implication that any of the interviewees are actually lying or deliberately withholding information.

What lessons can we draw? First of all, a rational biology and psychology of memory is possible: we can point to places in the brain where changes occur that support the consolidation of memory over time, and we can decompose the processes underlying memory at a functional level. We can point to where these changes occur in the brain—mainly at the synapse. In turn, this means that we can now start to understand the processes that are responsible for the instantiation and consolidation of memories in the brain. We can also tease apart how different brain regions support memory. This also means that we are now starting to understand how memory loss from disease or aging might be attenuated or prevented. It also means that we are starting to understand the factors that impinge on memory: in particular, how insult (disease, stress, infection, torture, or head injury, for example), the mere passing of time, or even recalling previous memories can affect the acquisition of memories, on the one hand, and the recall of previously learned information, on the other. This should be the first point of concern for prospective interrogators: that what they say can and will be incorporated automatically into the memory of the person being interrogated or interviewed.

Regrettably, public debate about interrogation is almost completely ungrounded in what we know about memory. The lay assumption is that probing suspects' memories is a more or less straightforward affair—that repeated questioning of captives will not cause distortions in memory, or forgetting, inconsistencies in recollection through time, changes in accessibility of a memory over time, or failures to remember, and so on. This assumption is fallacious and incorrect (unless of course extreme care is taken). It is remarkable that these issues are ignored in the protorture affirmations provided by those who support the use of torture to extract information from the long-term memories of detainees. There is also the profound problem of interpreting what has been said by the captive, for what is not said (deliberately or otherwise) may be just as important in understanding what the verbal protocols collected actually mean. In other words, there is the difficulty of detecting and deciphering the meaning of the *absence* of a signal, as well as the *presence* of a signal. This is where theories of interrogation meet the brain but also meet social context. And all of this is before getting into the area of mutual incomprehension caused by language issues, when the interrogator and the person being interrogated are not native speakers of the same language and do not show a common cultural understanding of what words mean. After all, would it not be much easier if we could invent a machine that would unequivocally tell when someone was lying? Or develop a drug that would force someone to tell the truth? Then all the messiness of trying to understand if there are sins of memory occurring, or lying or simple misinterpretation, would just go away. It is to this simple wish, founded on a simpleminded exasperation with understanding the complexity of human conduct, that we turn to next—lying and how we might detect lying in others.

3

Can We Use Technology to Detect Deception?

Worried politician: It's very tough conducting full evidential investigations. Here's an idea: Can we invent a machine to directly interrogate the brains of captives, making lying a pointless tactic during interrogation? Because we could, you know, see their thoughts?

Vested interests: I don't know, but let's try. It'll cost a lot. Who will pay?

Disinterested party: Everyone. Wasted time. Wasted resources. Wasted hope.

Lots of money and lots of hope has been spent over the past century on the promise of new technologies that will make it easy to detect reliable indicators of lying and deception or even to go further—to reveal the actual thoughts held within the privacy of a person's mind. Revealing actual thoughts would be a most remarkable violation of cognitive liberty and of our assumed rights to cognitive privacy. The use of lie detectors during interrogations has been, and continues to be, controversial. Lie-detector technologies (and especially the polygraph) assume that lying causes activity in the autonomic nervous system and that this activity, when appropriately correlated with probe questions or challenges, will reveal an underlying pattern of lying. However, there is little good evidence that polygraph-based lie detectors are of any use at all to detect lies, because they both are easy to countermand and lack diagnostic sensitivity and specificity. A second issue with the polygraph lies in its theoretical underpinnings: it posits a relationship between underlying autonomic nervous system function and lying—a relationship that is not well founded experimentally or theoretically. A final point here is the institutionalized life that such tests can assume despite their uselessness. The former senior CIA counterterrorism figure Jose Rodriguez (2012) comments in his autobiography that polygraphs are widely used by the CIA, which is remarkable for a technique that has so little empirical support. It plays a role more akin to security theater—it has no real function at all. And into this void slips an even larger and more impressive machine: brain imaging.

Functional magnetic resonance imaging (fMRI) is a remarkable technology. Ostensibly, you can *see* the brain at work; apparently, you can even *see* the networks supporting thought in the brain. Lots of money has been spent on this technology, with high-flown promises of what it can reveal. The truth is, of course, more prosaic. These technologies are not silver bullets to detect lying and reveal truth as their proponents suggest them to be. Picking up a thread that runs through this book, the reliance on naive introspection, sometimes by people who should know better, is what provides the justification for using these devices in this context, despite lack of evidence for their efficacy, validity, or reliability for detecting lies or deception. We will discuss here specifically the use of fMRI as a technologically based lie-detector tool for interrogations, describe what they are alleged to measure, including their supposed relationship to lying, and show how they are not capable of fulfilling this purpose or promise.

Aldert Vrij and his colleagues describe and review the current state of the technological art to detect lying in the following terms:

> Nowadays, technology is used to measure physiological (and neurological) reactions—particularly the polygraph; voice-stress analyzers; electroencephalograms (EEG); and most recently,

functional magnetic resonance imaging (fMRI). The promotion of such tools can be aggressive. For example, companies have begun to offer fMRI deception-detection services to investigators. Two companies—Cephos Corporation in Massachusetts and No Lie MRI, Inc. in California—claim to know with at least 90% accuracy whether a subject is telling the truth (Stix, 2008). However, a very small number of published studies have examined brain function during deception, and such claims lack strong empirical foundation. (2010, 2).

This is quite a telling critique for anyone seeking a shortcut technofix for a complex and difficult problem (see Spence 2008 for a similar argument). It should also allay at least some of the worries that have been raised about the use of fMRI in the courtroom (Greely and Illes 2007). We will now examine the details of these differing claims.

There has been a century or longer quest to devise technologies that will unequivocally detect the presence of a lie on the part of the person who is interrogated. The polygraph in particular, a device that has been used principally in the United States over the past seven or eight decades, has been used in an attempt to detect the presence of lying. Laterally, with the advent of brain imaging, fMRI machines have also been used in this effort. There is one limit case that needs to be stated clearly here: assume, for a moment, that there is an unequivocal biomarker that is clearly, reliably, and only associated with lying (there is not, but let us pretend there is). Furthermore, this biomarker is present only when the participant tells a lie and is not associated with false positives (that is, it is not sometimes present during truth telling). Now, I emphasize that no such biomarker exists—but let us assume the counterfactual that it does. Then what? The answer is again straightforward: the presence of the biomarker does not provide any verdict of the content of cognition whatsoever: knowing that it is present provides you with a correlation between a brain state and a cognitive state but does not provide direct access to the contents of that cognitive state. So knowing there is a brain state suggesting that the interviewee is lying tells you nothing about the contents of the lie itself: the context of the lie, the intentions associated with the lie, underlying cognitive biases that may affect the content of the lie itself, or just straightforward faulty cognitions, misperceptions, or whatever, on behalf of the liar.

Imaging the Working Brain

Brain-imaging technologies are a ubiquitous tool in modern neuroscience institutes. At the Institute of Neuroscience at Trinity College, Dublin (where I work), we have several functional brain magnetic resonance imaging (fMRI) systems. These are quite remarkable machines. Our key human-brain-imaging system weighs approximately 4,600 kilograms and is about three meters high, three meters long, and about two meters wide. MRI machines do not come cheap and are not cheap to run. They require specialist personnel (physicists, radiographers, radiologists, and other medical and paramedical personnel), in addition to the workaday neuroscientist investigating the brain. Between the specialist construction works required at the site (water filtration, electrical, heat handling), the electromagnetic shielding, the MRI itself, specialized imaging coils, changing rooms, image readers, computers, the helium fill required to keep the magnet supercooled, and quench pipes, there will not be much change out of a few million dollars or Euros. Then add ongoing secretarial and administrative support, insurance costs, patient scheduling and time-tabling costs, research conduct costs (for example, ethics committees, subject recruitment, financial management costs associated with running research grants). And then add ongoing maintenance and upgrade costs, and opening the door for a medical-grade, modern, research-standard MRI facility is not cheap.

To imagine what an MRI looks like, picture a large rectangular box with a long, body-shaped tunnel in the center and an electrified, movable bed that can travel in and out of this tunnel. The hollow center tube is known as the bore, which contains the bed on which you lie while the MRI does its work. The bore is typically about 130 centimeters or so across, so space is at a premium. This is not a pleasant place to be if you suffer from claustrophobia. As a result, MRIs are usually supplied with panic buttons, and the operator will usually be in constant microphone contact with the patient or research participant. The MRI machine sits in a room within a room—an electrically isolated, temperature-controlled room lit with muted colors. There is a constant low-level hum and, occasionally, louder noises still. This machine can take very high-quality, thinly sliced pictures through any part of the body. The quality of these images is something to behold. Short of actually dissecting the brain, these images are probably as good as you can routinely obtain. A structural scan of this type takes about ten to fifteen minutes to perform. This kind of imaging is known as structural imaging—the taking of images or pictures of the structure of the brain and body. Structural MRI scans are a routine part of medical technology and diagnostic medical investigations. They are safe and noninvasive and do not involve radioactivity. The MRI generates very strong spinning magnetic fields, focused around the part of the body that a picture is needed of. These scans allow physicians to see the internal structure of the body quickly and easily. Structural scans can allow the detection of, for example, the exact location of fractures, soft-tissue injuries, or certain tumors. There are very strict protocols for using these machines. Research participants must remove all sources of metal from their persons—keys, coins, glasses, wallets. The presence of metal is dangerous because it can both heat up and be accelerated by the magnetic fields present. Fragments of metal in the body might be induced to move, causing injury. Tattoos containing extensive amounts of iron oxide have been a worry for some clinicians, given the possibility that they might heat up during the imaging procedure.

Functional magnetic resonance imaging, or fMRI, lies at the heart of the modern attempt to detect deception or lying by a third party. fMRI relies on changes in the hemodynamic response, that is, changes in local or regional blood flow in specific brain areas that are observed during the performance of some neural activity. The principal method that is almost universally relied on is the blood-oxygen-level dependent (BOLD) contrast. This contrast relies on the idea that neural activity requires energy, which is supplied by oxygen uptake in a brain region. Tasks requiring more effort will require more energy, or tasks that require greater levels of activity will require more energy (I simplify). Statistical analysis and experimental design in fMRI studies are not straightforward affairs. After data acquisition, the data must then be subjected to a variety of quality checks to ensure that there is little by way of artifact present, including from the subject's own motion, respiration, and heart rate. Trials may have to be excluded, or indeed subjects may have to be excluded for a variety of reasons, including equipment failures, subject noncompliance, or other reliability issues with regard to the execution of the experiments. The dramatic images that we see of brain-area activations (what is sometimes referred to as blobology) are the end stage of a long series of decisions that are made by a variety of involved individuals. Thus, initial decisions revolve around the form of experimental design: will this be event related, or will this be a block design (these are the most common experimental designs)? Or will it be a more exotic experimental design? Both of the common experimental designs require the presentation of appropriate challenge stimuli in a particular temporal sequence. Averaging of neural responses on the basis of the timing of the presentation of those stimuli is then conducted. Thereafter, there are a series of decisions that are required in order to analyze the data. These include decisions about the size of the voxels (cubes of brain tissue within which neural activations are measured). Voxels that are too large or too small risk either false positives or false negatives in the data. Then there need to be decisions made about whether analyses of a particular region of interest should be conducted. These decisions in turn will determine the degree of statistical correction that needs to be applied in order to ensure that false, though statistically significant, outcomes are not obtained. Then a decision must be made about which statistical analysis package to use (such as SPM, AFNI, Brain Voyager, or a homegrown suite of tools). Then the relevant experimental contrasts must be chosen and the analyses performed, and the data acquired from an individual must be then translated into a common brain projection, typically the Talairach coordinate space (there are other such neural coordinate spaces too). At this point, problems of theory and interpretation begin. In order to make sense of the data that have been acquired, you must have an underlying theory of the cognitive processes that a particular neural circuit will support. Note that you do not have access to the contents of the information being processed in that brain circuit: what you have is access to inferences about what may be going on in that brain circuit. These are not the same thing. Furthermore, the BOLD signal itself is not causal. It is the end-stage readout of a series of prior neurophysiological and haemodynamic processes.

I have belabored the analysis points here (and, by the standards employed in the field, have merely sketched them in very preliminary outline) in order to convey a sense to the uninitiated about how nonstraightforward brain imaging is. The naive, and especially the experimentally naive, might assume that these are all settled issues. They are not. The BOLD signal was first described as recently as 1990, and there is a fevered debate within cognitive neuroscience about precisely what activations observed under any particular set of circumstances denote. The key point to convey here is that this is a young science. It has made great strides in a comparatively short span of time, but those who have expert knowledge in the field (as opposed to superficial acquaintance and naive expectations) are very clear about what is and is not possible to achieve using these techniques. The problem in a nutshell is that without a mechanistic and causal account of the underlying psychological processes that are used in lying and deception, it will be very difficult to relate changes in neural activation to any particular psychological state. The assumption here that technology will easily and reliably provide the answer to the question of whether a particular individual is lying is simply misguided.

Imaging the Exact Cognitive Contents of the Lying Brain: A Fool's Errand

The popular and technical press have run sometimes very substantial articles that discuss the possibility of brain-imaging-based lie detection. Margaret Talbot had a substantial piece in the *New Yorker* (2007), for example, in which she says (correctly), "Maybe it's because we're such poor lie detectors that we have kept alive the dream of a foolproof lie-detecting machine." She notes further that entrepreneurs have jumped into the area, hoping to sell services for lie detection, perhaps to the private sector or to government agencies. Talbot also (correctly) damns the polygraph because the false-positive rate is far too high. The polygraph's uselessness as a lie detector has been dealt with extensively elsewhere, and I therefore will not deal with it here, apart from making a few points that apply similarly to brain imaging. First, false positives and false negatives are a profound problem for the polygraph: a false-positive rate of 10 percent is substantial and in the medical diagnostic domain (for example, for cancer detection) would be sufficient to invalidate the test (see below). Given the poor quality data available because of the difficulty of actually operationalizing lying and its relationship to autonomic nervous system reactivity, it is difficult to comment meaningfully on either the sensitivity or specificity of the test.

David Colquhoun (2014a, 2014b), a mathematical biomedical scientist, provides a useful discussion that is of direct relevance to the use of these tests. Colquhoun uses a specific example—a widely publicized test for mild cognitive impairment (MCI), a condition marked by memory deficits that are substantially greater for a given age within the relevant age-risk group than would otherwise be expected. MCI is regarded as an imperfect predictor of the future probability that someone will subsequently succumb to Alzheimer's disease: estimates suggest that in a given population of people with the MCI diagnosis, approximately 25 percent will convert to Alzheimer's disease within twelve to twenty-four months. Tests for MCI are therefore vitally important and medically necessary. Colquhoun discusses a particular test for MCI with a specificity of 95 percent (implying that 95 percent of the healthy will get a correct negative test) and a sensitivity of 80 percent (implying that 80 percent of people with MCI are correctly diagnosed). Now, here is the problem: for MCI, with an estimate of the population affected by the disease, when you do the calculations, the false-positive rate is actually 86 percent. This is because sensitivity, specificity, and population prevalence (base rates) are different concepts with different outcomes, but at least they can be estimated for this condition. The point here is that this test for MCI—a condition that involves a substantial impairment in a central component of ongoing cognition, namely, memory—is actually pretty poor. Lying and deception involve several cognitive processes, as will be discussed later. One might, not unreasonably, expect that such a substantial cognitive impairment, prodromal to a devastating neurodegenerative condition, namely, Alzheimer's disease, would reveal itself easily and obviously through diagnostic testing; but this is not necessarily the case at all. What is the likelihood, then, of such a subtle cognitive process as lying and deceptive intent being detected so easily?

A similar sensitivity, specificity, and base-rate analysis has been performed by Martha Farah and her colleagues (2014) in relation to detecting lying and deception using brain imaging. They examine a study by Andrew Kozel and colleagues (2009) that uses fMRI to attempt to detect a mock sabotage crime. Kozel and colleagues claimed to correctly detect deception in 100 percent of participants in one condition but also mistakenly detected deception when it was not present on 67 percent of occasions in another condition. This false-positive rate indicates that while the sensitivity might be high, the specificity is low. Now consider the missing element here—the base rate for deception or lying in the relevant population. A simple calculation shows that in a population of 101, with 1 liar and 100 truth tellers, this test would detect 68 as liars (1 actual liar and 67 honest individuals). This shows that the chances of the test disclosing the liar are about 1 in 68 (or less than 1.5 percent), and conversely, the likelihood of incorrectly detecting deception when it is not present is greater than 98 percent. This is the paradox underlying these forms of diagnostic tests—they are performed on populations from which estimates can be derived, against which an individual diagnosis can be estimated, and then confirmed or not against other evidence (for example, cell samples, blood, or whatever). No such body of reliable and replicable data exists for lie detection with fMRI (or indeed with the polygraph).

As noted earlier, since the advent of brain-imaging techniques, there has been the hope that brain imaging would provide, in some way or other, unequivocal evidence that a person is engaging in deception. Unsurprisingly, there has been a great experimental effort to try to demonstrate that this is so. There are, as has been already noted, a great number of difficulties with the use of brain imaging as a tool for detecting deception. The first is a straightforward conceptual one: the simple fact that an activation is observed in a particular brain area does not tell you anything about the cognitive processes that are occurring in that area. This problem is exacerbated by the fact that the typical output of fMRI studies represents a group-averaged brain, rather than the brain of an individual. These images will have been generated by averaging across individuals and standardizing the image into a single space that is not necessarily representative of any particular brain that may have been studied. A second issue that has bedeviled the brain-imaging literature generally, and the fMRI literature in particular, is a statistical issue, namely, that of whether studies have been adequately statistically powered to detect changes that are statistically significant, not arising as a result of chance, and that have a meaningful effect size associated with them (and this having put to one side the unsolved issue of the relationship among the cognitive processes that are involved in generating a lie, in uttering a lie, in holding that lie online while it is being generated, and in supporting any other form of behavior).

There have been many reports in the literature claiming some degree of success in discriminating groups that may have engaged in deception, on the one hand, and groups that have not, on the other (for example, Ganis and colleagues 2003). There are two significant problems here. The first is that brain imaging has been subject to a significant false-positive problem (arising in part because experimental designs are statistically underpowered). The second is a significant file-drawer problem. A file-drawer problem arises when nonsignificant results are not published, with the consequence that we are unable to tell whether an effect is truly present or truly absent because we have no reliable estimate of base rates. This is a problem that has really come to the fore in a whole variety of domains with regard to biomedical science in the past few years, because of the bias in the literature toward the publication of positive results.

A very important article by Katherine Button and her colleagues of the University of Oxford (2013) places the power issue in stark relief. It suggests that, given the problem with false positives and the looseness of statistical fit and statistical modeling that can occur in fMRI studies, we need to ignore, or at least treat with a very high degree of caution, studies that have been conducted with less than approximately twenty to forty subjects per condition and in which a hypothesis about a particular region of interest has not been stated.

Additionally, we can probably include the criterion that we should treat with a great degree of caution reports that do not conduct an independent replication within the same study to ensure that the effect found is real or for which the effect is not easily replicated by other research groups or in which there have not been other measures taken (for example, of respiratory or cardiac function or other variables) for which the underlying physiology is already well understood. These caveats, unfortunately, remove probably most, if not all, of the previous studies conducted in this area. This leaves us with a small core group of studies that claim, at the population level, that it is possible to distinguish truth tellers from liars. We will discuss some of these studies here, but bear in mind during the course of the discussion the tremendously unsophisticated paradigms that are used, in contrast to humans' capacity for engaging in differing types of lies. Finally, we will also discuss measures that can be taken that obviate the effects found in these experiments.

Lying in the Real World

Humans are remarkably bad at determining if another human is lying to them, but humans are also remarkably good at lying. How else can we account for the astonishing rise of the confidence trickster Bernie Madoff, who amassed and spent a staggering fortune through a modern-day Ponzi scheme? The evidence that he was generating consistent 20 percent year-on-year returns for his clients was taken, by those who wanted to believe him, as evidence of his financial genius and acumen. For others, and especially for the whistle-blower Harry Markopolos, the consistency of his returns was actually evidence that something was afoot, that some form of wrongdoing was ongoing. It took eight years (from 2000 to 2008) from Markopolos making his initial presentations suggesting that Madoff was running an old-fashioned Ponzi scheme to Madoff finally confessing to what he had done. Madoff appears to have hoodwinked about 4,800 clients to the tune of perhaps $17 billion over a thirty-year period. Think of this for a moment: what an astonishing period to lie over, what an astonishing number of people who were taken in by his lies, and how astonishing that his lies were not detected over this time! Being rich does not confer immunity against gullibility, and of course, plain human greed nursed the lie, as it often does.

But then humans are just pretty poor at detecting when other people lie to them. One of the most extensive reviews of the experimental literature on the detection of lies (an analysis of 206 studies) showed that people detected lies on 54 percent of occasions—when chance was set at 50 percent. This means that laypeople can just about detect lying on some very few numbers of occasions, but they would be nearly as well off guessing when they think someone else is lying. Paradoxically, however, laypeople believe they are good at detecting lies—another good example of when confidence in one's abilities and one's actual abilities are greatly at variance with each other. At least part of the reason people believe in their lie-detecting abilities is because they believe that if you are good at doing something that of its essence is covert and unobservable, then you are good at detecting whether someone else is doing that same thing. This, of course, may be true for external behaviors—for example, it would be surprising if a good soccer player could not detect if another soccer player was any good. In this case, though, the objective and consensual criteria for being a good soccer player are well understood. These range from being a consistently good goal scorer to how well you play on the team and are able to merge your playing game with that of others on your team. We can judge how the quality of someone else's speech—its clarity, its emotional content—affects us in some way. But when matters of lying about fact are concerned, we are on very shaky ground indeed. We can lie easily; therefore, we should be able to detect lying easily. But the very fact that we can lie easily, and that the lie can go undetected, should cause us to think that perhaps others can lie easily too. And how would we know? Professional lie detectors (for example, police officers, who should know better), when they are tested experimentally using, for example, videotapes of people telling lies and the truth, are more confident than are laypeople of their ability to judge who is lying but are no more successful at detecting lies.

Lying is an emergent and spontaneous behavior. Children learn to tell lies from a very early age, and they learn to do so spontaneously. Studies indicate that in a normal child, the average age at which they start to conceal information from their parents is from about the age of three or so. There may be a straightforward adaptive value to lying—it allows a transgressor to avoid punishment, if he or she is successful. Victoria Talwar and Kang Lee (2011) of the University of Toronto have found that three- to four-year-old children educated in a punitive school (compared to a nonpunitive school) were about twice as willing to lie and better able to conceal the lie. Children were left alone in a room with a toy that they were asked not to peek at. The punitive schoolchildren were much more likely to lie about peeking, compared with the non-punitive schoolchildren. Follow-up questioning showed that the punitive schoolchildren were better at monitoring the deception, compared to the nonpunitive schoolchildren. Here is an outcome that folk psychology does not predict: spare the rod and spoil the child. Adults are not likely to be much different, are they?

The psychologists Maria Hartwig and Charles Bond (2011) make the point that there are two major classes of lie, which they classify as "self-oriented" and "other-oriented." Self-oriented lies are lies that are designed to increase one's own social desirability, for example, or to decrease the risk or severity of punishment because of some transgression or other. Other-oriented lies are lies to protect feelings in others or to protect the nature of social relationships with others. Lying is therefore a very complex behavior, involving cognition, emotion, motivation, and even motor behavior. The motives for lying and the consequences of lying may not be clear, even to liars themselves. Furthermore, lying has a contextual and transactional component: excluding the case when one has to lie or when one fools oneself, there is a context within which lies occur (lying to particular people and for some particular reason). Furthermore, lying may be by omission or may be even more subtle than that—the result of allowing someone else to believe something through a combination of elusion, inexactitude, and dissimulation.

In Ireland, we have recently been introduced to the concept of mental reservation by churchmen attempting to explain their responses to the unfolding dynamics of scandals regarding child sexual abuse and their particular individual and institutional roles in responding to what is by any measure a straightforward outrage perpetrated against children. Mental reservation is not an explicit act of lying, as it relies on elision, omission, and the acute understanding that you are allowing somebody to believe something to be the case that may not be true or accurate and are not correcting their belief about it. The phrase *mental reservation* derives from Catholic theology and was introduced into public discourse by Cardinal Desmond Connell during the controversies regarding the role of the Catholic Church in protecting child sexual abusers. Connell stated in 2010 that "the general teaching about mental reservation is that you are not permitted to tell a lie. On the other hand, you may be put in a position where you have to answer, and there may be circumstances in which you can use an ambiguous expression realising that the person who you are talking to will accept an untrue version of whatever it may be—permitting that to happen, not willing that it happened, that would be lying. . . . It really is a matter of trying to deal with extraordinarily difficult matters that may arise in social relations where people may ask questions that you simply cannot answer. Everybody knows that this kind of thing is liable to happen. So, mental reservation is, in a sense, a way of answering without lying" ("Pope Must Answer" 2010). This answer reflects the extraordinary difficulty encountered by interrogators or interviewers when questioning suspects. Are the suspects lying? How will we know? Do they believe what they are saying? If so, how can we tell if they are lying? How do we distinguish lies from the seven sins of memory, in which sins of omission and commission distort recall without any intention to lie? How can you distinguish the one from the other?

The concept of mental reservation is a particularly interesting one because it is not overtly lying in the sense that somebody is willfully telling an untruth or is withholding information and actively distorting it. Instead, what the person is doing is allowing the other person to whom he or she is speaking to become complicit in the continued belief in something that happens not to be the case. This illustrates a very interesting and important reality about lying. Lying requires two people: it requires certain complex mental acts on the part of liars. It involves filtering the truth, as they see it, in certain ways, but also it involves the person to whom the lie is being told and that person responding in particular ways to what it is that he or she is being told. The matter becomes ever more complex when—as is palpably the case with certain lies and certain liars—the liars themselves believe what it is that they are saying.

The search for an unequivocal marker of an underlying biological process is known as biomarker discovery and is one of the hottest topics in all of neuroscience. It would be revolutionary if it were the case that we had biomarkers that unequivocally predict the future onset and course of, for example, pathological conditions such as Alzheimer's disease. It would be even more impressive if we had a suite of biomarkers that become modified as the result of the disease progression and that can be changed as the result of treatment for the disease. However, the search for biomarkers, which provide unequivocal neural signatures relating to underlying grossly pathological conditions of the brain, has proven to be astonishingly difficult. The problem, therefore, of detecting neural signatures associated with subtle changes in cognition that are required during lying is going to be very difficult indeed. Lying, as we have noted already, is not a unitary psychological phenomenon. People can engage in outward compliance—they can state something to be the case while actually not believing it to be the case—and one might expect that there might be predictors of that. But more subtly, people might simply not dissent from a particular judgment or a particular statement made during the course of an interrogation by an interrogator, despite the fact that they may not believe the statements that are being made. In other words, they engage in covert dissimulation (or mental reservation). And here the lie is manifest as the absence rather than the presence of a signal in behavior.

I argue here that these technologies are more or less impotent at detecting whether a person is lying. As mentioned earlier, a major problem in the detection of lying is deciding what it is that constitutes a lie per se. Having decided what a lie is, one must then have a theory that relates how a lie is told to the underlying brain state or states from which that lie is generated, to the cognitive mechanisms that are used to detect the changes that are nominally associated with lying. But as we have already discussed, lying is a complex matter, and humans are poor lie detectors but, paradoxically, are accomplished liars. Some surveys claim, for example, that 40 percent of people report telling a lie in the past twenty-four hours. Indeed, everyday life would become very difficult indeed if people were baldly and bluntly engaged in truth telling to each other at all times. After all, saying "I'm fine" is easier than burdening someone else with your daily tale of woe. Furthermore, what people believe to be true changes and often changes without people being aware of these changes. In Chapter 2, we discussed the study by Gregory Markus in which people's attitudes to their own political beliefs were tracked over the course of a decade, and it was found that people who had shifted their political beliefs along the political spectrum to the more conservative end believed themselves to have been more conservative eight or nine years previously than their own recorded responses indicated at that time. Does this mean that these people are lying, that they are telling an untruth about what it was that they formerly believed and what they now believe? Any fair reading of the data could not conclude that. The subtle evolution and adaptation of people's opinions over time and their lack of awareness of precisely how their own opinions have changed does not constitute active lying. But there is a difference in what people state they believe to have been true of themselves in the past and what was actually true of them at that time.

Cognitive distortions and cognitive biases of one form or another are therefore central to understanding what it is that people are saying that they believe to be true. The fact that people might subtly incorporate information presented to them in the form of leading questions, which leads over time to their stating something different from what they might have stated at the start of an interrogation session, does not indicate that they are lying. It simply indicates that cognition is frail, cognition is bounded, and our memories are very imperfect and subject to unconscious updating and revision. In addition, what we can recall from our memories at any one time differs from occasion to occasion. In a famous article, the psychologists Saul Kassin and Katherine Kiechel devised a simple paradigm to induce false confessions simply and easily in the lab; participants were induced to accept guilt for a crime they were not responsible for. Inducing false confessions under duress is remarkably easy, as the sad history of forced police confessions shows. Kassin and Kiechel asked participants in their study to press a key on a computer in a fast-reaction-time task or in a slow-reaction-time task (the ostensible object of study). Participants were then accused (falsely) of damaging a computer key, which all of them denied doing. A confederate then stated (falsely) that she had either seen (or not seen) the participant hit the key. Participants in the fast-reaction-time group were more likely to sign a short statement admitting the damage (measured on a self-report scale) and to incorporate false details into their memory of having committed the act. The ease with which a false confession can be elicited, and the ease with which events that did not occur can be incorporated into memory, should provide a warning about how interrogators proceed and how confessions are extracted.

These examples of false confessions do not mean that people are lying, but it makes the detection of brain signatures that are unequivocally associated with lying difficult to detect. Even if it were the case that such brain signatures or biomarkers were available, it is still impossible, given any current technology, to know what the content of that brain signature is signaling, in terms of the nature of the underlying lie. If we see a particular pattern of activation in area x in the brain in somebody we believe to be lying, that is all that we have. We do not have any greater access to what the person is actually thinking than the knowledge that area x or network y appears to be activated during the course of the interrogation more than had been the case during other, prior states, but we still do not know what the activation in that area indicates. This is a profound problem in attempting to understand the nature of human conscious thought, because activations occur in all sorts of brain areas without the person actually being aware of them or what they signify. Lots of the activity of the brain is preconscious, or nonconscious. You, the reader of this text, are sitting, lying, or standing, I hope, in a comfortable position. You are not aware of the activity in your semicircular canals, which are helping maintain your posture relative to the earth's gravitational vertical. You are not aware of the activity in primary and secondary visual cortices in any direct sense—but you are aware that you can see. You have the experience of seeing, and you automatically convert marks on a page, arbitrary symbols, into meaning, into language. This training took many years for your brain to achieve—perhaps a decade of schooling for the brain networks involved to become very fine-tuned and responsive to these sorts of perceptual symbolic-semantic transformations. However, these issues do not present difficulties for those who would like to believe that somehow, some way, a technology must exist that allows the unequivocal detection of lying.

Why Are We So Bad at Detecting Lies?

We have previously mentioned the work of Aldert Vrij and his colleagues, and especially their publication of what is probably the most comprehensive analysis available in the literature to date on lying, published in the journal *Psychological Science in the Public Interest,* present a simple conclusion: "cues lie detectors are encouraged to examine and interpret are faint and unreliable" (2010, 15). They show that lie detectors (the human kind!) fall into one or more predictable pitfalls when trying to detect lying. The pitfalls made can be classed into approximately three groups. The first is a lack of motivation to detect lies. This occurs when the lie detector does not want to test the possibilities that might uncover a lie, especially if the lie will cause the lie detector to disconfirm a pet theory. A second class of pitfall involves the difficulties associated with lie detection. There are no truly reliable and repeatable behavioral cues associated with lying, not even, as is popularly believed, gaze aversion, that is, the moving of the eyes away from the person that you are speaking to. Many people believe that gaze aversion provides a reliable route to the detection of lying. It does not, however. Averting one's eyes periodically during a conversation, or during interrogation, can happen because of differences in status, differences in cultural background, or simple nervousness arising from the fact that one might be innocent but has been accused of a crime for which one is not guilty. Gaze-aversion estimation is an interesting issue. It can be relatively easily measured under laboratory conditions using eye-tracking devices—when the target is known and deviations from visually tracking that target can be measured. Gaze aversion during conversation is much more problematic, though. To accurately estimate whether there is a disproportionate amount of gaze aversion during a conversation or interrogation, the interrogator must estimate, on the fly, what proportion of time the suspect averts his or her gaze. This means the interrogator is dividing his or her attention (in effect dual tasking) between engaging in questioning and the proportional estimation of the amount of gaze aversion presented by the person being questioned. Such estimates are inherently unreliable (regardless of how confident one is in making them). Even estimating this proportion reliably is useless by itself, unless you know to what extent the person engages in gaze aversion during normal conversations with people of differing status and rank (this is the base rate problem again). Then you need to estimate how gaze aversion may be affected by the difficulty of the question and the emotional state of the person. These effects may not be independent of one another. You also need to be able to estimate the stability of any of these putative effects through time. Finally, there are common errors made by humans acting as lie detectors. They give differential weight to the wrong cues; for example, they believe that liars fidget. They make the mistake of overemphasizing nonverbal cues, especially focusing on the demeanor of the person they are questioning: "there is a tendency to interpret nervous behaviours as suspicious without taking individual differences into account, puts several people at risk, including introverted individuals and people who are socially anxious" (Vrij and colleagues 2010, 12).

How do you overcome these problems? These will be discussed in more detail in Chapter 8. But we will mention here Vrij and colleagues' first set of conclusions regarding errors to be avoided while questioning: First, avoid examining the wrong cues—pay attention to what is said, as well as to what the person is doing. Second, do not rely on nonverbal cues alone. Take the speech content into account, including the presence or absence of fillers (such as "um" or "ah" or "eh"). Third, consider other explanations for the presence of emotional responses and cognitive load in the person who is being interrogated; for example, a fear arising from a false accusation would probably show some form of behavioral leakage. The person will be nervous, will fidget, and may overreact or show an enhanced startled response during the course of questioning. Interrogators should also avoid relying on their own biases, heuristics that may suggest there is a single gateway to the truth. Finally, interrogators should take account of inter- and intrapersonal differences. For example, our ability to recall things varies over the course of the day, according to how relaxed we are, how hungry we are, and how much sleep we have had. There are also substantial differences between individuals. Some people have a better memory than others. Some people may respond better to one approach rather than another, where questioning is concerned.

People lie not only about their experiences, but also about their opinions. Determining the veracity of such conceptual representations may not be important in typical police suspect interviews, because they are mainly concerned with detecting lies about transgressions. However, it can be important in many security settings such as, for example, when deciding whether an informant is (a) indeed as much anti-Taliban or against Muslim fundamentalism as he or she claims; or (b) truly entering the United Kingdom or the United States solely for the purpose of university study. Incorrect veracity judgements can do irreparable harm in such situations, as demonstrated by the loss of seven CIA agents in Afghanistan on December 30th, 2009. The CIA agents were killed via a suicide attack by a man they thought was going to give them information about Taliban and Al Qaeda targets in Pakistan's tribal areas. The CIA agents had used polygraph tests to check the man's sincerity and were aware that he had posted extreme anti-American views on the internet. However, it was decided that the views he had expressed were part of a good cover, and the possibility that they were his real views was discounted. (Sharon Leal and colleagues 2010, 323)

One strategy here is to ask the person who is being questioned to tell his or her story in reverse order, from the present working backward to the past. This is a difficult thing to do; it disrupts the normal linear order of our cognitive schema of the world. It requires us to engage in mental time travel in a direction the reverse of the one we normally engage in. Experimentally, this strategy does seem to work: it enhances the detection of lies somewhat (on up to 60 percent of occasions, which is some improvement over the normal situation). Another tactic is to impose a simple cognitive load, namely, asking the subject to maintain eye contact at all times during the questioning. This is known as dual tasking, and there is a substantial literature showing that the effects of such dual tasking can be very demanding indeed, especially on memory. The task of the liar here will be threefold: to answer questions, to fabricate a story, and to maintain eye contact. The task of the truth teller is simpler: it is to answer questions and to maintain eye contact. The demands of an additional task should, under some circumstances at least, cause failures in online task monitoring such that liars, on occasion, will trip themselves up.

Another tactic has already been hinted at. This is the asking of irrelevant or unanticipated questions, jumping from a current set of questions to an entirely new set of questions and perhaps jumping back again. These multiple shifts between different cognitive structures representing different aspects of memory will also be costly, and doing this while asking suspects also to maintain eye contact, thereby imposing additional cognitive burdens, may cause them to reveal inadvertently aspects of information stored in schemas in memory that they did not intend to do. There is, however, little by way of good experimental data demonstrating which of these methodologies (if any) will be best under any particular set of circumstances.

There is another difficulty too. Vrij and his colleagues also make the very interesting and telling point that the literature on lying revolves almost in its entirety around actions in the past or intentions in the past; in other words, questioning is usually about something that has already occurred or something that somebody was attempting to do in the past. However, the experimental psychology of deceptive intentions is almost wholly undeveloped. This is an area that, for law enforcement, for the prevention of terrorist outrages, is something that needs to be developed very vitally. The forestalling of a future criminal or terrorist act is surely as important as solving or understanding an act that has occurred in the past. Vrij and colleagues note that in one experiment, those who intended to actually do something used a greater degree of concreteness in their descriptions of what it was they intended to do—that is, they provided actual concrete details of what they were about to do—compared to those who did not intend to do it. Questioning of this type—the "where are you going?"; "what are you doing?"; "who are you meeting?"; "where are you staying?" types of question—could prove very useful indeed, where the detection of those who are possibly going to engage in criminal acts is concerned.

A final topic that Vrij and colleagues suggest also needs focusing on is the issue of lying in networks—that is, when two, three, or more people rehearse a story together about something that they have done or that they intend to do, as a cover for something that they are actually doing (alibi generation and its validation with reference to another individual). There is almost no empirical literature available as a guide in this area. Regrettably, under these circumstances, human lie detectors would be left to rely on hunches or heuristics to guide them. We have previously mentioned transactive memory. Group processes (or transactional processes) in memory are also very important. Memories differ between different members of a group because group members tend to specialize in different things. Too great a degree of similarity about past events or future indications might be indication of rehearsal—and hence a group process designed to provide a cover story (and hence to subvert a human lie detector). This hypothesis needs to be tested, however.

Limitations of Brain-Imaging Technology for Lie Detection

We can think of there being several major limitations to brain-imaging technology in the context of attempting to use brain imaging as a route to lie detection. The first area of limitation is straightforward. The vast preponderance of studies in the literature have been conducted with normal participants. By this I mean psychiatrically, psychologically, or neurologically normal participants, usually young adult males and females. There has been a welcome tendency to conduct brain imaging in other populations, including those suffering from neurological conditions such as Alzheimer's disease or psychiatric conditions such as depression. However, there has been either no or extremely limited testing of these lie-detection paradigms in populations that might actually be of special interest, such as individuals suffering from personality disorders, borderline personality/conduct disorder, and conditions resulting in gross deficits in empathy, such as those that are widely held to underlie conditions such as sociopathy and psychopathy. Another interesting and unexplored group is that of pathological fabulists, perhaps resulting from head injury: individuals who lie easily, elaborately, and with great propensity. Finally, meaningfully representative studies on individuals who are extremist in their ideology have not been conducted. Indeed, studies of groups like this have been profoundly limited by the problem of accessing such individuals. Committed jihadists are unlikely to respond to a plea for volunteer participation in fMRI studies.

Gentler forms of political extremism, of course, have been studied, with contested results. Some researchers have argued (for example, Drew Westen and Jonathan Haidt) that individuals who are ideologically committed liberals or conservatives (in the American sense of these terms) differ fundamentally in their worldviews and how they frame approaches to understanding problems of morality and political ideology. Of course, comparisons between opposite tails of any distribution are going to give you reliable differences. However, for the somewhat less committed in the middle, these statistically evident differences may disappear. As an aside, while people sometimes assume that views of this type are more or less fixed allegiances derived from one's personality, clever experiments have shown that it is possible to flip a person's political allegiance with a manipulation of responses that they themselves believe they have made about their own political positions only a few moments previously (Hall and colleagues 2013). In these experiments, participants stated their voting intentions (which were recorded in front of them) and were presented with right-wing/left-wing dividing issues and asked for their opinions (which were again recorded in front of them). A sleight-of-hand altered their replies to place them in the contrary political position. Participants again discussed their attitudes on the manipulated issues. Remarkably, only 22 percent of the manipulated replies were noticed, and 92 percent of participants accepted and endorsed the altered political survey score for themselves. Thus, there is a plasticity of response present and a capacity to change one's own political position quite rapidly—despite the general idea that political affiliations might be enduring reflections of some underlying, unchanging, and enduring personality trait.

Countermanding techniques for lie detection are easy to implement. We might, for present purposes, divide these into two categories: cognitive strategies and somatic strategies. Cognitive strategies are straightforward, relying on the modulation of cognitive processes via differing but easy-to-implement strategies. These may include practice effects (a skilled liar may practice a lie to the point that it becomes second nature, and therefore a lie is retrieved as easily as the truth); dual tasking (where, in addition to engaging voluntarily in whatever interrogation is being imposed on the person, the person also imposes an extra mental load by, for example, engaging in a subtraction task); and finally (but not exclusively) stimulus-response imaging (where the person simply imagines associations between items of information and some other extraneous or irrelevant piece of information to generate superfluous activations). Somatic strategies can be defined as strategies that are based around manipulations of one's own bodily state in order to impact on the brain images that are collected. There are many of these strategies. In order to acquire an artifact-free and reasonably reliable scan, subjects are requested to voluntarily suppress a wide variety of behaviors, and these behaviors can be used to occlude the natural response to challenge questions. A nonexhaustive list would include subjects moving their eyes whenever a stimulus is presented; holding their breath; clenching the anal sphincter; biting the internal surface of the cheek; engaging in small but repetitive finger or toe movements; blinking the eyes excessively; and engaging in subtle but discontinuous movements of the body trunk, of the limbs, or of the head. And then the person may also interpose either a variable delay or an irrelevant movement between the question and its answer.

There are other problems too, and there needs to be a sense of realism on the part of investigators regarding how irrelevant the paradigms that they have generated are to the real-world circumstances of criminal investigation. To make the matter more explicit, the challenge here is for brain imagers to devise a protocol that would allow them to reliably draw inferences about the underlying state of a participant's brain circuits and subcircuits, on the basis solely of the questions that are presented during a structured clinical interview. In these circumstances, there will be questions of variable duration, referring to instances of memory performance in the past, and there will be variable response times from interviewees depending on their current psychiatric state. Further, interrogation sessions are often of several hours' duration, necessarily being fatiguing for both the questioner and the questioned. Inevitably, there will be, within the subject, baseline drift arising as a result of long periods within the scanner, and these periods of baseline drift might vary from stress and anxiety from being in an enclosed space for substantial periods of time all the way through to periods of fluctuations in conscious state and to sleep itself.

The issue of how realistically one can compare the challenge paradigms that are used in brain imaging to real-world circumstances is one that has simply been given insufficient consideration by investigators. The problem for brain imaging is straightforward: somebody who is being questioned in connection with an incident will be questioned in narrative terms, with narrative answers being supplied to the questions asked. Investigators may have complete knowledge of what has happened, or they may have very incomplete knowledge, due for example to simple ignorance, language barriers, conflicting testimony between differing individuals, or lack of reliable forensic-science information. The role of the questioner in these circumstances is completely different from the role of the experimenter, so much so that there may in fact be a simple category error here: experimenters are comparing apples with oranges in terms of the external validity of the experiments that they are conducting. For these experiments to work, you must already know what the subject does or does not know. You know the stimuli that subjects have been exposed to, and you are not blinded to the conditions that they are exposed to; nor is it likely that any experiment involving brain imaging could allow blinding to occur and still allow for the possibility of acquiring meaningful data. Furthermore, these experiments do not work when lying is a transactional problem, when there is no overt or covert attempt to lie; all that the questioned person is attempting to do is to lead the questioner (perhaps in a Socratic fashion) astray or to a set of conclusions that in some way the questioner might find congenial. Finally, people under stress during interrogation might reply to questions in a wide variety of fashions. They may be sarcastic, they may speak ironically, they may be aggressive, they may go to great efforts to suppress their own feelings of aggression, they may be nervous, and the like. It is therefore little wonder that the same set of brain structures may be persistently activated across all of these cognitive states—namely, brain systems concerned with executive control (those contained within the prefrontal cortices), implying that there is little possibility of engaging in meaningful differential diagnosis.

Another Approach: Using Truth Serums

Truth serum is a phrase used semiseriously to denote the possibility that there may be pharmacological agents that in some way facilitate information retrieval or extraction from a subject undergoing interrogation. By definition, these agents are psychoactive and may induce hypnotic states in which compliance with questioning is assumed to be possible (narcoanalysis). The American Psychological Association (APA) in a 2004 workshop entitled "Science of Deception: Integration of Practice and Theory" (subsequently removed from their website, but web-archived) asked the following question in one session: "What pharmacological agents are known to affect apparent truthtelling behavior?" The outcomes of this workshop have not been publically released, but the fact that the question would even be posed by the APA points to a neuropharmacological naivety that is surprising. I have been unable to find any large-scale, double-blinded, reliable and replicable, randomized controlled trials that have systematically sought to investigate the efficacy of putative truth serums. I suspect that such trials simply do not exist for the simple reason that they have never been conducted, because there are no theoretical or experimental grounds from neuropsychopharmacology to posit their existence. Truth serums appear occasionally in films and in television programs as plot-driving devices. Jack Bauer, in the series *24,* used on occasion some form of truth serum to facilitate the release of information from suspects who were being interrogated. In a seeming reflection of fiction into fact, the Constitution Project report states, "Several Guantánamo detainees have alleged that doctors or psychologists administered psychotropic drugs for purposes of interrogation. A DOD inspector general's report on these allegations, released in response to a Freedom of Information Act request filed by Task Force staff, and others found that detainees had not been administered drugs for interrogation purposes. However, the same report found that detainees who were diagnosed with schizophrenia and psychosis received involuntary injections of Haldol and other powerful antipsychotics, and were interrogated while experiencing the effects of this treatment. This raises questions about the reliability of those detainees' statements under interrogation" (2013, 24). One wonders why an antipsychotic medication used for the treatment of schizophrenia and other related psychiatric conditions would be thought to be in any way capable of reducing deception or lying, to be compliance inducing or otherwise motivational. The sense here again is of people with little experience or knowledge trying things out to see what will happen.

The sometime neuroscientist and polemicist Sam Harris imagines an entirely fictional and counterfactual ticking-time-bomb scenario and then introduces a fanciful, imagined, and make-believe "truth serum" (demonstrating that a little domain-specific knowledge acquired during the course of a Ph.D. does not prevent counterfactual revenge fantasies): "To demonstrate just how abstract the torments of the tortured can be made to seem, we need only imagine an ideal 'torture pill'—a drug that would deliver both the instruments of torture and the instrument of their concealment. The action of the pill would be to produce transitory paralysis and transitory misery of a kind that no human being would willingly submit to a second time. Imagine how we torturers would feel if, after giving this pill to captive terrorists, each lay down for what appeared to be an hour's nap only to arise and immediately confess everything he knows about the workings of his organization. Might we not be tempted to call it a 'truth pill' in the end?" (2011). Having treated us to this psychopharmacological counterfactual, Harris fails to elaborate on its logic. Why would inducing extreme neuropsychiatric distress and paralysis be assumed to facilitate motivated reliable and veridical recall? No rationale is offered other than the folk intuition that this must be so. Harris unfortunately does not offer any further elaboration in terms of brain mechanisms or psychological processing for how imposing this extreme stressor state will facilitate the release of withheld information. Harris's perorations on this topic are completely bereft of any meaningful body of citations to the scientific literature (or, incidentally, to the vast ethical, philosophical, or legal literatures on torture either). He has also presented arguments in favor of the use of torture to facilitate information extraction from suspects. The torture methods themselves are not elaborated on, nor are their likely effects on brain function, despite the knowledge that Harris presumably possesses as a Ph.D. in cognitive neuroscience from the University of California–Los Angeles.

Three compounds have been experimented with as truth serums in nonblinded and nonsystematic studies, and they are mentioned in some case reports. Sodium amytal is a drug that has been in use for at least fifty years. It has mildly hypnotic and mildly sedative effects similar to those that might be found under hypnosis. Scopolamine is a drug that has effects on the cholinergic system of the brain, and its effects on learning and memory have been very well quantified over the past twenty-five or thirty years, particularly in terms of the effect that it has on the underlying physiology of the brain. In general, scopolamine has amnestic effects—in other words, it induces amnesia or simulates amnesia, rather than promoting recall. Sodium pentobarbital is a poor anesthetic, not much used in the clinic any-more: at certain low doses, it can induce something of a hypnotic and sedative state. The use of an anesthetic is supposed to facilitate compliance and the induction of psychological states that predispose one to being unguarded. This is a slightly more sophisticated version of the old adage *in vino, veritas*. But anyone who has spoken with a drunk knows that getting sense from them is hard. It needs to be said bluntly that the quest for a truth serum is a fool's errand. They exist in fiction and imagination but have absolutely no existence in reality.

Propensity to Lie during Interrogation

There is a simple and reliable way to disrupt torture, at least tem-porarily: to talk, to do so at length, and to provide information of seemingly great specificity and lots of colorful detail. Blending a mix of commonplace truths and half lies with appropriately modulated pauses (allowing some control of the conversation to be assumed by the captive) will also help forestall torture. Keeping the signal-to-noise ratio appropriately low will also help—sorting wheat from chaff takes time. This brings us to a particular flaw in the protor-ture argument: that it will reliably elicit veridical information from the captive's long-term memory. This is commonly asserted by many media commentators in the context of the ticking-time-bomb sce-nario or in the case of a major imminent threat in which lives could be saved. But a pragmatic antitorture argument is that torture will not elicit veridical information, that it is as likely to elicit false as it is true information, and that separating the one from the other will be difficult. Advance planning of the sophistication required to place major bombs in urban locations will also involve the use of decoys, and resources will have to be spent checking out the possible leads that the captive has given up under torture. You cannot assume that the signal-to-noise ratio is high—that the captive has provided the single piece of easily verifiable information required to forestall the imminent explosion. Rehearsals and dry runs for the attack will inevitably involve planning for the capture of individuals and the rehearsal and simulation of alternative stories.

The protorture position assumes much about the behavior of the confreres of the detainees also. In the geographically contained and physically small provincial environment of Northern Ireland, where many people were to known to each other on all sides of the political divides, "former paramilitaries argue that rather than saving lives the use of torture in Northern Ireland actually aggravated and prolonged the terrible violence. Tommy McKearney [an IRA activist] says: 'Torturing prisoners will provide a very short-term gain. In the medium term it's of doubtful value. The IRA quickly moved people and weapons and cars, and abandoned safe houses, once they realised their people were being tortured' " (Cobain 2012, 203). This is a persistent feature of terrorist operations (the lone-actor scenario aside): detainees are embedded in a complex social, fiscal, implicit, and explicit rule-governed network, and their disappearance from the network sends an important signal to the remaining members of the network that they are likely to have been compromised. Sophisticated terrorists are embedded within a social infrastructure and network that enables their activities, and this network is responsive to their behavior. Confusing this network-centric view of terrorist activity with the lone-actor or near-lone-actor activities of an Anders Bering Brevik, a Timothy McVeigh, or a Ted Kaczynski leads to important errors of policy and action.

A reading of the testimonies of those who have been tortured provides ample confirmation, if it were needed, that under torture people will say what they think their interrogators want to hear in order to terminate the torture session. John McCain, who suffered torture while imprisoned in Vietnam, writes about the trail to Osama bin Laden, as well as about what prisoners will reveal under torture, as follows:

I asked CIA Director Leon Panetta for the facts, and he told me the following: The trail to bin Laden did not begin with a disclosure from Khalid Sheik Mohammed, who was water-boarded 183 times. The first mention of Abu Ahmed al-Kuwaiti—the nickname of the al-Qaeda courier who ultimately led us to bin Laden—as well as a description of him as an important member of al-Qaeda, came from a detainee held in another country, who we believe was not tortured. None of the three detainees who were waterboarded provided Abu Ahmed's real name, his whereabouts, or an accurate description of his role in al-Qaeda.

In fact, the use of enhanced interrogation techniques on Khalid Sheik Mohammed produced false and misleading infor-mation. He specifically told his interrogators that Abu Ahmed had moved to Peshawar, got married and ceased his role as an al-Qaeda facilitator—none of which was true. According to the staff of the Senate intelligence committee, the best intelligence gained from a CIA detainee—information describing Abu Ahmed al-Kuwaiti's real role in al-Qaeda and his true relation-ship to bin Laden—was obtained through standard, noncoercive means.

I know from personal experience that the abuse of prisoners sometimes produces good intelligence but often produces bad intelligence because under torture a person will say anything he thinks his captors want to hear—true or false—if he believes it will relieve his suffering. Often, information provided to stop the torture is deliberately misleading. (2011)

The former intelligence officer Malcolm Nance provides an account of torture in Cambodia by another torture survivor:

On a Mekong River trip, I met a 60-year-old man, happy to be alive and a cheerful travel companion, who survived the geno-cide and torture . . . he spoke openly about it and gave me a valuable lesson: "If you want to survive, you must learn that 'walking through a low door means you have to be able to bow.'" He told his interrogators everything they wanted to know including the truth. They rarely stopped. In torture, he confessed to being a hermaphrodite, a CIA spy, a Buddhist Monk, a Catholic Bishop and the son of the king of Cambodia. He was actually just a school teacher whose crime was that he once spoke French. He remembered "the Barrel" version of waterboarding quite well. Head first until the water filled the lungs, then you talk. (2007; ellipses in original)

Khalid Sheikh Mohammed provided the following testimony to the International Committee of the Red Cross: "During the harshest period of my interrogation I gave a lot of false information in order to satisfy what I believed the interrogators wished to hear in order to make the ill-treatment stop. I later told the interrogators their methods were stupid and counterproductive. I'm sure that the false information I was forced to invent in order to make the ill-treatment stop wasted a lot of their time and to several false red-alerts being placed in the US" (ICRC 2007).

Mohammed el Gorani in 2011 described being tortured in Karachi (the dates are uncertain) prior to being transported to Guantanamo at about the age of fifteen:

In the beginning there were interrogations every night. They tortured me with electricity, mostly on the toes. The nails of my big toes fell off. Sometimes they hung you up like a chicken and hit your back. Sometimes they chained you, with your head on the ground. You couldn't move for 16 or 17 hours. You peed on yourself.

Sometimes they showed you the ugly face: torturing, torturing without asking questions. Sometimes I said, "Yes, whatever you ask, I'll say yes," because I just wanted torture to stop. But the next day, I said: "No, I said yes yesterday because of torture."

My first or second interrogator said to me: "Mohammed, I know you're innocent but I'm doing my job. I have children to feed. I don't want to lose my job."

Classical conditioning is a form of associative learning that was first systematically studied by the Russian physiologist Ivan Pavlov (hence the term *Pavlovian conditioning*). In abstract terms, classical conditioning refers to how stimuli may signal biologically relevant events. Pavlov focused on how neutral stimuli that precede feeding (such as the preparatory behaviors involved in food preparation and food serving) generate salivation and gastric changes. He took a seemingly banal observation and showed that it is central to a variety of forms of behavior. A particularly clinically relevant form of this learning has been intensively explored over the past two decades: fear conditioning. In fear conditioning, human volunteers or animals are exposed to a signal (say a sound) that indicates the onset of an unpleasant event (for example, a mild but unpleasant electric shock). After a few tone-shock pairings, the response that would have been elicited by the shock is now elicited by the tone. This process goes by a variety of names, but for present purposes conditioned aversion or conditioned aversive stimuli will do. Stimuli may also signal periods of safety from noxious or aversive events—these are known as conditioned safety signals, as they signal a period in which no noxious or aversive events will occur.

In a torture situation, the interrogator and captive differ in their motivations: the interrogator wants the captive to speak, thereby disgorging information from long-term memory. The captive wants to escape the extreme stress of torture while not revealing anything significant of what he or she knows. Here, the detainee's own words provide the safety signal: "If I'm speaking, I'm not being tortured." The truth of what detainees say does not provide a safety signal, just the fact that they are talking because speech acts signal periods of safety. The interrogator must perforce suspend the waterboarding in order to hear what it is the captive is saying. The conditions of such torture are incompatible with speech acts occurring. Equally, when the captive is talking, the interrogator's objective has been attained because if the captive is speaking, he or she may reveal useful information. Further, because the captive is speaking, these speech acts also provide a safety signal to the interrogator. Making the captive talk, rather than the truth of what the captive is revealing, might mark the end of the torture. As long as the captive is talking, the interrogator can avoid using torture (we will explore in Chapter 7 just how difficult it can be for one person to impose extreme stress on another person). It is likely to be difficult or perhaps impossible to determine during interrogation whether the information that a suspect reveals is true: information presented by the interrogator to elicit responses during interrogation might inadvertently become part of the suspect's memory, especially because suspects are under extreme stress and are required to tell and retell the same events that might have happened over a period of years. Other factors exacerbate this problem. Confabulation (the pathological production of false memories) is a common consequence of frontal lobe disorders, and as already noted, prolonged and extreme stress has a deleterious effect on frontal lobe function. Thus, distinguishing between confabulations and what is true in the verbal statements of tortured suspects will always be difficult.

4

What Do Stress and Pain Do to the Brain?

Worried politician:	We aren't getting enough information from these guys. I don't want you to torture these guys, but, you know, push them hard, be tough, don't leave any marks. You can nearly drown them and make them suffer. I have a memo from a lawyer saying it's okay to make them suffer, because suffering alone isn't torture.
Untrained young military interrogator:	Er, okay, I guess. So long as it isn't torture, right, I can be tough. Like Jack Bauer?
Worried politician:	I think it's a no-brainer. And here's that memo from the lawyer.

For the one who is tortured, stress, fear, and pain are at the heart of the experience. For the one who would torture, the imposition of stress, fear, and pain are the tools by which the captive is to be manipulated. This chapter discusses the brain's experience of stress, fear, and pain in the context of the effects that these noxious conditions have on memory, cognition, and psychological states more generally. Stress is a diagnostic and descriptive term that has become ubiquitous in modern life. Stress-related illnesses, for example, account for a disturbingly high proportion of occupational disability in the Western world. One European Union estimate suggests that work-related stress (defined as "a pattern of emotional, cognitive, behavioural and physiological reactions to adverse and harmful aspects of work"; European Commission 1999, p. v) costs €20 billion a year in time and health bills; it is the second-most-common occupational health problem (after back pain). A different estimate from the European Agency for Safety and Health at Work (2014) reported that stress-related illness cost EU companies more than €13 billion in 2010. An estimate reported by the American Psychological Association (2008), using a different method of calculation, suggests that job stress costs U.S. industry an estimated $300 billion a year in absenteeism, turnover, diminished productivity, and medical, legal, and insurance costs (Rosch 2001). These are disturbing consequences of the kinds of work conditions that at least some people feel themselves under in the modern world. The stress response was originally identified by Hans Selye. Selye took the term *stress* from engineering, where it has a very precise definition: the load experienced by a structure when it is subjected to some sort of force, for example, a weight—the stress load on a steel beam, for example. Other terms in the stress literature have been taken directly from mechanical engineering, such as *breaking point* and *brittleness*.

Jeansok Kim and David Diamond suggest that the experience of stress causes heightened excitability or arousal in the brain and body; that it also causes a perception that present or future events will be unpleasant; and finally that this perception is also combined with a lack of controllability over these events. Experiencing stress causes release of stress hormones (cortisol and catecholamines, such as noradrenaline). Stress hormones provoke and control the fight-or-flight response. If overly prolonged, the fight-or-flight response results in compromised brain function. As we will see, prolonged stress can even result in tissue loss in certain brain regions. The hippocampus and prefrontal cortex are particularly rich in receptors activated by stress hormones. The primary stress hormone, cortisol, increases the excitability of brain cells. If prolonged, this can compromise the normal physiological functioning of brain cells. Catecholamines modulate many sites in the brain (including the hippocampus and prefrontal cortex) and have many effects, including provoking glucose release and increasing blood pressure and heart rate. These responses can be beneficial and adaptive in the short term, as they allow a rapid response to threats to bodily integrity. However, they can cause long-term damage to the brain and body if this state of hyperarousal is maintained over the long term. Furthermore, the amygdala (involved in the processing of fear- and threat-related stimuli) can become enlarged, creating a negative feedback loop that amplifies the effects of subsequent stressful events.

Contemporary thrillers regularly use torture as a plot device. Torture is frequently used as *the* method of choice to extract information in films, especially action-adventure films and thrillers. The extraordinarily successful television series *24* featured scenes of torture, imminent threat of death (experienced as explicit and overt predator threat), mock executions, and the threatened execution of children and spouses. Predator stress—the physiological and psychological stress experienced when your life is threatened—is perhaps the most extreme form of stress that it is possible to experience. The brain mobilizes activity in a coordinated fashion, creating the fight-or-flight response—the immediate and rapid preparation by the body and brain for action in response to threat. Predator stress activates a wide range of structures in the brain. As we will see (but we already know through experience), watching another person being subjected to extreme duress causes an immediate and relatively uncontrolled autonomic response. The autonomic nervous system (ANS) controls many reflexive automatic and nonconscious functions. Among other things, the ANS controls, directs, or affects breathing, heart rate, gastric transit and digestion, secretion of certain fluids (for example, urine, saliva, perspiration), and dilation of the pupils. As we will see in Chapter 8, seeing another human being in distress or experiencing extremes of stress causes powerful activations of circuits in the brain concerned with the cognitive and emotional aspects of pain. These circuits control, in turn, aspects of our own stress response—they turn on surges of stress hormones involved in the fight-or-flight response.

Sometimes, it is useful to distinguish the classes of information that are conveyed to the brain. Generally, two classes are distinguished. The first is general somatic information—information about touch, pressure, pain, temperature, position, vibration, and the like. The second class of information is general visceral information: information from the visceral organs is transferred via nerve conduction to the brain. There are sensory receptors scattered throughout the body: in the skin, in the muscles, in the joints, and in the internal organs. A sensory receptor has the job of transforming input from within or without the body into an electrical signal that can be conducted along a nerve pathway to the brain. Think of the relationship of the eyes to the brain, for example; the eyes convert light photons into electrophysiological signals that travel via the optic radiations to the visual parts of the brain. This activity gives rise to the experience of vision. There are three general types of sensory receptor. The first are exteroceptive; that is, their job is to bring information from outside the body that arrives on the surface of the body, on the skin or the sensory organs such as the eyes, the ears, or the nose, and transform it into an electrical signal so that it can be conducted into the brain. The second class are interoceptive. The job of the interoceptors is to bring information from the viscera, that is, the internal organs of the body, to the brain. The final class of sensory receptors are concerned with proprioception, that is, information about the position of the joints of the body—for example, the position of the ankles, the orientation of the elbows, the position of the hands. There are several subclasses of sensory receptors. The first are nociceptors. These are concerned with pain and extremes of temperature and are found in the skin, in muscle, and in other tissues. Mechanoreceptors are concerned with the sensation of touch, pressure, and similar phenomena. Mechanoreceptors are found in the deep parts of the skin, in the roots of hair, in ligaments, and in joints; they are scattered throughout the internal organs as well. The final class is muscle and tendon mechanoreceptors: these are all found in skeletal muscle. These differing receptors perform different functions, and transmission of signals from each of these receptors is segregated from transmission from the others. The key job of all of these receptors is to bring vital information from the organs that they service to the spinal cord; the information rapidly travels via the spinothalamic tract to the thalamus (a deep brain structure that can act as a relay between the spinal cord and higher-order brain areas). Finally, sensation is transmitted to higher brain regions, where it may enter consciousness.

Pain and its manipulation are central tools in torture. Causing pain, the threat of pain: these are seen, rightly or wrongly, as tools that can be used to loosen the tongues of the unwilling. Pain can be decomposed into a number of components. There is a sensory component—the mechanisms by which noxious stimuli are transmitted to the brain. There is an affective component—the emotional response to the experience of the painful stimuli. There is a cognitive component—the evaluation of the painful stimuli. There may also be motor components—as in the rapid withdrawal of the hand when it touches a hot surface. Together these different components are regulated by a complex network of areas in the brain, sometimes referred to as the pain matrix. The pain matrix has been the subject of extensive studies in both animals and humans over the past century or so. Brain-imaging studies have explored the brain areas associated with different types of pain. A prototypical experiment might involve asking volunteers to endure a series of systematically applied electric shocks to the extremities and then imaging the parts of the brain activated by the intensity and frequency of the electric shocks. This kind of experiment provides a good model of acute and sharp pain. Other kinds of experiments might involve placing small amounts of capsaicin (the active ingredient in chili peppers) via an injection just below the skin of volunteers. This creates a sensation of acute and diffuse burning that can last a period of time. Other experiments again might take advantage of chronic pain conditions—as might be found in patients with back injuries, for example. These and other experiments have allowed the identification of a network of brain areas that support the experience of pain (the secondary somatasensory cortex, the insula, the anterior cingulate cortex, certain brain areas concerned with movement—in particular, the cerebellum, and the secondary motor cortex—and finally the thalamus and primary somatasensory cortex). These differing areas perform a variety of sensory, cognitive, and motor functions during the painful experience from evaluation to attempts at defensive and escape movements. We will encounter these areas again in Chapter 7, where we explore the mechanisms that underpin the experience of empathy.

Torture perpetrated via the teeth is a fantastic cinematic plot device: who does not know toothache? The well-known film *Marathon Man* famously included such a plot device, used to attempt to force an innocent to speak on matters of which he had no knowledge. Teeth consist of an outer, calcified surface, known as the enamel; an inner layer of dentin; and a root canal containing pulp. Pulp contains blood vessels and nerves and is astonishingly sensitive to painful stimuli, such as excesses of heat, cold, dental caries, or trauma. The pain from such a procedure is something that anyone who has undergone dental treatment can easily identify with, if only by imaginative extension. So prevalent is our fear of dental pain that dental phobias (properly known as dentophobia) affect, in Western societies, somewhere between 7 and 13 percent of the population. The head possesses a set of specialized nerves called the cranial nerves. There are twelve pairs of these nerves in total, emerging directly from the brain. These nerves serve functions such as the sense of smell (olfactory nerve), vision (the optic nerve), and eye movements (the oculomotor nerve). Teeth are served by subdivisions of the trigeminal nerve (cranial nerve V). The trigeminal nerve is the largest of the cranial nerves. It is a complex nerve, divided into three major components—ophthalmic, maxillary, and mandibular. The trigeminal nerve has sensory functions, as it conveys inputs from the face, the teeth, and the tongue to the brain. It also has motor functions, assisting the chewing (mastication) of food and the movement of the tongue. It sends a major projection to the trigeminal nucleus of the pons, located in the brain stem. This nucleus contains a homunculus, which is a map of the surface of the body in the brain. This map of the body represents the component parts of the body, from which it receives inputs. These inputs in turn are relayed to the highest centers of the brain—to the thalamus and the cortex, from which stimuli rapidly enter consciousness, especially stimuli that are associated with pain. The application of a drill to the unanesthetized tooth will cause terrible, immediate, and inescapable pain. Some brave human subjects in Switzerland have undergone brain imaging so that we can understand how the brain processes the pain associated with trauma to the teeth (Brügger and colleagues 2011). Remarkably, twenty-one healthy volunteers allowed themselves to have electrical stimulation of the canine teeth and the incisor teeth while lying in a brain scanner. A constant current was applied to the particular tooth, above the pain threshold for that tooth, as measured by a perceived pain intensity scale. Pain thresholds and intensities are easily measured through numeric estimates provided by participants. Scales can be used in which participants rate a stimulus on scale from 0 (no pain at all) to 10 (the worst pain imaginable). Humans are superb at calibrating their own sensations of pain—for obvious adaptive reasons. Electrical stimulation of the teeth produced a wide range of activations throughout the brain and, in particular, widespread activation of the pain matrix (the brain structures involved in the processing of pain). Other brain areas were observed to have been activated as well and especially parts of the brain particularly concerned with cognition and emotion. The subjects were, in many cases, able to subject themselves to remarkably high levels of stimulation.

Pain is a signal from the body to the brain that something bad, noxious, unpleasant, or aversive is occurring. Pain is also the usual vehicle by which torture is represented in movies. How pain is presented and how pain is experienced in films is unrealistic in many regards. A first and simple example of this is that people typically underestimate their own capacity to endure pain. Studies show that people typically underestimate both the intensity and duration of pain they can actually impose on themselves (for example, in tasks where they must voluntarily keep their hands in iced water). People are capable of reducing the feeling of pain markedly by engaging in a variety of strategies. One recent, clever study showed that people were able to keep their arms in a bucket of iced water for forty seconds longer if they were allowed to engage in a simple verbal strategy: they were allowed to swear out loud (see Stephens, Atkins, and Kingston 2009). However, this effect was only present in people who did not swear much during the course of their everyday lives. Another simple method for reducing the experience of pain is to forcibly direct one's attention to a body part that is not currently hurting. These are obviously short-term strategies, but they do show that central, controlled cognitive processes can modulate the experience of pain.

Signaling by brain cells involves all-or-none transmission of signals known as spikes or action potentials. Action potentials result from the stimulation of nerve cells and are conducted, in the case of pain, away from the periphery via the spinal cord to the brain. There is a limit to the capacity of brain cells to signal the presence of any stimulus, irrespective of its origin, whether it is painful, visual, auditory, or whatever. This is a given of the nervous system itself. The limit varies somewhat from place to place in the nervous system, but it has a very important consequence. It means that there is a maximum rate at which spiking can occur. This, in turn, limits the experience of pain. And who has not discovered this for themselves? If you catch your finger in a door or break a bone, it hurts almost overwhelmingly at first and then it numbs. This is because signals are capable of being processed to a particular point, and beyond this point, feed-forward mechanisms prevent any greater signal being transmitted to the brain. A central analgesic response may also occur under circumstances mediated by, among other factors, the central opioidergic system of the brain—the same system activated by drugs such as morphine and heroin. Additionally, local inflammatory responses may cause some indirect analgesia at the site of damage. The final result may be a period of numbness that can last from seconds to minutes to hours. If the pain is severe enough, the person will faint, thus limiting his or her capacity to experience further pain. Here you have what we might describe as the torturer's paradox— maintaining pain that is just intense enough to cause intense suffering, fear, and anxiety but not so much that, because of physiological design, it causes transmission to the brain, or of the pain matrix of the brain itself, to cease processing pain-related stimuli for a period of time.

Television and films provide many examples of the extremity of suffering caused by the crushing of body parts. On the face of it, we imagine the extremes of pain produced to be almost unbearable. However, the crush of a significant and sensitive part of the body not only results in pain signals being generated from the periphery; it also results in the release of large quantities of stress hormones, as well as the initiation of an analgesic response in the brain (as mentioned earlier). This system is activated by morphine, heroin, and similar opiates, but it is also activated by the release of opiates that are endogenous, that is, native to the brain itself. This results in a further dampening down of the pain response, irrespective of the body part that is challenged (witness a boxer continue a fight despite having fractured teeth). The reality is that pain is a phasic response, which waxes and wanes over time, in a partly predictable and partly unpredictable fashion. Pain management is a notoriously complicated process in surgical and other contexts, partly because of this variability.

We have discussed at several points the ticking-time-bomb scenario; those who talk about it as a likely scenario will invoke catastrophe as being one hour hence. Yet the Senate Torture Report (and collateral testimony provided by Ali Soufan) stated that the estimated times required for torture techniques to work started out at thirty days (for white tortures such as sleep deprivation). Furthermore, Philip Zelikow (a senior lawyer within the Bush administration who opposed the use of torture) notes that the initial decision to apply the palette of coercive techniques to the first captive took about three months to emerge (2012, 23). Clearly, little of the ticking-time-bomb urgency influenced this initial decision. Some people might think that an immediate resort to painful stressors of an extreme sort will work more quickly than will the slow metabolic stress involved in waterboarding or sleep deprivation. But I think it is probable, on the basis of what we know about the neurophysiology of pain, that there is no technique for inducing pain that is sufficiently severe so as to cause a well-conditioned and well-prepared individual to rapidly want to reveal information without being able to resist for sufficiently long before the brain and body go into a pain-induced shock or dissociative state. And there is certainly no such technique that will work within the minutes required in order to find the hidden bomb and test the deactivation codes that were provided under duress. If you find this assertion difficult to accept, I invite you to attempt to remember a colleague's telephone number voluntarily after you adventitiously and accidentally cause yourself some (mild) extremity of pain (even a bad paper cut will do). The implication is clear: supervening states of pain impair the directed recall of items of information from memory. Orla Moriarty and colleagues have provided a comprehensive review, exploring this contention in chronic pain patients and in deliberate pain-evocation paradigms in humans and in animal models. They conclude that "cognitive function is impaired in chronic pain patients compared with controls and with the general healthy population" (Moriarty, McGuire, and Finn 2011, 391). Furthermore, Moriarty and Finn state that "neural substrates involved in cognition and pain processing are linked, and that the two systems modulate one another reciprocally. Increased pain would then impair cognitive function, and an increasing non-pain-related cognitive load could reduce perceived pain" (2014, 130).

Chronic, Severe Stress Impairs Psychological Functioning

There are numerous reviews available in the literature of the effects of chronic stress on cognitive functioning and on psychological well-being. These reviews are based on a variety of data. The first important category of data is derived from experimental and observational studies of patients suffering from hypercortisolemia or hypocortisolemia—an excess or a deficiency of stress-hormone production. The second category of patients are those suffering neuropsychiatric disorders—typically stress and anxiety disorders, depression, or posttraumatic stress disorder (PTSD). The third category comprises individuals in the normal population suffering from some form of occupational or other work-related stress disorder. The fourth category is patients that have other medical conditions (for example, chronic insomnia) that cause changes in stress-hormone levels (as does, for example, aging or senescence too). Finally, there are numerous studies of stress, fear, and anxiety conducted in animal models—typically on experimental organisms such as rats or primates (for example, New World primates such as marmosets). This final category of experiment is typically focused on understanding the underlying neurobiological mechanisms that support the stress response and of the consequences of inducing or modulating the stress response.

There have been hundreds (if not thousands) of studies conducted across these different categories. It is possible to draw some important and well-supported conclusions from all of this work. A reasonable overall conclusion is this: prolonged chronic stress impacts negatively across a wide range of brain systems and bodily organ systems, causing deleterious long-term changes that are associated with neuropsychiatric, neuropsychological, and neurological conditions, as well as end organ inflammation and dysfunction. Thus, the experience of stress, in particular its intensity, chronicity, and uncontrollability, is implicated in depression, anxiety disorders, and impaired psychological well-being. Additionally, stress of this type impacts negatively on cognitive processing more generally. This conclusion is sometimes referred to as the neurotoxicity hypothesis, originally advanced by Robert Sapolsky and colleagues as far back as 1986 and recently restated with even greater supporting evidence by Sonia Lupien and colleagues in 2007. Marie-France Marin and colleagues summarize the overall data as follows: "[Stress hormones] have access to the brain and more particularly to brain regions responsible for memory, emotions and emotional regulation. It is [therefore] not surprising that chronic exposure to elevated levels of [stress hormones] has an impact on cognition and the development of different psychopathologies" (2011, 590).

The undoubted psychopathological effects of stress are of great interest in their own right. However, we will focus here on summarizing the effects of stress on a special case, namely, episodic memory. Episodic memory retrieval is at the heart of the interrogative process and of witness evidence. It is therefore of paramount importance to understand how the deliberate exogenous application of high levels of stress, especially predator stress, might impact on memory function in somebody who is undergoing an interrogation. There have been many experimental investigations of the effects of stress on memory. We will summarize the overall pattern of findings here, and then we will examine the effects of stress on cognitive and psychological function in two special populations—combat soldiers and victims of torture.

There have been many full-length reviews of the effects of stress (and especially stress hormones) on cognition. The stress hormone cortisol (in humans) binds to glucocorticoid receptors (GCRs) and mineralocorticoid receptors (MCRs) in the brain and with particular affinity and with profound effect in the part of the brain most implicated in episodic memory, namely, the hippocampal formation. This is a particularly important finding for, as Lupien and colleagues note (2007, 215), this means that the effects of stress hormones on episodic memory can be attributed to the effect of these stress hormones on the brain systems that support episodic memory and not as a result of collateral effects on brain systems supporting, say, vigilance or attention. Lupien and colleagues' overall conclusion is that "the majority of studies performed in human populations tend to confirm the rodent literature reporting acute negative effects of glucocorticoids on hippocampal dependent forms of memory" (216). This is a reasonable and uncontroversial summary of the vast preponderance of the literature. It should be noted in passing that while chronically elevated levels of stress hormones have a profoundly deleterious effect on memory, as we will discuss in the next section, very mildly elevated levels of stress hormones can actually facilitate memory function, confirming that for stress hormones, as for other hormonal and transmitter systems in the body, there is an optimal inverted-U-shape curve governing their action. Too little is deleterious and too much is profoundly deleterious, but there is an optimal point between these two extremes. This optimal point, of course, it needs to be emphasized, is far below that experienced during chronic, unpredictable, uncontrollable stress.

That there may be a somewhat positive effect of mild stressors on memory (both recall and encoding) is not particularly well appreciated. It might well be the case that the levels of arousal and stress caused by capture, transport, captivity, and loss of control are sufficiently high to overcome these positive effects (this is an empirical question). A key part of the interrogation process will have to be ensuring that the levels of stress and anxiety experienced by captives are reduced to levels that both are humane and facilitate optimal levels of recall. This is not a straightforward task. We will below examine the effects of extreme stress in a well-motivated and highly trained human population, that of combat soldiers, and then in actual torture victims themselves.

Stress Induced by Cramped Confinement and Shackling

Cramped confinement is a form of extreme stressor in which prisoners are kept in small boxes that allow little movement and that, because of limited ventilation, quickly become unpleasantly warm. The trapped body heat causes perspiration, and the loss of body fluid in turn leads to rapid dehydration and debilitation of brain and body. The body of a seventy-kilogram male is about 50–70 percent fluid by weight. Total body water turnover is about 5–10 percent per day, implying fluid losses of two to four liters per day. Death will occur after seven to ten days of water deprivation at normal room temperatures. The design of the box can vary. It might be sealed so that there is relatively little air exchange with the external environment, or it may be ventilated passively through holes, or it may be actively ventilated through some form of air conditioning. But the key point is that movement is restricted or impossible and that the conditions of confinement themselves are, at a minimum, socially isolating, deindividuating, uncomfortable, and inescapable. The logic underlying the use of cramped confinement is the use of claustrophobia (the sense of dread and fear of being trapped in confined spaces) to force the loosening of tongues. Again, the strange logic of folk psychology rears its head: the guess or surmise that the fear of enclosure and confinement will be so great that it will induce captives to reason that if they speak, they will be released.

In other words, the threat of the confinement—or the actual use of confinement—will be enough to loosen the tongue. The fear of cramped confinement is of course very real. Claustrophobia is an anxiety disorder recognized by the *DSM*—the *Diagnostic and Statistical Manual of Mental Disorders* of the American Psychiatric Association. It is a reasonably common phobia, which can be decomposed into two differing fears. One is the sensation of being trapped and unable to move, and the other is fear around the inability to breathe. Some estimates suggest that about 5 percent of the population at large, in Western societies at least, suffer from claustrophobia. The proportion of individuals suffering from claustrophobia is possibly higher than this, though.

The folk psychology here is the reasoning that inducing an underlying fear of the situation will facilitate recall because the captive will be motivated to escape the situation by complying with the ongoing questioning of the interrogator. Thinking through the logic, though, leads you to at least two different possibilities. If the box is large, then it may actually become a place of refuge and will be sought after. After all, if you are inside the box and you are comfortable in the darkness, you might, because of the sensory deprivation involved, get to sleep for a while. This would be a welcome respite from a concurrent program of sleep deprivation. Minimally, at least, you will not have to see your captors, and you probably cannot hear what they have to say terribly well. If the box is small, however, then what might occur could be quite the contrary. If it is dark, the position that you have to adopt is stressful and uncomfortable, and if it is unventilated, so that you become excessively hot, then it will become a situation from which you will wish to escape. Confinement, under either of these circumstances, of course, is involuntary—that is, you have no control over your environment or what is being done to you. The smaller box, by definition, will be aversive, and as a result, a phobia—claustrophobia—may develop. Phobias can be chronically disabling, especially if they are severe, prolonged, and generalized to a wide variety of environmental contexts—that is, if the rooms and places that you are in all trigger the phobic response because you have suffered cramped confinement in them or in rooms that are very similar to them. A noteworthy feature of anxiety disorders (including phobias) is clinically significant deficits in memory function.

Restraints are often used during interrogation. These may be shackles used to chain the prisoner to the ground or to a chair; they may be handcuffs used to chain the prisoners' hands to a table, to a body belt, or merely to each other. Restraint procedures such as these are common and may be claimed to be necessary because of the danger that the prisoner may pose to themselves or to others. The other context within which restraints have been used is in the case of psychiatric patients. The straitjacket is one formerly very commonly used form of restraint, in which the arms are crossed in front of the body and tied at the rear, so that they are pinned to the torso, thereby greatly restricting the range of potential movement possible in patients. The phrase *chemical straitjacket* (sometimes *liquid straitjacket*) refers to the use of psychoactive drugs as an alternative form of restraint in such patients. Sedative drugs may be used to calm the patient. These drugs, of course, are inappropriate operationally in an interrogation procedure. The sedative effects of these compounds will, minimally, prevent the captive from engaging coherently with the context of interrogation. Higher doses may render the captive completely unresponsive. I have been unable to find any articles in the literature that measure stress hormones in voluntarily restrained humans before and after the manual or physical restraint procedure. There is a large literature on the use of physical restraint in psychiatric patients, but these patients, by definition, are at the end of a spectrum of disturbed responsivity. A review of the available data suggests that manual restraint in Old World monkeys increases the production of stress hormones and also causes many other widespread physiological changes (Reinhardt, Liss, and Stevens 1995). Furthermore, the monkeys do not adapt over time to being restrained. Given the similarities in responsivity of the autonomic nervous systems in human and nonhuman primates, forced manual restraint will cause similar and probably much more widespread changes in humans. Nonrestraint methods during interrogation are desirable, and the design of the physical environment within which the interrogation is to take place may facilitate the use of nonrestraint (see Chapter 8).

For ethical reasons, restraint stress is usually only studied in nonhumans. As noted, it is rarely studied in nonhuman primates but has been frequently studied in small laboratory animals such as rats and mice. In a typical procedure, rats or mice are restrained by placing them into a confined space that limits movement. This might be a small Perspex container that allows them to be visible to the experimenter. They are unable to walk about, they are unable to engage in personal grooming, and they may have to urinate or defecate in the position they are in, thereby soiling themselves. The procedure seems to be very effective, unsurprisingly, at inducing severe and high levels of stress. How do we know that the animals are indeed stressed? There are a couple of methods for knowing this. One is to sample blood periodically from the tail vein and to measure the levels of the stress hormones that may be present, such as corticosterone. Cramped confinement of this type causes, in this animal model, great increases in the levels of stress hormones, to typically three, four, or five times above the levels that are found in the nonrestrained condition (e.g., Lakshminarasimhan and Chattarji 2012).

The levels of hormone peak in the hour or so after the initiation of confinement and are then maintained at near maximal levels for more or less the period of confinement. This means that adaptation to the stressor does not typically occur. Does this procedure have any other effects besides an increase in circulating stress hormones? A particular interest of many researchers has been to examine the interaction between these stress-inducing procedures and learning and memory.

There are many ways that we can measure memory function reliably in rats and mice. One of the most effective is a very simple apparatus known as the water maze, a device that has been used extensively since the early 1980s. It was invented by Richard Morris, a fellow of the Royal Society and professor of neuroscience at the University of Edinburgh in Scotland (Morris 1981; see also D'Hooge and colleagues 2001). Rats are placed in a circular pool of water, typically one and half to two meters in diameter. Hidden in a quadrant of the pool is a platform just below the surface. This platform offers a place of refuge from the water. Rats are preternatural swimmers: they know how to swim despite never having been trained to swim. When placed in a pool of water like this, they will typically circle around the circumference of the pool, looking for an escape route (a behavior named thigomataxis). After a few minutes, they will make short and small excursions across the pool. Eventually, they will, by chance, blunder into the hidden platform, find that it is a stable refuge, and climb on top of it. Here they will groom themselves, shake themselves, and dry themselves off. On their first exposure to the pool, it may take them perhaps a minute or so to find the hidden platform. After ten or twenty exposures to the pool, perhaps over a few days, normal young adult rats will find the hidden platform in a matter of a few seconds—perhaps five to eight seconds. Aged animals take a much greater period of time to find the hidden platform. Aged animals that have been treated with certain procognitive drugs (drugs that enhance cognition) might find the hidden platform more quickly and will remember its position for much longer periods of time. Animals that have been treated with drugs that may be amnestic in their effects will take much longer to learn the position of the hidden platform. Unsurprisingly, given the ease of the water maze's construction and the simplicity of its use, the pharmaceutical industry has widely adopted it as a simple behavioral screen for drugs that might be thought to be of use in the treatment of disorders of memory such as Alzheimer's disease.

The brain structures responsible for this type of learning have also been explored in great detail. Learning to find a refuge in an environment is an example of spatial cognition—the cognitive processes required to recall where you have parked your car, where your office is, where the spaghetti is usually located in your local store—in other words, any of the processes that are required to support thinking and remembering about where you currently are, where you have been, where you would like to go (and perhaps what you might like to do when you get there). Damage to the hippocampal formation causes grave and enduring deficits in animals in the water maze. If the hippocampus is damaged (by surgical or other means), these animals are typically incapable of ever learning where the hidden platform is. If the hippocampus is removed posttraining, they will also suffer deficits. Restraint stress is another method for inducing grave and enduring deficits in the water maze and indeed in other forms of (spatial) cognition. A general, reasonable, and well-founded conclusion from the empirical restraint literature is that exposure to this form of stress on a chronic basis (that is, day after day) causes grave deficits in learning and memory. These deficits typically do not resolve during the period when the animal is exposed to the stressor and typically can take many weeks to disappear—if they do at all—after the experience of the stressor is removed. The deficits in memory caused by this form of restraint stress extend far beyond merely being unable to learn the water maze satisfactorily. Daily exposure to this stressor, for as little as a couple of hours a day for a few days, can cause a decrease in the volume of the hippocampus itself. We know this because we can measure the volume of the hippocampus in anesthetized animals using structural magnetic resonance imaging, from which we can make estimates of the reduction of the total volume of the hippocampus as a result of restraint stress. The volume of the hippocampus can also be measured using the techniques of neuroanatomy. In this case, on completion of the experiment, the animal is killed by an overdose of general anesthetic, the brain is removed and sectioned into very thin sections, and then the sections are mounted onto glass slides, which are then examined using a microscope. An enduring, stress-induced decrease in brain tissue surely constitutes organ damage and organ failure, a criterion specified, ironically enough, in the Torture Memos as an intervention rising to the standard of torture.

Neurogenesis and Apoptosis: The Birth and Death of Brain Cells

A series of studies first conducted in rodents and monkeys and then later extended to humans have shown that neurogenesis, the birth of new brain cells, occurs in certain brain areas (in particular, in the hippocampal formation). These new brain cells are born right throughout the course of life. Neurogenesis is affected dramatically by conditions that cause disturbances to memory function; these include, in particular, conditions related to neuropsychiatric distress (depression, stress, and the like), as well as other causes (such as chronic sleep deprivation) and the effects of certain drugs. Many contemporary theories suggest that interrupting neurogenesis is materially related to, if not causally related to, the genesis of many neuropsychiatric disorders (such as depression) that in turn negatively affect mood, memory, and cognition.

The experimental procedure used to investigate neurogenesis is straightforward. A chemical (with the shortened chemical name of BrDU) is injected into the body. This chemical is taken up only by cells of the body undergoing division; BrDU has been used as a marker for the continued division of cancer-causing cells. BrDU passes into the brain, and it passes from the brain without leaving any trace of its presence, with the exception of a number of limited areas, where it stains a small but reliable number of cells a distinctive brown color. Careful experimentation over the past two decades or so has shown that this label is present only in newly born brain cells. Almost without exception, the universal observation in the literature is that a severe, chronic, repeated stressor, irrespective of its origin (whether it be from restraint stress or social challenge by a dominant other or a predator or from a neurochemical source such as circulating stress hormones), inhibits the production of new brain cells in the hippocampus. This reduction of the production of new brain cells has been widely observed in just about every animal model of stress and also in models of depression. Recent data indicate that this reduction in neurogenesis also accompanies profound and enduring deficits in learning and memory. These data go further— they show also that the reduction in neurogenesis is also accompanied by a reduction in the production of growth factors in the brain. These are factors that assist the growth of neurons and whose function is most often associated, in the adult brain, with the stabilization of the synapse and with the behavioral expression of memory. Loss or inhibition of the growth of tissue in the body is referred to as hypotrophy. The effect of chronic stress on the hippocampus is hypotrophic—it causes the hippocampus to shrink, along with deficits in the function it supports (namely, memory).

Stress also can cause the enlargement of organs in the body and in parts of the brain. This is known as hypertrophy. In particular, enlargement of the adrenal glands can occur; these glands secrete stress hormones. A similar effect can occur in the brain. Stress can cause hypertrophy of the amygdala, a structure particularly associated with the processing of information about fearful events; it becomes hyperresponsive under conditions of stress, fear, and anxiety. Amygdalar hypertrophy and hyperresponsiveness are often found in patients with posttraumatic stress disorder. When the prefrontal cortex becomes hyporesponsive, it begins not to respond to stimulation, and there may be decreases in tissue volume in this area of the brain. Benno Roozendaal and his colleagues (2009) in a very important review article summarize the effects of chronic stressors as follows: the hippocampal formation becomes reduced in volume and shows reduced neurogenesis; prefrontal cortex becomes hyporesponsive and may show some degree of tissue loss. The amygdala becomes hyperresponsive; it becomes more likely to respond and actually undergoes enlargement (hypertrophy). As we have already noted, the hippocampus and prefrontal cortex—particularly involved in the intentional control of memory and in the long-term storage of information in memory—can, as a result of the changes in the areas of the brain responsible for memory, become less responsive. The amygdala, by contrast, undergoes a degree of enlargement with the imposition of extreme and prolonged stress.

How does all of this relate to torture? A common argument in favor of torture is that it will reliably elicit veridical information from the captive's long-term memory, without any effect on memory itself. The underlying contention is that repeatedly imposing profound stressors during coercive interrogation does not have any substantive or profound effect on memory. The key point here, however, is that the repeated imposition of such stressors impacts in a terrible way on the very brain systems responsible for supporting mood, memory, and cognition. While understanding the effects of stress in animal models is useful, it would be much more useful to study the direct effects of stress in humans—and better again to investigate the effects of stress on memory. This kind of work is particularly important because the effect of stress on recall in humans who are motivated to cooperate will show directly, without any motivational effects. And it is thus to the effects of stress in combat soldiers that we will turn next. However, the evidence presented thus far suggests just the opposite of that common argument in favor of torture: the imposition of extreme stressor states does not facilitate memory function and does not enhance recall, even under conditions of motivated recall. The evidence shows that extreme stressors significantly impair recall of information in a time-dependent retrograde fashion, as well as in an anterograde fashion. Indeed, extreme stressors affect particularly deeply fluid accounts of recently acquired information (about what happened when and to whom and about the relationships among the principal actors). The effects are deepened when the stressors are imposed repeatedly, when inappropriate questioning techniques are used, when leading information is supplied, and when (as is common in torture scenarios) the veracity of what information is provided is denied. Under these circumstances, people will naturally and correctly start to doubt their own judgment regarding what it is they think they know.

Stress Dramatically Impairs Memory, Mood, and Cognition in Combat Soldiers

Charles Morgan and his collaborators at Yale University have conducted a series of very important studies focused on extreme stressors in combat soldiers. They have examined the effects of military survival training on the human stress response and on the recovery from the effect of the stressors encountered during such training. These studies are remarkable because the stressors used arise during the course of training, are of an extreme nature, are imposed on physically fit young humans, and finally, are conducted with assays of a wide range of psychological variables (for example, learning, memory, and attention) without a substantial supervening effect of motivation. Motivational variables are a key component of folk reasoning regarding the use of torture. The reasoning goes that captives are motivated to withhold information. Motivational variables of this type will not be at play with combat soldiers, and thus the pure effect of extreme stress on a variety of psychological variables can be investigated directly without the confounding effects of motivation or compliance on recall of episodic and semantic information from memory (something that is true also of animal models). We will now examine some of these studies here. In general, these studies use a pre-post experimental design: soldiers are assessed on a variable or set of variables of interest, are then subjected to some element of combat training for some period of time, and are then assessed further. Any changes in performance can then be attributed to the effect of the intervention—in principle, there may be a positive or negative effect, or there may be no change, and these changes may occur in different directions simultaneously for the differing measured variables. Thus, these studies provide a particularly powerful way of quantitatively investigating the effect of extreme stressors on memory, cognition, and other psychological variables. Finally, these studies can also be used to investigate the effects of such stressors on a variety of so-called wet biomarkers—changes in hormones and the like—usually from blood or saliva samples.

In one study, Morgan and his colleagues (2001) examined changes in the level of neuropeptide Y (NPY) in soldiers undergoing military survival training. Secretion of NPY reduces anxiety levels somewhat, as it functions a little like benzodiazepines such as valium, which also have antianxiety effects. NPY is naturally occurring and is secreted in response to the effects of stress; for example, it is secreted when one suffers from metabolic stress during exercise because of oxygen restriction, buffering the effects of stress somewhat. Morgan and colleagues found that in soldiers subjected to military-style interrogation, NPY levels increased as a result of the imposition of the acute psychological stress.

In another study, Morgan and his colleagues (2009) focused on levels of DHEA (dehydroepiandrosterone), which is secreted in response to the stress-hormone precursor ACTH (adrenocorticotropic hormone). DHEA is also involved in the response to stress: it tends to decrease in response to illnesses, including psychiatric illnesses such as depression and schizophrenia (and even anorexia). Morgan and his colleagues examined DHEA levels in military personnel undergoing survival-school training, in order to examine the relationship between the production of DHEA, stress hormones, and perceived stress and resistance to stress on the part of the individuals undergoing this training. The researchers took saliva and blood samples to measure DHEA levels at a baseline, preintervention. Subjects were also administered the CADDSS—the Clinician-Administered Dissociative States Scale. This test instrument measures the extent to which individuals are currently in touch with their environment or the extent to which they are dissociated or distracted from engagement with their environment. The study involved the use of a mock prisoner-of-war camp, where the trainees underwent interrogations, were forced to engage in a variety of problem-solving dilemmas, and were sleep deprived and food deprived. As expected, levels of the stress hormone cortisol rose, average heart rates were higher, subjective distress increased, and the male sex hormone testosterone was decreased. Military survival-school training increased psychological dissociation to moderate levels. These were levels at which a clinician would be required to attend to a patient and to regard the patient as at risk, in order to ensure that nothing further goes wrong with him or her. The researchers also examined the ratio of DHEA to cortisol, in order to investigate what happens in individuals in whom there are high levels of DHEA relative to cortisol and in individuals in whom there are low levels of DHEA relative to cortisol. Individuals who had a high DHEA-to-cortisol ratios performed better on independent measures of overall military performance, and they showed lower levels of dissociation. The researchers found the reverse in individuals who had a low DHEA-to-cortisol ratio. These data point to the fact that the response to a severe but acute stressor that lasts a couple of days varies between individuals; some individuals are much better at coping with the effects of an imposed stressor than are others. Individuals who are better at coping with these stressors are less likely to show clinically significant signs of psychiatric problems.

These studies show that an externally imposed or exogenous chronic stressor (military training) can cause important changes in circulating hormones and peptides and that these changes are associated with changes in the psychological state of at least some individuals. Such studies do not directly address the key issue in this book, however—the effects of the imposition of severe stressors on quantitative changes in memory, mood, and cognition. Fortunately, such studies are also available. A particularly important and pertinent experimental model of the effects of stress on memory was devised by Morgan and his colleagues (2006), in a study of special-operations soldiers being subjected to prisoner-of-war conditions. The soldiers were exposed to extreme bouts of food and sleep deprivation and to extreme temperature variations (hot and cold). Morgan and his colleagues showed that extreme behavioral stressors caused grave memory *deficits:* in particular, impairments in visuo-spatial capacity and recall of previously learned information. The key point here is that these soldiers were not motivated to withhold information from their interrogators; they were impaired in voluntarily recalling the information sought by their interrogators, despite their motivation to reveal the learned information. This point can hardly be overemphasized: there was no motivation to withhold information in these participants, but yet there was still a substantial decrement in performance on event-memory tasks of about one-third (Morgan and colleagues 2006). In other words, exposure to a substantial period of stress is sufficient to induce deficits in the recall of recently learned information from memory in humans who are especially selected for their capacity to withstand stress and who are in great physical condition. And yet even these soldiers show a profound decrement in memory after being exposed to substantial and sustained stressor states.

As we have already seen, standard torture techniques involve combinations of the manipulation of differing metabolic states. These might include restricting food and liquid intake or other dietary manipulations, sleep deprivation, and temperature manipulations. These are extreme and inescapable interoceptively generated stressors that are imposed exogenously. Systematic manipulations of this type are difficult to perform in a volunteer group of participants but again can be investigated in the context of military training. Morgan and colleagues have examined the effect that combining stressors such as sleep loss, heat, dehydration, and undernutrition might have on cognitive performance, mood, and hormonal status in an elite military unit on a combat training exercise (see Lieberman and colleagues 2005). They measured, in thirty-one male volunteers (who had, on average, about nine years' active military service each), three times over five days, the effect of the combination of simulated combat with sleep deprivation, heat stress, physical stress, and a restricted diet on cognitive performance, mood, physical activity, and hormonal status. They also measured reaction times, vigilance, memory, and reasoning. They also administered a mood-profile questionnaire and measured sleep using an actigraph (an activity monitor). The soldiers all had free access to water, so hydration was (initially) not believed to be a problem. The researchers also measured body composition using a DEXA scanner (used clinically to measure bone density). Finally, they measured from saliva the stress hormone cortisol, testosterone, and melatonin. Over the test period of five days, they found that simulated combat (and the severe stressors associated with it) caused a dramatic reduction in natural sleep rhythms. The soldiers slept for approximately three hours over this period of time, usually in short bursts of about twelve minutes or so. These periods were never sufficient to repay accumulated sleep debt. They found that the soldiers lost substantial amounts of weight—approximately four kilograms on average over the period of five days. The weight loss consisted mostly of water loss; it did not appear to be muscle mass or fat, despite the soldiers having free access to as much water as they required over the period of time. They also found that on all tests of cognition the soldiers were severely impaired. Their mood also disimproved dramatically, as did their hormonal status. Surprisingly, "even well trained leaders exhibit significant degradation in cognitive performance and mood when exposed to severe multi-factorial stress." (Lieberman and colleagues 2005, 427).

Other data confirm these findings. For example, Harris Lieberman and his colleagues examined (in a 2006 NATO report) the effects of battlefield-like stress on cognitive and endocrine function in captains from the U.S. Army Rangers (with an average of nine years' service). Participants were exposed to multiple stressors related to combat conditions (for example, short preparation times, unexpected location deployment, little food and liquid, simulated combat, and high humidity). Two very important findings were made: first, battlefield-like stressors caused a severe degradation in psychological status (vigilance, reaction times, learning, memory, and logical reasoning were all impaired, and mood states such as anger, confusion, and fatigue were exacerbated); second, cortisol levels did not show a spike, indicating that extensive pretraining can buffer the classic stress response, despite the negative changes in psychological status. Interestingly, in a previous study, Morgan and colleagues (2000) did not observe this buffering effect on cortisol in a nonelite group of soldiers with a shorter duration of service (seven years on average).

The question naturally arises: why would anybody imagine that this significant degradation in cognitive performance and mood, induced by the imposition of severe stressors such as sleep deprivation, heat, dietary restrictions, and other variables, would in some way facilitate recall, enhance memory, and improve motivation? The experimental evidence systematically obtained in a well-motivated group of highly trained, highly experienced individuals shows quite the contrary. The effect of imposing such extreme stressors causes a significant degradation in cognitive performance. There is no basis for expecting that imposing such stressors, especially in combination, is going to facilitate recall by people who are being subjected to interrogation. We can say this with confidence because we see across a wide range of stressors imposed on these soldiers a significant decrease in baseline performance, that is, when the humans are not required to learn any material for subsequent recall. We also see this fall in performance when the soldiers are required to learn some material for subsequent recall. Here, motivation and compliance are not an issue. Participants in studies of this type are already motivated to perform, and yet they perform anywhere from poorly to catastrophically badly.

Social Isolation and Sensory Deprivation as Forms of White Torture

Social isolation and sensory deprivation are not the same thing, but they can have and do have similar effects. Sensory deprivation was formally inaugurated as a field of study in the 1950s by Donald Hebb, a Canadian neuropsychologist. Hebb, in a series of groundbreaking experiments (see Hebb and Heron 1955; Hebb, Heron, and Bexton 1952), brought volunteers into a laboratory, gave them comfortable, loose clothes to wear, placed large mitts around their hands, placed blindfolds over their eyes and earmuffs over their ears, and had them lie down in a darkened room on a comfortable bed. Most volunteers fell into very deep and relaxing sleep, typically lasting between forty-five minutes and about two to three hours. Thereafter, though, virtually all of his volunteers reported strange and unusual psychological phenomena occurring to them. They would hallucinate, experiencing sensory input from the visual system or the auditory system that was not there; they would imagine themselves to be weightless and to be floating in space; or other similar phenomena. As the period of sensory deprivation became extended, most volunteers reported feeling extremes of emotion and occasionally quite terrifying phenomena, many reminiscent of the kinds of intrusive auditory and visual input that occurs in certain psychoses (such as schizophrenia). Hebb was interested in the effects of perceptual isolation on cognitive and affective function, and not in developing such techniques for the particular purpose of torture per se (see Brown 2007 and McCoy 2007 for a differing interpretation). His research work was conducted on volunteer university students, and not on prisoners undergoing interrogation. Social isolation is a somewhat different manipulation. As a form of incarceration, it has been practiced more or less as long as prison cells have been in use. Placing a prisoner under isolation without access to social interaction has long been recognized as a great and profound punishment, one at best to be endured. In this section, we will deal with the use of sensory deprivation and of sustained social isolation as forms of extreme stressors that are used as methods to "enhance" the efficacy of an interrogation regime.

We deal first with sensory deprivation. Formally, sensory deprivation means to deprive one or all of the senses (seeing, hearing, touch, balance, taste, pain) of their natural and normal input. In practice, the two senses that are most easily disrupted are vision, by means of blindfolding, and audition, by means of earplugs and/or earmuffs. In these cases, the deprivation is to remove the input. There is another possibility, which is to attempt sensory overload, for example, by keeping prisoners in cells where supranormal levels of light are used and into which loud sounds are played (apocryphally, loud music in recent years has been used—some appears to be from a variety of death metal bands). By now, the neuroscience of sensory deprivation has become very well understood, and we will explore it by looking at the consequences of sensory loss or impairment for normal brain function, especially during the development of the nervous system. We will further focus on the effect of deliberate insult designed to remove sensory input in the mature nervous system, and finally, we will look at some case studies of individuals who have been subject to extreme sensory deprivation.

Sensory deprivation has been studied intensively in a variety of animal models and in occasional human cases since the 1960s. The classic experiments involve removing visual input from one eye by means of blindfold or eyelid suture during the early period after birth and over the first months of life. The conclusion of these studies is straightforward: deprivation of monocular input (that is, input from a single eye) has profound and dramatic effects on the organization of the visual system. The parts of the visual brain that should have received these inputs do not develop normally, and their function is not restored, even if subsequent visual input is allowed by means of removal of the eyelid sutures or of the eye patch. These kinds of findings have given rise to the idea that there are critical periods in the development of the nervous system when sensory input is required in order for the nervous system to develop appropriately. What is true of the visual system of cats is similarly true of the language system of humans. Occasional cases come to light of humans subjected to horrific deprivation in the early months and years of life. Children who are not exposed to an appropriate language community between the period soon after birth and up to approximately six or seven years of age do not learn to speak in anything resembling the language used in the language communities that normal humans would display. This gives rise to the idea that sensory input across all of the sensory channels is vital for the normal development and function of the nervous system and that this so-called activity-dependent set of changes will not occur unless these inputs are present at the appropriate time. The effects of sensory deprivation on the mature or developed nervous system are not the same, by any means, as the removal of inputs during development, but it is clearly the case that the removal of these inputs profoundly affects the structure and function of the mature nervous system—but in reliably and predictably different ways to those found in the developing nervous system.

Social Isolation and Solitary Confinement

Humans, like many other species, are social animals, and deprivation or isolation for sustained periods from our fellow human beings (with rare exceptions) is usually very deleterious for our normal psychological functioning. A very profound example of this is given by an instructive case study in Alzheimer's disease. There is an active debate, which we do not need to dwell on here, on the causes of Alzheimer's disease, but it is becoming clear that one of the key variables in predicting the onset of Alzheimer's disease in the elderly is the social network within which the individual is embedded. To put it bluntly, the lonelier you are and the more socially isolated you are, the more likely you are to succumb to the effects of Alzheimer's disease. In a particularly elegant study by David A. Bennett and colleagues (2006), it was shown that the amyloid burden, when brains come to postmortem, could be identical in different individuals, but the clinical diagnosis of Alzheimer's disease premortem was not. This is because although the presence of amyloid in the brain is thought to be a significant predictor of the presence of cognitive dysfunction, the density of one's ongoing social connections and social network is a significantly moderating variable regarding whether one would succumb to Alzheimer's disease and show the related pathologies of cognition. In other words, social connections matter, and they matter to the extent that they can moderate significantly the pathology induced by Alzheimer's disease.

Social isolation is something that we persistently underestimate in terms of its effects on ourselves or on others. But it is easy to demonstrate the consequences of social isolation by means of a simple thought experiment. Which would you prefer, to break a limb or to be excluded from a peer group that you value? The answer here is not obvious. Most people will choose social isolation over the breaking of a limb. However, and most peculiarly, the pain from limb breakages does not persist, usually, past the resetting of the bone, but the pain induced by social isolation does. Humans can be obsessed by incidents of what appear to be unfair social exclusion or social isolation, the effects of which may rankle for years past the time when they occurred. Who among us does not think back to slights during our past and ruminate on them? It should therefore be of no surprise that traumatic incidents inscribe themselves on the brain.

What Changes Occur in the Brains of the Tortured?

There is a small but very important literature exploring the long-term effects of torture on torture survivors. We will briefly review some of the findings of this literature here, as these findings underpin the data found in elite performers—the combat soldiers. At least three different types of evaluation of torture survivors are available in the literature. The first are clinical psychological or psychiatric assessments, in which the effects of torture are assessed in order to arrive at a psychiatric or psychological diagnosis. Epidemiological studies indicate that perhaps somewhere between half and up to 90 percent of survivors suffer from posttraumatic stress disorder (or at least meet the *DSM* criteria for PTSD); absent any treatment, this condition can persist for decades. A second type of study will have torture survivors voluntarily participate in provocation paradigms in which the survivors are presented with stimuli that may evoke symptoms of one sort or another. For example, survivors might be presented with a series of faces with differing expressions and asked to judge the expressions that are on those faces—if the faces are fearful, happy, or sad. Another form of investigation involves examining changes in brain function in these survivors, typically using either brain scanning or EEG studies, and estimates are made of the differences in function in differing parts of the brain in the torture survivors, relative to a nontorture group. There have been several recent comprehensive reviews of the literature (for example, Johnson and Thompson 2008; Campbell 2007; and especially the collected papers edited by Weierstall, Elbert, and Maercker 2011). A reasonable summary of these extensive literature reviews is as follows: (a) torture survivors, in the main, continue to suffer the psychological effects of torture for many years and perhaps decades after their experience; (b) the psychopathological effects of torture manifest themselves in a variety of ways, ranging from insomnia, flashbacks, and the like to full-blown psychiatric disorders such as PTSD, depression, and a general behavioral syndrome that involves a perpetual state of environmental awareness, hypervigilance, and inappropriately strong processing of putative threat-related stimuli; (c) there are individual differences in the response to having been tortured—some individuals suffer terribly indeed, while others show a greater degree of resilience; (d) there can be intergenerational effects too, as the children of torture survivors may manifest a variety of conduct and other psychological problems as well; (e) there has been some (limited) degree of success in treating survivors with cognitive-behavior therapies and other psychological/psychiatric techniques.

Iris-Tatjana Kolassa and colleagues (2007) investigated differences in the brains of ninety-seven torture survivors compared to ninety-seven controls. The torture survivors met the *DSM* criteria for post-traumatic stress disorder, and most of them also met the criteria for major depression. The researchers found, at rest, substantial differences present in the brains of the torture survivors compared to controls. Alterations were found in the electrical oscillations of the brain compared to normal controls. In particular, there were more slow waves, especially in the left temporal brain region, the bilateral insula, and the right frontal area. The insula are implicated in multimodal convergence from all of the senses, and they are also involved in attention, pain, and other functions and also they play a role in speech and language. The insula in particular seems particularly implicated as a key brain structure involved in the induction and maintenance of posttraumatic stress disorder in torture survivors. Other studies (for example, Catani and colleagues 2009; Defrin and colleagues 2014; Mollica and colleagues 2009, Ray and colleagues 2006) all confirm a similar pattern of findings across ethnically, gender-, and age-diverse groups: there are profound and enduring changes in the brains of the tortured that relate precisely and specifically to the imposition of torture. These changes in the brain may vary from structural abnormalities (which can be visualized using brain-imaging techniques) to persistently abnormal activity in certain brain regions, to extreme and long-lasting sensitivity to pain, among other changes.

Phobic Stressors

The suggested use of a person's phobias in order to manipulate him or her revolves around the idea that, to be effective, the fear induced by a phobia has to be unrelenting and unremitting and that exposure to the fearful stimulus (for example, the close-confinement cabinet) must evoke depths of fear and anxiety that are overwhelming to the individual. These depths of fear must occur to the point that, when people are anticipating what is about to happen to them, they would sooner reveal what they know than endure the feelings that will occur as a result of the experience of the fearful stimulus of the cramped confinement cabinet. Here, of course, the naive psychological inference is deeply wrong, for it presumes that the phobia itself is enduring and is therefore the point of leverage. We encounter an additional variant on this reasoning with the proposal (never implemented) to expose captives to insects. Insectophobia (or entomophobia) is common and is not predictable in terms of its outcomes. A more subtle attempt at coercing some captives has involved suggesting to them that their phobias will be used to manipulate them into revealing information. The essence of these proposals is the attempt to increment the effect of the stressors that the prisoners are exposed to.

Phobias can be extremely disabling. People develop them for a variety of reasons and often in an age-dependent fashion. Often the stimuli themselves are not, in themselves, life threatening. Blood phobias, for example, typically develop much earlier than do social phobias (which, on average, start to occur during those most acutely self-conscious of years, around puberty). Treatment for phobias is generally based around principles derived from cognitive-behavior therapy (occasionally supplemented or augmented by drug therapy in certain cases). Cognitive-behavior therapy has been found to be extremely effective in reducing the symptoms of phobia. For claustrophobia, two types of treatment are likely to be used. The first is known as flooding therapy, and the second is known as systematic desensitization therapy. Flooding therapy involves the well-founded idea that it is difficult to maintain an anxiety response for very substantial periods of time in the face of a stimulus that induces the phobia. In this case, the person will be exposed to the phobic stimulus in a fully experienced fashion. Ethically, this may seem a dubious route to treatment, but there is sufficient evidence to suggest that being exposed to the fear-inducing stimulus without the possibility of escape may decrease the phobic response over time. Systematic desensitization can take a similar route to exposure to the fear-inducing stimulus, but it does so in a systematic and graded fashion. People undergoing therapy might be at first asked to visualize a small cramped space, while they are being carefully monitored. They may then be asked to approach, but not physically stand in, a confined space (such as an elevator). They may then, again through graded exposure, cross the threshold into the elevator and then count for a short time before stepping out, with the count incremented on each occasion. They might then travel a short distance,

along with the therapist, in the elevator. Finally, they may undertake a more substantive set of journeys by themselves in elevators of
differing sizes and capacities. The ultimate test of the therapy might
involve having the patient lie in the narrow bore of a brain-imaging
machine or some other similarly small space.

Cramped confinement is probably more akin to the experience of
flooding therapy than it is to systematic desensitization. Prisoners
will likely be forced or manhandled into the box. The box is locked,
and they may struggle to release themselves from the box but after
a while give up the struggle if the box is inescapable. Their stress-
hormone levels will peak, perhaps in minutes to perhaps an hour of
confinement in the box, but will thereafter start to diminish. The
analogy with flooding therapy here is clear. Repeated confinement
in the box will, all else being equal (assuming no other stressors such
as electrocution or temperature manipulation are involved), result
in a diminution of the phobic response to the box. The irony here, of
course, is clear. There is a predictable outcome to the use of cramped
confinement, but not one that its proponents are aware of. It is
likely, if repeated sufficiently frequently, to cure captives of any
phobia they may have of being confined in a small environment. Similar principles apply in terms of flooding therapy and systematic
desensitization where insect phobia is concerned. The phobia can be
trained out as it was trained in, if the prisoner is indeed exposed repeatedly to the insect in question. This of course will not be true for
insects whose stings or bites are severely injurious or fatal, but only
a very foolish interrogator would take a risk of this type. So again
a naive psychological analysis proves to be unhelpful in the quest to
find ways to manipulate prisoners. A rudimentary knowledge of contemporary treatment methods for psychopathologies would have
obviated this suggestion. Common sense clearly prevailed in the case
of terror suspects after 9/11, as this latter method of coercive interrogation, while suggested and discussed seriously, was not used on
any prisoner.

A similar lack of sophistication is seen in the application of learned helplessness theory as a potential basis for interrogations. Learned helplessness is a theory originally developed by Martin Seligman (1975) as a potential explanation for how depression develops in humans. It most certainly was not developed as a theory to be applied to the abuse of prisoners during interrogation. The Senate Torture Report (and many other confirmatory sources) details how psychologists involved in interrogation misapplied the theory of learned helplessness to interrogation: "On the CIA's behalf, the contract psychologists developed theories of interrogation based on 'learned helplessness'" (SSCI 2014, 10); similarly, a footnote states, "'Learned helplessness' in this context was the theory that detainees might become passive and depressed in response to adverse or uncontrollable events, and would thus cooperate and provide information" (32n19). This is a startling misapplication of the theory, which suggests that the lack of control over the current situation and the inability to control outcomes are crucial to developing depression. Learned helplessness theory has been enormously fruitful as a source of theory and empirical investigation of depression in humans (and in relevant animal models). It has certain well-recognized problems (it does not account especially well for individual differences in depression liability, for example, whereas other variables may do so; see Swartz and colleagues 2015 for one such example). Learned helplessness may also be a psychological process underlying other problems such as social anxiety or phobias. It has no relevance to interrogation, although it may underpin the induction of stress and anxiety disorders that result from torture.

What Happens in the Human Brain during the Experience of Threat and Fear?

There is by now a large experimental literature involving human volunteers who have willingly undergone experiments in which they were exposed to threat and anxiety. We will here examine the procedures involved in a well-known experiment to provide a detailed picture of the procedures involved and the conclusions that follow. The logic underlying this kind of experiment is discussed in some detail as well. Afterward, I provide a consensus summary review of the literature. Dean Mobbs (now at Columbia University) and his colleagues (2007) examined what happens in the brain in response to predator threat (see also Mobbs and colleagues 2010). They devised a simple computer game in which the participant's character or avatar is chased by a predator. If the predator catches the participant's character, the participant gets an electric shock to the back of the hand. The pain of the shock varies from high (three shocks in quick succession) to low (one shock). The game offers the possibility of escape from the predator but also varies proximity to the predator or, more correctly, varies the proximity of the predator to the player's character. This varying of the distance between the predator and the player's character, and hence an increase or decrease in the likelihood of being shocked, is a way of simulating the imminence of the threat to bodily integrity posed by the predator. The closer the predator is to you, the more likely he will catch you and therefore the more likely you will be electrocuted; the level of the threat posed varies depending on the condition. By simultaneously conducting brain imaging and getting participants' ratings of their current subjective feelings of fear and dread with regard to the predator, experimenters were able to investigate if there are shifts in the activity of the brain depending on whether the predator was near (shock was imminent) or far (shock was not imminent). A clear and consistent pattern of results was observed: when the threat was perceived as being far away (that is, not immediately present), frontal regions of the brain were activated—especially brain regions concerned with the evaluation of stimuli. However, when the threat was proximal and immediate—when the chances of being electrocuted were high—activity shifted profoundly to regions of the brainstem concerned with reflexive and defensive behaviors, the anticipation and attempted mitigation of pain, and fear and anxiety. These latter areas, especially the brainstem periaqueductal gray, are not areas implicated in conscious, deliberate, and evaluative cognitive processing; rather, they are largely nonconscious and provide an override mechanism that inhibits the conscious, cortically supported, cognitive processing in favor of brain systems that support immediate anticipation of threat and promotion of survival-related behaviors. The reverse pattern of activation was observed when the threat was distal—that is, far away in time and space. The authors conclude that their "observations concur with the proposition of hardwired forebrain-midbrain network" (Mobbs and colleagues 2007, 1082).

The implication here is straightforward: when the threat is immediate, present, and profound, then deliberative conscious mentative cognitive processes supported by cortical areas will be suppressed or overridden in favor of brain areas that support immediate, nonconscious, reflexive survival promotion. This suggestion of a shifting axis of activity from conscious, deliberative cognitive processing (primarily cortical and cortical frontal in nature) and of a brainstem-mediated axis of activity (supporting reflexive and automated nonconscious reflexive responding) is quite profound. It suggests that when one is experiencing threat, especially predator threat, which profoundly threatens one's bodily integrity and which is associated with pain, conscious regions are to a very large extent overridden. These data, by implication, suggest that prisoners interrogated under extreme duress and exposed to repeated sustained chronic predator stress would not be capable of engaging in meaningfully conscious directed recall of individual episodic memories. They suggest further that episodic recall would be quite profoundly inhibited and that the verbal protocols generated under these circumstances would be poorly constructed and sparse in information content. Given this very strong likelihood, the dilemma experienced directly by torturers and their overseers is explained. It is apparent from the various reports that there was surprise at the lack of intelligence gathered using these methods. The belief prevailed nonetheless that the prisoners surely must have known more. However, we have a framework to explain why it is that they revealed so little and why it is that coercive interrogation does not work. Activating a principally brainstem-based reflexive network that is directed toward immediate survival and that has a principal function of suppressing activity in brain areas that are unrelated to immediate survival, including brain areas concerned with directed search through memory, will, of design, leave a prisoner being tortured incapable of saying much that is useful.

The Effects of Chronic Stress on Cognition, Subjective Well-Being, and Mental Health

By definition, torture involves the imposition of extremities of stress on an individual for variable and perhaps substantial periods of time. For example, the Constitution Project report states that "a publicly released interrogation log, dated from November 23, to January 11, 2003, shows that al Qahtani's treatment only became harsher after Miller's appointment. . . . Al Qahtani was interrogated for approximately twenty hours a day for seven weeks; given strip searches, including in the presence of female interrogators; forced to wear women's underwear; forcibly injected with large quantities of IV fluid and forced to urinate on himself; led around on a leash; made to bark like a dog; and subjected to cold temperatures. Not surprisingly, his condition deteriorated further. On December 7, 2002, al Qahtani's heartbeat slowed to 35 beats per minute and he had to be taken into the hospital for a CT scan of his brain and an ultrasound of a swollen leg to check for blood clots" (2013, 39). Twenty hours a day for seven weeks is approximately 980 hours for the application of the described stressors, including the loss of about 196 hours of sleep over this period of time. In other evidence in the Constitution Project report, waterboarding was found to have been applied for thirty days and then continued for another thirty days, as it was (predictably, given the argument of this book) not working (207–212). Similarly, sleep deprivation was applied for 180 hours, implying sleep deprivation of twenty-two days straight at eight hours per night (if calculated purely on a sleep-lost basis). These extreme lengths of time of course obviate any ticking-time-bomb argument in favor of torture; as Ali Soufan puts it, "coercive interrogations are . . . slow" (2011, 425). And yet the Torture Memos state, "The 'waterboard,' which is the most intense of the CIA interrogation techniques, . . . may be used on a High Value Detainee only if the CIA has 'credible intelligence that a terrorist attack is imminent'; 'substantial and credible indicators that the subject has actionable intelligence that can prevent, disrupt or delay this attack'; and '[o]ther interrogation methods have failed to elicit this information [or] CIA has clear indications that other . . . methods are unlikely to elicit this information *within the perceived time limit for preventing the attack*'" (Cole 2009, 231). The estimated times for coercive techniques to work are therefore of the order of weeks to months, something their proponents do not acknowledge, while they continue to argue for their usefulness (even though they demonstrably do not work). John Yoo, for example, stated in December 2014 that rapport-based "methods can take weeks, if not months, if they work at all." Yoo, ostensibly trained to be part of an evidence-based profession, provides no evidence at all to support his assertion and in fact inverts the facts here. There is a profound inconsistency at work here: the protorture argument says that torture is rapidly effective; the assertions of the practitioners are that these coercive techniques actually take from weeks to months to work, and in the meantime the ticking time bomb has fizzled out, only to make a new appearance when the protorture camp needs to reach for an intellectually dishonest argument to bolster a position they have arrived at for other reasons. The Senate Torture Report underscores this point: in a clear demolition of the logic for the immediacy of a ticking time bomb, it is clear from the logs maintained on the captives that, prior to the imposition of coercive techniques, one captive was subjected to forty-seven days of isolation prior to the start of coercive interrogation (SSCI 2014, 40). Despite the oft-stated claims that the information was required urgently, it clearly was not required that urgently if a captive could be allowed to sit unquestioned for forty-seven days. Lapses like this in matters so serious are really quite astonishing to behold.

5

What Does Sleep Deprivation Do to the Brain?

Interrogator:	I need a method of interrogation to motivate the detainees that makes their senses befuddled, that stops them thinking straight, that will make their injuries more difficult to heal, that will damage the fabric of their brains, make them confabulate and occasionally suffer transient episodes of psychosis. Because this will make them remember.
Superior officer:	I seem to remember that Menachem Begin had this done to him. Must be okay.
A lawyer:	Here's a memo approving this procedure.
Silent voice in all heads:	That time I stayed up all night and didn't eat, I nearly crashed the car the next day. But that's okay. Driving is not a cognitive thing: I don't need to remember where I am, where I am going, understand the intentions of others, or have sharp reactions to drive a car.

We all have some subjective sense of what sleep deprivation is like. Anyone who has been jetlagged by a long intercontinental flight or who has stayed up working on a major project or tended for an infant or a loved one over a period of nights knows the effects of sleep deprivation. It leaves you unable to think and remember, unable to focus and to pay attention. And jetlag can last for days. The desire for sleep becomes overwhelming and similar in strength to the hunger for air or food. A sleep debt builds up, and this debt must be paid. Sleep deprivation has been used as a form of so-called white torture. Some former prisoners who have been subjected to sleep deprivation have written eloquently and at length of its effects on the psyche. One is the former Israeli prime minister Menachem Begin. In his memoir, *White Nights,* he describes what it is like to be sleep deprived, as follows: "In the head of the interrogated prisoner, a haze begins to form. His spirit is wearied to death, his legs are unsteady, and he has one sole desire: to sleep. . . . Anyone who has experienced this desire knows that not even hunger and thirst are comparable with it. I came across prisoners who signed what they were ordered to sign, only to get what the interrogator promised them. He did not promise them their liberty; he did not promise them food to sate themselves. He promised them—if they signed—uninterrupted sleep! And, having signed, there was nothing in the world that could move them to risk again such nights and such days" (1979, 107–108).

Alexander Solzhenitsyn, the Russian novelist and dissident, described sleep deprivation in the *Gulag Archipelago:* "Sleeplessness (yes, combined with standing, thirst, bright light, terror, and the unknown—what other tortures are needed!?) befogs the reason, undermines the will, and the human being ceases to be himself, to be his own 'I.' . . . A person deprived of sleep acts half-unconsciously or altogether unconsciously, so that his testimony cannot be held against him" (Solzhenitsyn 1974, 112).

Arthur Koestler, the important midcentury political novelist, also writes with great subtlety about sleep deprivation in *Darkness at Noon,* one of the most important political novels of the twentieth century. Koestler describes the ever-present cognitive fog, the deficits in recall and reason, the blurring of the sense of linear time. He describes the sudden onset of microsleeps—periods of a second to perhaps a few tens of seconds when Koestler's character Rubashov disappears below consciousness—only to find the world still present when he resurfaces. These authors catch something central regarding the overwhelming presence of this most profound biological hunger, the deep physiological hunger for a deep and prolonged sleep: that it is one that overwhelms all others eventually. Beyond the cognitive fog, Koestler hints at something more profound: Rubashov longs for sleep in order to "come to his senses." Here, Koestler recognizes something very important about sleep. Extended periods of sleep deprivation result in profound distortions of perception but also of cognition. These changes resemble those found in certain psychiatric patients and in people showing the decline in cognitive function that may attend aging, as well as those who may have suffered a mild head injury.

Sleep is a biological universal. Virtually all animals sleep. Bats, for example, sleep an average of eighteen hours a day, whereas donkeys and horses tend to sleep somewhat less, something of the order of three to four hours a day. What is sleep itself? One definition is that sleep is a "reversible behavioural state of perceptual disengagement and unresponsiveness to the environment" (Carskadon and Dement 2011, 16). Sleep serves many functions: these include obvious ones like conservation of energy and repair and restoration of the body. Less obviously, during those long periods of sleep as an infant and teenager, most of your growth occurred—approximately 80 percent of growth hormone is secreted during sleep. Sleep therefore has important homeostatic functions, and sleep deprivation is a stressor that has consequences for the brain, as well as for many body systems.

Initial breakthroughs in the study of sleep occurred in the period after the invention of the electroencephalogram (EEG) by Hans Berger in the 1920s. Berger and the generations of physiologists who followed him attached electrodes to the scalps of people while they were sleeping. They discovered that sleep is a complex phenomenon with cycles of electrical activity that occur repetitively through the night. These cycles vary between rapid eye movement (REM) sleep, associated with a characteristic form of activity on the EEG, and slow-wave sleep (SWS), in which the rhythms appearing in the EEG are slow in nature and during which rapid eye movement is absent. During REM sleep, the body is very active. Rapid eye movements behind the closed eyelids are visible, and muscle tone tends to be rather low. During non-REM sleep, the body is relatively quiescent, and there are characteristic differences in the brainwave signatures that are seen between these two conditions. Sleep itself is controlled by a nucleus deep in the brain—the suprachiasmatic nucleus (SCN). The SCN is genetically programmed to act like a pacemaker. If you place SCN neurons in a petri dish and keep them alive in a special oxygenated fluid, they beat according to their own rhythm, rather as if they have an internal clock. In turn, this clock is responsible for what we know as sleep and wakening. Light plays an important role in the regulation of sleep and wakening. There is a direct pathway from the eye to the SCN, which allows light to pace the activity of the SCN over a twenty-four-hour period—hence the central importance of light for the control of sleep and waking and an explanation for why flooding the cells of prisoners with very bright light is such an effective stressor.

Subsequent investigations have disclosed underlying changes in the microstructure of the EEG associated with the different stages of sleep. During non-REM sleep, a transition occurs as alpha waves at the start of the sleep cycle, when there is a relative degree of alertness, which gradually transition to a form of desynchronized activity known as delta waves, which are relatively slow in their recurrence. These delta waves appear at the deepest phase of sleep. There is an alternation between REM and non-REM sleep over the course of the night, typically on a ninety-minute clock cycle. The depth of sleep during successive phases of this cycle between non-REM and REM sleep gradually diminishes, until wakening occurs. Sleep scientists generally suggest that there are two principal determinants of sleep. The first is a homeostatic component. This is a self-regulating component of sleep in which sleep debt, which has been built up as a result of a prolonged period of sleeplessness, is compensated for. The effects of prolonged wakening are erased over the course of sleep. There is also a circadian component (the one that we are all very used to) in which alertness varies over the course of the day: from being very alert in the morning to a reduction of alertness immediately after lunch, an increase in alertness again over the course of the early afternoon and evening, and then gradually a reduction in alertness and preparation for sleep toward the latter part of the evening and the early night.

In general, during non-REM/slow-wave sleep, there is a reduction in brain activity across the whole brain so that there is less activity than during the waking period. In contrast, during REM sleep, there are marked differences in the activity across the different regions of the brain. For example, activity in the dorsolateral prefrontal cortex (DLPFC; regions of the brain that are on the convex outer surfaces of the frontal lobes) is greatly decreased, whereas cortical midline structures (the anterior cingulate cortex) and the area of the brain immediately above the orbits of the eyes (medial orbital frontal cortices) show marked increases in activity. Furthermore, there are marked increases in the centers of the brain that are involved in the processing of fear and anxiety, namely, the amygdalae. During REM sleep, dreams are very vivid. They tend to have a very emotional quality and are experientially bizarre. Sleep paralysis is usually present in REM sleep, and there are changes in autonomic functions, including a change in core body temperature, as body temperature drops over the course of the sleep cycle from approximately 37°C (98.9°F) to about 36.5°C (98°F). Other functions continue during the course of sleep: gastric transit (the passage of food through the gut), kidney function, and the like. Sleep disorders are common in the population at large. Approximately one-third of people reporting clinical levels of depression and anxiety report sleep disruption, including chronic insomnia. People with drug addictions (such as alcoholics) often report chronic insomnia. A small proportion of the population at large also report a phenomenon known as rapid limb movement, in which in particular the lower extremities—the legs— undergo kicking and other rapid movements, sometimes with an intensity that can cause the sleeper to wake up.

The experimental investigation of sleep has undergone a revolution over the past twenty or so years. Experimental approaches to sleep in humans have revolved around recording behavioral observations of activity during sleep; recording changes that occur in autonomic responsivity during sleep; recording changes in the brain associated with the different phases of sleep; and examining the interaction between prior interventions and the subsequent quality of sleep. These interventions might be simple: having people observe stimuli of some description and then waking them when they are dreaming and asking them to describe the content of those dreams. It seems, for example, that playing Tetris for an hour or two prior to sleep may cause you to dream about falling or to dream about objects falling down. A different intervention might be to ask somebody to learn some prose, to read a complex passage and recall the contents of it, to learn some new motor act (such as a sequence of finger tapping), and then to require that person to play the sequence or recall the memory under differing experimental conditions. These might include being allowed to sleep, having sleep interrupted during slow-wave sleep or during REM sleep, or having sleep abolished entirely for a complete cycle by being required to stay awake in a sleep laboratory.

Sleep-Deprivation Methodologies

The primary method of sleep deprivation involves the use of shackling to keep the detainee awake. In this method, the detainee is standing and is handcuffed, and the handcuffs are attached by a length of chain to the ceiling. The detainee's hands are shackled in front of his body, so that the detainee has approximately a two-to-three foot diameter of movement. The detainee's feet are shackled to a bolt in the floor. Due care is taken to ensure that the shackles are neither too loose nor too tight for physical safety. We understand from discussions with OMS that shackling does not result in any significant physical pain for the subject. (165)

A consistent theme through the Torture Memos is a discussion of, and an intended resort to, sleep deprivation as a tool to facilitate interrogation. Sleep deprivation is mentioned many times through the series of memos and is discussed at great length. The discussions are extensive, and the guidelines for the use of sleep deprivation are, seemingly, very precisely and exactly stated. The relevant memo states, "the maximum allowable duration for sleep deprivation is 180 hours, after which the detainee must be permitted to sleep without interruption for at least 8 hours" (Cole 2009, 167–168). This is a very substantial period of time to be forcibly sleep deprived. Regrettably, there has been little public disclosure regarding what actually occurred, as the actual interrogation logs that would verify the course of conduct are not in the public domain.

Two methods to induce sleep deprivation are described in the memos. Both involve shackling with chains of the detainee in positions in which sleep is rendered impossible. Shackling is to occur either in a standing position or in a seated position, on a small, three-legged chair. Toilet breaks are not permitted, and the detainee therefore is required to wear an adult diaper (Cole 2009, 165–166). There is an outline attempt to discuss some of the physiological effects of long-term sleep deprivation. A book published some fourteen years previously (Horne 1988) is cited—this memo was drafted in 2002. The memos conclude, "we understand that experts who have studied sleep deprivation have concluded that 'the most plausible reason for the uneventful physical findings with these human beings in [*sic*] that . . . sleep loss is not particularly harmful' " (from Cole 2009, 184; quoting Horne 1988, 23–24). The discussion of sleep deprivation is thin, badly researched and uninformed, and forms a very poor basis for making a serious policy prescription for deciding whether sleep deprivation is a useful interrogational device. The memos do note that there is a valid contrast to be drawn between studies of the outcomes of sleep deprivation in volunteers and what might happen in captives, but they also remarkably slide into this discussion permission to couple sleep deprivation with caloric restriction (to, as we have already seen, 40 percent of the normal recommended daily allowance for adults) *and* the use of the waterboard. Disingenuously, the memo then states, "we understand that there is nothing in the literature or experience to suggest that sleep deprivation would exacerbate any harmful effects of the waterboard" (220). No serious attempt to explore the literature is presented at all, despite the fact there was available a substantial literature on the effects of sleep deprivation and how it interacts with other variables. Paul Naitoh and colleagues of the U.S. Naval Health Research Center, for example, note that one consequence of sleep deprivation is an increase in circulating stress hormones (1990, 210). They also note, "all of us could develop psychomotor-type epileptiform discharges under the combined influence and other stressors" (218). Finally, they review studies of the interaction between stressors, sleep deprivation, and aerobic capacity (VO2 max, which is presumably directly relevant to lung function during waterboarding; 218–219). A specimen result indicates "that cardiovascular endurance was not affected by total sleep deprivation of 30 hours, *but it was affected by food and water deprivation of the same duration*" (219, emphasis added). In other words, contrary to the assertion in the memo, there was evidence available that sleep deprivation (a stressor) combined with caloric restriction (another stressor) and waterboarding (another profound stressor) will affect respiratory-cardiovascular function. The relevant data were available within the military itself, if anyone had looked for it or thought to ask if it were available.

A close reading of the relevant sections of the memos indicates that the interrogators had been given permission (across several differing pages) to conduct sleep deprivation over a very substantial and unclear period of time, to do this in the context of shackling while the captives are wearing adult diapers, while undergoing substantial involuntary caloric restriction, and all the while being waterboarded. Here, we see what Rejali and others have warned about so often. An escalation of coercion becomes permissible when early attempts to extract information via more limited coercion (more or less predictably) fail. There is another issue here: the expectation that there would be something published in the biomedical literature looking at the consequences of the interaction between involuntary waterboarding and forced periods of extended sleep deprivation is entirely grotesque. Such experiments could only be conducted on humans under conditions that previously would have obtained in prison camps, for which the United States and its allies engaged in prosecution against the supervising and attending physicians for the commission of war crimes. It is difficult to understand what motivated this statement. It can only have been presented as a way to avoid responsibility in the event that something catastrophic went wrong and the captive were to die as a result of the combined and escalated coercive interrogation regime.

It could be argued that the authors of the memos did not have access to the understanding of the dangers of sleep deprivation that appeared subsequently in the extensive literature that developed on sleep deprivation since the 2002–2005 time period when the memos were written. This is simply not true. The literature available for the period 1990–2001 is both extensive and replete with descriptions of the profound problems caused by extended periods of sleep deprivation. I cite here a few examples of relevant review articles that were published during this time period examining the neuropsychological and other health effects of what were commonly mild episodes of volunteer sleep deprivation. I ignore for present purposes the vast literature on the effects of sleep deprivation on preclinical models in experimental animals such as the laboratory rat, literature that was concurrently available. Naitoh and colleagues, for example (mentioned earlier), published an extensive review of the health effects of sleep deprivation, which concluded that while the effects of limited-duration sleep deprivation (typically a single sleep-wake cycle) in controlled laboratory conditions in young, healthy volunteers were reliable but small, there were "caveats" (1990, 225), especially when physical fitness, long-duration sleep deprivation, stressors, and disease status were considered. A review published ten years later considerably amplifies these concerns, stating, "Experimental evidence is in favour of the stressful nature of sleep deprivation in humans. Chronic sleep loss may therefore accelerate the development of metabolic and cognitive consequences of glucocorticoid excess, such as cognitive deficits and decreased carbohydrate tolerance" (Van Reeth and colleagues 2000, 209; see also Leung and Becker 1992). A review by the Canadian military recognized a substantial problem with performance in complex tasks as a result of sleep deprivation, suggesting that alerting drugs might be used to ensure no loss of performance as a result of sleep deprivation (McCann and Pointing 1995; see also McLellan and colleagues 2003–2004 for a further review from the same source—and note that two of the coauthors are U.S.-military-related personnel; see reference for further details). June Pilcher and Allen Huffcutt (1996) combined 143 studies using the statistical aggregation and inference method of meta-analysis, coming to three important conclusions: first, sleep deprivation strongly impairs human functioning (with mood being more affected than cognitive or motor performance); second, repetitive partial sleep deprivation has a more profound effect on functioning than does short- or long-term sleep deprivation; third, the effects of sleep deprivation might have been underestimated in some narrative reviews (especially concerning partial sleep deprivation). The partial deprivation effect might relate to the phase of sleep disrupted (slow-wave or REM) and hence to the induction of sleep inertia (Tassi and Muzet 2000). Yvonne Harrison and James A. Horne, in a review of the effects of sleep deprivation on decision making, suggest that sleep deprivation "impairs decision making involving the unexpected, innovation, revising plans, competing distraction, and effective communication" (2000, 236). Jones and Harrison (2001) note that sleep deprivation results in impaired performance on frontal-lobe-dependent executive-function tasks (such as verbal fluency, creativity, and planning).

Other articles reviewed the relationship between sleep and traffic collisions in drivers; unsurprisingly, sleep deprivation causes increases in vehicle crashes and other occupational hazards (Horne and Reyner 1999). One of the first brain-imaging studies of short-term sleep deprivation found that it produces global decreases in brain activity, with larger reductions in activity in the distributed cortico-thalamic network mediating attention and higher-order cognitive processes (Thomas and colleagues 2000). A review of brain-imaging data from this period suggested that sleep is required for normal memory function (Smith 2001). Drew Dawson and Kathryn Reid (1997) compared the performance of volunteers who were given progressively greater quantities of alcohol to volunteers who underwent progressively greater periods of sleep deprivation over the course of a night. Subjects performed a computer-administered test of hand-eye coordination, which involved a certain degree of unpredictability in the tracking task. The deficits in performance induced by alcohol and sleep deprivation were statistically indistinguishable. Sleepiness during the performance of complex motor tasks, such as driving, is as dangerous as is drinking alcohol. More generally, sleep deprivation decreases daytime alertness and increases daytime sleepiness. These two phenomena, in turn, cause decreases in cognitive performance across all domains. They cause impairments in motor skills and also cause mood changes in the short term in particular, resulting in increases in irritability. Further experimental data suggested that "moderate sleep deprivation produces impairments in cognitive and motor performance equivalent to legally prescribed levels of alcohol intoxication" in a population of transport employees and soldiers (Williamson and Feyer 2000, 653–654). In short, there has been a systematic and sustained effort to understand the effect of sleep deprivation on a variety of measures of human performance.

Other studies from this time period investigated physiological effects of sleep deprivation. Masahiko Kato and colleagues (2000) examined the effects of one night's sleep deprivation on the functioning of the cardiovascular system. This was a particularly well-conducted double-blind, randomized, controlled trial, and the data indicated that mild sleep deprivation results in increased resting blood pressure, decreased muscle sympathetic nerve activity, and no change in heart rate. Other data showed that sleep deprivation impairs the immune system, leaving the sleep deprived more susceptible to pathogens and infections. Michael Irwin and colleagues (1996) found that a (modest) partial night of sleep deprivation reduces natural killer cell and immune responses in humans (see also Irwin and colleagues 1994). Finally, in a particularly important review, Olivier Van Reeth examined the interactions between stress and sleep, in the laboratory and in the clinic, concluding that "shift workers, chronic insomniacs or patients suffering from mental disorders show abnormal hypothalamo-pituitary-adrenal secretory activity and concomitant sleep disturbances" (2000, 201).

A search of the literature from the relevant period will disclose many more relevant experimental articles and reviews. Contrary to the thinly researched and poorly discussed impression provided by the memos, there was available a large and extensive literature about sleep deprivation in healthy volunteers, in chronic insomniacs, and in shift workers and other occupational groups. The literature of this time converges on a strong and consistent message: that sleep deprivation causes deficits across a wide set of affective, cognitive, physiological, and immune functions and that the effects are dose dependent. The more sustained the period of sleep deprivation, the greater the effects. It takes little by way of an act of empirical imagination to surmise that the periods of sleep deprivation proposed in the memos—far in excess of those usually employed in the volunteer experimental literature—might be likely to have substantially greater effects than those previously observed. The relevant literature was available at the time for anyone who wished to look. It would have given an answer contrary to the one required, however, which presumably is why it was not reviewed in any meaningful way.

Cognitive Pathologies Induced by Sleep Deprivation

Sleep deprivation has been a commonly used method of white torture. It is all too easy to trivialize or minimize the effects of extended periods of sleep deprivation and to suggest that sleep deprivation is not torture. The testimonies of those who have been subjected to it attest otherwise. However, we will set the definitional issue aside here. Instead, we will examine the question of whether short or long periods of sleep deprivation affect learning, memory, and cognition generally and whether this deprivation enhances motivation to comply with instructions (whatever the source). These are not the same thing and may indeed be opposed to each other. The Torture Memos (almost) acknowledge this fact. The memos define the purpose of sleep deprivation as follows: "to reduce the individual's ability to think on his feet and, through the discomfort associated with lack of sleep to a maximum of eleven days to motivate him to co-operate" (Cole 2009, 108). There is a surreal undercurrent that the author does not wish to acknowledge or is perhaps unaware of. Sleep deprivation reduces the ability to think on your feet—but thinking is what you want the subject to do! You want the subject to speak of the past, to recall the past, to recall events, places, and things that he or she has encountered. You want the subject to recall prior plans and intentions that he or she might previously have had. But the consequence of sleep deprivation is a cognitive pathology—one of inducing a deficit in the capacity to think—in order to make the person comply. But comply with what? Surely, it is the instruction that subjects think about the past, the persons, events, places, and things they have encountered, as well as the plans and intentions that they might previously have had, one must presume. Inducing a deliberate pathology in the capacity to engage in thinking will not enhance this capacity. Here, there is a clear unwillingness to think through the consequences of one's own position, even on one's own terms. But then there is a peculiar cognitive process associated with the decision to torture—it acquires an internal logic that is not based on reason and evidence.

There is now a substantial body of data on the effects of chronic sleep deprivation both in human volunteers and in animal models. We will first summarize the general effects of chronic sleep deprivation on the general function of body systems and then specifically discuss its effect on cognition in humans. The approach we will adopt here is examining the changes in mood, alertness, and cognition in people who have been sleep deprived, as the result of either some disorder, such as insomnia, or some experimental behavioral intervention or the influence of a stimulant that prevents them sleeping fully. Indeed, a sedative can have similar kinds of effects to sleep deprivation; alcohol, for example, is notorious for interrupting the normal sleep cycle because it interferes with the normal REM–non-REM cycle. Chronic insomniacs provide a particularly interesting population for investigating the effects of sleep deprivation on cognition. These are patients for whom sleep is difficult, and if sleep comes, it comes fitfully; for these people, the sleep debt is very rarely fully repaid. Depriving human beings of sleep in a laboratory is not easy. Laboratory assistants themselves must stay awake, and they must ensure that the test person stays awake. Laboratory assistants will have overwhelming sleep urges and usually must resort to working in shifts.

Bruce McEwen, in an important review, suggests that the "changes in brain and body further evidence that sleep deprivation is a chronic stressor and . . . can contribute to cognitive problems which can in turn further exacerbate pathways that lead to disease" (2006, S20). Further, McEwen concludes that chronic sleep deprivation in healthy volunteers increases appetite and energy expenditures; decreases parasympathetic and increases sympathetic tone; and increases blood pressure, cortisol levels, and blood glucose. Sleep deprivation affects the most basic energy-use demands of the body: the uptake and metabolism of glucose by the cells of the body. Concurrently, there are effects on the cardiovascular system, placing it under some degree of stress. There is also a dysregulation of the immune system, rendering the individual more susceptible to infections and other conditions (such as impaired wound healing). The key point to emphasize here, however, is that the vast empirical literature showing these deleterious effects is uncited in toto in the Torture Memos (see Lim and Dinges 2010, for a further review). There are also structural changes in the brain caused by sleep deprivation: Dieter Riemann and his colleagues (2007) compared hippocampal volumes in patients who are good sleepers and patients who are suffering from primary insomnia. Insomniacs are an important comparison group, as they are chronically and involuntarily sleep deprived. Chronic insomniacs have on average a reduction of several percent in hippocampal volume, compared to normally sleeping subjects. This indicates that sleep deprivation is associated with structural remodeling of the brain.

There are many pathologies of cognition associated with insomnia and other disorders of sleep. One of the most common is the condition known as obstructive sleep apnea, in which snorers (for it is typically them) are unable to breathe for short periods of time during sleep. This has consequences for daytime functioning, including sleepiness during the course of the day, impairments in attention, and sometimes even depression. Sleep apnics typically wake up on multiple occasions during the course of the night, often without any conscious recollection that they have done so (a well-known form of sleep-associated amnesia). Narcolepsy is another sleep pathology: the sudden occurrence of sleep in individuals who should normally be awake. The condition can vary in terms of its intensity and frequency, from a gradual feeling of sleepiness or drowsiness that overcomes the sufferer to a sudden onset of sleep within which there may be very intense dreaming, sometimes sufficiently intense that it causes the person to start awake with a great degree of fright.

A large literature has investigated the interaction between sleep, learning, and memory over the past twenty or so years. One lesson is simple and straightforward: sleep deprivation, after one learns something, impairs subsequent recall for that something. This is irrespective of whether the to-be-remembered material is a motor skill or verbal material. Similarly, sleep deprivation causes grave deficits in recall of previously learned and consolidated material, and the deficits induced increase in magnitude with the time since the last bout of sleep. The key conclusion is that sleep itself is vital for the consolidation of learning and memory and not merely because of the passage of time. Sleep deprivation, therefore, is an excellent tool for inducing amnesia. This is not necessarily an obvious conclusion, and we will discuss some of the data backing up this conclusion shortly. But the key point to capture here is that a naive psychological model of the interaction between sleeping and memory would suggest that sleep deprivation and recall of previously learned information should not interact with each other. This assumption could not be further from the truth.

Similarly, claims that extended and prolonged periods of forcible sleep deprivation induce compliance, which in turn will facilitate recall, could not be further from the truth. There is an important difference between resistance and compliance. It may well be the case that prolonged periods of sleep deprivation do reduce individuals' capacity to resist the physical and other demands that may be imposed on them, and it may be that they will be more likely to comply with simple behavioral commands. Inducing obedience to these commands, though, will come at a great cognitive cost, because such obedience will require effortful attention and concentration on the part of the individual who is being commanded to comply in some way. This in turn depletes the reserve capacity of individuals to reply meaningfully to other commands or questions. Furthermore, it will reduce individuals' ability to actively search through memory in order to provide answers to questions that they have been asked. This directed, intentional search function is principally controlled by the dorsolateral prefrontal cortex. It is a capacity impaired by sleep deprivation, and it is recharged as the result of sleep. The key thing to emphasize when looking at these studies is that recall, in the case of normal human participants in a nontorture situation, is voluntary and appropriately motivated. So the issue of "enhancing" motivation by the imposition of a stressor is irrelevant. Nonetheless, large and sustained deficits in recall occur as a result of the imposition of sleep deprivation.

Jessica Payne and her colleagues at Harvard University (2012) have conducted a study that, in terms of the logic of how sleep impacts on learning and memory, uses a particularly appropriate experimental design. They investigated how the explicit memory for semantic- (or meaning-) related and unrelated declarative information benefits from a period of sleep and how memory is negatively impacted by a period of wakefulness. The researchers systematically varied the impact of sleeping, wakening, and time of day on the processing of declarative information with strong semantic links in a group of volunteers. The words to be remembered were closely related to each other, or they were paired with novel associations. The researchers found that sleep deprivation negatively and substantially impacted subsequent recall of the learned material. The consequences of sleep deprivation were therefore to induce a dose-dependent cognitive pathology: the greater the period of sleep deprivation, the greater the induced pathology. Less obvious, too, is that learning and memory are regulated by sleep, and memories of what has happened during the course of the day are consolidated during sleep.

There are many other such studies available in the literature, all revolving around the same theme: that sleep deprivation impairs mood, as well as general cognitive and psychomotor function in a dose-dependent fashion. Amy Reynolds and colleagues (2012) restricted sleep in volunteers on five nights to four hours (a partial sleep-deprivation regime) and then gave them one of six sleep-recovery sessions. All experiments were conducted in-house in a laboratory. The researchers measured psychomotor vigilance, subjective sleepiness, mood, and a set of other cognitive functions. Interestingly, while they found that partial sleep restriction is recovered by extra sleep, in proportion to the extra time allowed, a full recovery to baseline did not occur, even after ten hours of sleep. Alertness and subjective measures of sleepiness did not reach baseline measures after allowing the volunteers to sleep for ten hours. This suggests that partial sleep deprivation imposes a sleep debt that requires more than a single full session of sleep to allow it to be recovered (see also Reynolds and Banks 2010 for a major review of the literature).

Other data concur with these findings. Nadia Lopez and colleagues (2012) investigated the effects of sleep deprivation on a variety of measures of cognitive performance by U.S. Air Force pilots. They examined how thirty-five hours of continuous sleep deprivation affected performance on a variety of cognitive tasks, as well as performance on a flight simulator (to provide a real-world validation of any effects that might be detected using conventional paper-and-pencil means). They found that performance across all cognitive performance tasks slowed in a more or less direct decline in proportion to the amount of sleep deprivation imposed. Note that this was a highly trained and experienced group: training, in and of itself, did not overcome the effects of sleep-deprivation-induced fatigue. Furthermore, in the real-world task, flight-simulator performance also degraded. Overall, it is reasonable to conclude that sleep deprivation caused a decline in cognitive performance, which in turn substantially predicted performance deficits in a complex real-world task. Similarly, Jonathon Scott and colleagues (2006) investigated the effects of thirty hours of sleep deprivation and a concurrently imposed exercise regime on mood, as well as on cognitive and psychomotor performance, in healthy young volunteers. Sleep deprivation uniformly degraded performance across all categories of performance measured. Remarkably, concurrent exercise exacerbated the deficits caused by sleep deprivation: mood worsened even more, as did reaction times.

Finally, we note one other aspect of the developing literature. A profound and currently unmet clinical need is for drugs that act to ameliorate the effects of Alzheimer's disease and other dementias. A characteristic of such dementias is the development of a profound, progressive, and nonremitting amnesia—in other words, memory loss. A particular problem for pharmaceutical development is devising realistic models of amnesia in humans, as there are limitations to contemporary animal models of these neuropathologies. Sleep deprivation is currently under investigation as a potential model for inducing mild cognitive impairment (MCI), a prodromal syndrome for Alzheimer's disease. Drugs under development for Alzheimer's disease, particularly for the therapeutic reduction in Alzheimer's disease symptoms, are being screened using sleep deprivation in normal volunteers to investigate if the cognitive pathologies induced by sleep deprivation can be reduced or remediated using the novel therapeutic chemical entity (Colavito and colleagues 2013). To spell out the implications a little further, sleep deprivation is proposed in the Torture Memos as a methodology to facilitate access to the contents of the long-term memories of captives, whereas sleep deprivation is being developed as a potentially viable model of cognitive pathology by the pharmaceutical industry to develop drugs that mitigate the amnesia associated with Alzheimer's disease and other dementias.

A pattern should be evident by now. Sleep deprivation causes a substantial and direct degradation in performance across mood, cognition, learning and memory, and psychomotor states, in direct proportion to the amount of time that the person has been sleep deprived. Typically, these studies are done in healthy, motivated volunteers. A fair and reasonable position would suggest that sleep deprivation reliably produces decreases across the full range of cognitive functions tested, from simple tasks involving stimulus-response reaction time to complex executive functions. Furthermore, extended periods of sleep deprivation cause changes in the very architecture of the brain that supports learning, memory, and executive function (particularly a loss of tissue volume in the hippocampus and a general blunting of frontal and temporal lobe function; see Torelli and colleagues 2011 for an analysis of structural and functional deficits in sleep apnea; and Stickgold and Walker 2013 for a more general review). The implications are straightforward: extended periods of sleep deprivation have exactly the opposite effects of those intended. Inducing an extreme of wakeful somnambulism in detainees might induce some form of surface compliance, but it will not assist in the directed and intentional retrieval of episodic memories; it will facilitate long-term structural remodeling of the brain systems that support the very functions that the interrogator wishes to have access to.

Sleep deprivation is therefore not a tool that should be used under any circumstances in which access to ongoing memory function in detainees is required. We now know that this is the regime imposed on captives on foot of the Torture Memos: extended sleep deprivation induced a variety of psychopathological phenomena. One captive started to hallucinate after fifty-nine hours of sleep deprivation, only to be told by a "psychologist that his reactions were 'consistent with what many others experience in his condition'" (Cole 2009, 132). Other captives experienced visual and auditory hallucinations (137–139, 165, 412). Remarkably, the CIA asserted that captives would be unlikely to experience hallucinations as a result of sleep deprivation; in fact, "multiple CIA detainees subjected to prolonged sleep deprivation experienced hallucinations" (412), and medical personnel did not intervene to restore sleep. There is no evidence presented that anyone committed to the use of sleep deprivation ever stopped to wonder if, in fact, inducing polysensory hallucinatory states in captives might not be a wise course of action, if securing reliable, veridical intelligence was the desired outcome. A catalogue of other effects of sleep deprivation are also described— slow wound healing, pooling and swelling of fluids in the lower extremities, changes in blood pressure, and so on—but nowhere is described what would be a signal achievement of the sleep-deprivation regime imposed on captives: the sudden spilling and release of intentionally withheld memories, useful intelligence, and information regarding previous and future plots and other information as a result of the psychophysiological extremity to which the captives were subjected. Unfortunately, the lack of results obtained through the use of sleep deprivation was an all-too-predictable outcome, if an honest reading of the literature had been conducted.

6

Drowning, Cooling, Heating, and Starving the Brain

Interrogator: I wonder, if we nearly suffocate the prisoner, and we do that lots of times, and maybe nearly kill him by making him too hot or cold, and not feed them properly, will that help him think straight? Maybe improve the quality of his memories?

A lawyer: I have written a memo that says it's okay. So long as you don't actually kill him. That *would* constitute organ failure.

Manipulating the fundamental metabolic physiology of the body offers an easy route to torture—especially torture that leaves no visible marks. Restricting diet, oxygen, and access to warmth offers possibilities for exposing captives to extreme stressors—ones that are essential to normal functioning—and offers possibilities for repeatedly bringing someone to the edge of death. The Torture Memos explicitly discuss manipulations of the core metabolic physiology of captives. Three manipulations are discussed: simulated drowning via waterboarding; core temperature manipulations via water dousing; and weight loss via caloric restriction. Creatively combined and titrated, these manipulations of our core metabolic physiology offer the possibility of exquisite extremes of stressor states to be imposed on a captive under interrogation. There is an extensive literature that bears on all of these manipulations—often generated by military sources, which are interested in maximizing human performance under these stressor conditions. This literature is of course uncited in the memos. In particular, there is no consideration given at all to the extensive biomedical literature on the inevitable pathologies of cognition and mood that are induced by pushing the metabolic limits of the core drives and needs of the body.

Simulated Drowning via Waterboarding

The "waterboard." . . . The detainee is lying on a gurney . . . inclined at an angle of 10 to 15 degrees to the horizontal, . . . on his back and his head toward the lower end of the gurney. A cloth is placed over the detainee's face, and cold water is poured on the cloth from a height of approximately 6 to 18 inches. *The wet cloth creates a barrier through which it is difficult—or in some cases not possible—to breathe. A single "application" [is] measured from the moment when water— of whatever quantity—is first poured onto the cloth until the moment the cloth is removed from the subject's face.* . . . If the detainee makes an effort to defeat the technique (e.g., by twisting his head to the side and breathing out of the corner of his mouth), the interrogator may cup his hands around the detainee's nose and mouth to dam the runoff, in which case it would not be possible for the detainee to breathe during the application of the water. In addition, you have informed us that the technique may be applied in a manner to defeat efforts by the detainee to hold his breath by, for example, beginning an application of water as the detainee is exhaling. Either in the normal application, or where countermeasures are used, we understand that water may enter—and may accumulate in—the detainee's mouth and nasal cavity, preventing him from breathing. (Cole 2009, 168; emphasis added)

Breathing (at the risk of stating the obvious) is central to life; air hunger is one of our deepest and most automatic drives. The lung capacity of the average adult human is about four to six liters (with some variations that depend on height, gender, altitude above sea level, aerobic fitness, and history of smoking). The average adult takes ten to twenty breaths per minute. There is an intimate coupling between the functions of the heart and the lungs, with the one serving to pace activity in the other. The lungs facilitate the uptake of oxygen by hemoglobin—the oxygen-carrying protein found primarily in red blood cells. A gas-exchange mechanism in the lungs allows carbon dioxide to be exhaled and oxygen inspired. Over the course of twenty-four hours, an adult will breathe approximately 11,000 liters of air, of which about 20 percent at sea level will consist of oxygen. Thus, the partial pressure of oxygen in an average breath corresponds to the availability of oxygen in inspired air. The body has an insatiable metabolic need for oxygen. Restriction of oxygen supplies (known as hypoxia or anoxia) to the brain causes rapid clouding and then loss of consciousness. Breathing is generally automatic and reflexive. Some volitional control is possible, and it is possible to voluntarily withhold a breath from seconds to, in a trained individual, minutes. The world breath-holding record, for example, is nineteen minutes and twenty-one seconds, held by the Swiss diver Peter Colat, under conditions of complete body immersion. Human breathing shows some degree of plasticity or adaptation under other circumstances. In trained divers, for example, there is some accommodation of breathing underwater over time that results in an enhanced capacity to use oxygen. Singers and wind-instrument players are also capable of modulating their breath for very long periods of time. It is not possible to hold one's breath to the point of killing oneself. Once you become unconscious from holding your breath, you will pass out, and automatic and nonconscious reflexes take over, causing a sudden gasp of breath. Manipulations of the fundamental physiology associated with such a basic need as air offer a method to induce the most profound and extreme life-threatening stressors that it is possible to experience. And the lack of any changes to the naked eye offers further advantages to the torturer, as the effects of the waterboard will be hidden—meeting the definition required for white torture. The ancients knew this, and this is why waterboarding as a torture technique has been used for centuries. It is cheap and easy to apply but has the capacity to induce extremes of uncontrolled panic and an associated feeling of doom. It works because it attacks our metabolism at its core— choking off the oxygen that is required for essential oxidative (oxygen-dependent) processes in every single cell of our bodies. It is a profound metabolic stressor.

The physiology of breathing has been under experimental investigation for more than 150 years. There is now a complex terminology associated with understanding breathing. One can do a breath-by-breath assessment of tidal volume (V_T): the total volume of air breathed out or breathed in on a single inspiration or expiration cycle. The inspiratory duration (T_I) is the length of time it takes to inhale; the respiratory duration (T_E) is the length of time it takes to exhale; respiratory frequency (F_R) is the number of times per unit time that breathing occurs. Oxygen deprivation triggers air hunger (dyspnea). This is the frantic and almost uncontrolled search for air and especially for oxygen. Behavioral panic under conditions of oxygen restriction is very common. Panic among people who are at the point of drowning is an especially common phenomenon. The brain centers that are involved in the control of breathing are now becoming understood. These comprise a network of areas that include the primary motor cortex, the premotor area, the supplementary motor cortex, and the cerebellum. The exquisite and extreme sensitivity of humans to air deprivation and oxygen restriction makes the respiratory system a wonderfully efficacious target for manipulation by torturers. Because such manipulations do not leave surface visible marks, they are a particularly effective form of white torture.

Repeatedly restricting breathing by placing the head in a plastic bag and sealing this bag against the nose and lips is a form of torture (allegedly) practiced by certain police forces. Whole-head immersion to the point of near drowning is a staple in many films, usually to make people "talk!" Of course, the images are compelling, and the narratives are convincing and driven by cruel necessity—the captive must talk and often does. However—and this point cannot be emphasized enough—it is still fiction, and the characters portrayed, just like Jack Bauer, *do not exist.*

Imaging the Breathing Brain

It has become possible in recent years to examine, using brain imaging, the network of brain regions that are associated with the volitional control of inspiration in humans. These experiments have a human participant lie in a brain-imaging scanner, wearing a breathing apparatus so that breathing can be measured. Participants wear instruments to measure heart rate, blood pressure, and other changes in the body. Participants will then engage in such behaviors as voluntarily withholding their breath when presented with a sound cue and holding their breath for as long as possible. In other experiments, participants give up control of their breathing, allowing themselves to be mechanically ventilated. In one such study, Karleyton Evans and colleagues (1999) conducted a study in which they compared mechanical ventilation (or passive breathing) to volitional inspiration (or active breathing). They found that there is a distributed network in the brain that is responsible for planning, coordinating, and performing motor activity during breathing. It is also responsible for providing feedback from breathing—in other words, the sensation of breathing itself, and to allow the stage with which these elements act to depend on the phase of the respiratory cycle. Active voluntary inspiration (breathing in) activates the superior motor cortex, the premotor area, and the supplementary motor area, and it also activates frontal regions of the brain during self-initiated motor acts, as opposed to passive breathing during ventilated respiration.

Asphyxiating and Drowning the Brain

Waterboarding is an ancient method of torture that has been used by many regimes over many centuries. In the Museo della Tortura in Siena, Italy, there is exhibited a medieval waterboard—this one used to force water into the esophageal, respiratory, and gastric tracts and thence into the stomach. It is a simple wooden device: a set of wooden traps for the feet, perhaps a meter or so from the ground; a narrow wooden block, perhaps a meter or a meter and a half distant from the foot traps; and finally a set of metal chains, a meter or so distant again. The feet are suspended above the level of the head in the traps; the back is supported by the narrow wooden block at the base of the spine. This is an adaptable device—the relative positions of the head and feet can be changed easily. A funnel rusts near a bucket, its work done. The description reads in part, "Among the most atrocious ordeals was and is the water torture. . . . The terror of drowning, endlessly repeated, is by itself an agonising torment. . . . The victim is tilted head-down, so that the pressure on the heart and lungs causes unimaginable anguish which the executioner [*sic*] exacerbates by beating on the abdomen."

In the modern form of waterboarding, the Torture Memos state that "the individual is bound securely on an inclined bench. . . . The individual's feet are generally elevated. A cloth is placed over the forehead and eyes. Water is . . . applied to the cloth in a controlled manner. . . . Air now is slightly restricted for 20 to 40 seconds due to . . . the cloth, . . . increas[ing] . . . carbon dioxide level[s] in the individual's blood. This increase in the carbon dioxide level stimulates increased efforts to breathe. This effort plus the cloth produces the perception of 'suffocation and incipient panic,' i.e., the perception of drowning" (Cole 2009, 109). The physical position of the body, with the feet elevated above the head while lying on one's back, is known as the Trendelenburg position. This position was originally developed as a strategy to enhance blood perfusion of the brain for surgical purposes, and especially for hypoperfusion of the brain resulting from low blood pressure. Current consensus suggests that the use of the Trendelenburg position is to be avoided in such cases (Bridges and Jarquin-Valdivia 2005) and that under cases of respiratory strain, high inspiratory pressure values may even enhance the risk of respiratory failure (Rubini and Carniel 2014). There is one other key point regarding the Trendelenburg position: it is a profoundly difficult position from which to clear obstructed airways, especially in the case of lung conditions (see, for example, McIlwaine 2007; Osadnik and colleagues 2012). The Senate Torture Report states "The waterboarding technique was physically harmful, inducing convulsions and vomiting. Abu Zubaydah, for example, became "completely unresponsive, with bubbles rising through his open, full mouth."(From the Senate Torture report: Findings and Conclusions, Point 3, p. 3). As we will see, brain-imaging data suggest that hypercapnia and associated feelings of breathlessness (dyspnea) cause widespread increases in brain activity, including brain regions associated with stress and anxiety (the amygdala and prefrontal cortex) and pain (the periaqueductal gray). These data suggest that waterboarding in particular acts as a severe and extreme stressor, with the potential to cause widespread stress-induced changes in the brain, especially when this procedure is repeated frequently and intensively. There is also a large literature on various aspects of the physiological responsivity of respirational breathing to water immersion (especially in divers) that is unreferenced in the Torture Memos. President George W. Bush subsequently publicly commented on waterboarding as follows: "No doubt the procedure [waterboarding] was tough, but medical experts assured the CIA that it did no lasting harm" (Bush 2010, 169). These "medical experts" have not been publicly identified. It would be interesting and purgative if they did come forward. Clarification by them on how their professional actions and professional ethical codes have not been violated by their participation in such procedures would be interesting to have. There are currently no articles listed in PubMed that directly investigate the physiology of waterboarding using the procedures described in the memos. Waterboarding leaves no visible injuries; it reaches deep into our physiology, mobilizing involuntary reflexes associated with drowning. Waterboarding is a profound stressor, inducing feelings of panic, dread, and imminent death. Why should it be assumed that inducing these intense reflex responses would in any way enhance a captive's willingness to engage in recall? The underlying, unarticulated logic is approximately as follows: the desire to escape the terror of the waterboard will overwhelm any active inhibition of the contents of memory that can be elicited by questioning. Furthermore, this inhibition will be unmoderated by the depth of affiliation that suspects have to their beliefs and their own peer group. The simple strategy to avoid being waterboarded, of course—if information elicitation is required—is to talk, lots of talk, at length and in depth. Trying to defeat waterboarding by breath cycling and holding is pointless. When the late Christopher Hitchens voluntarily underwent waterboarding, he was surprised to find that a firm fingertip probed his solar plexus to prevent any such strategies. Hitchens was told, sardonically, "We have all kinds of enhancements" (2008). (Of course, as Rejali 2007 notes, unauthorized escalation of torture is always a possibility. And where is the supervising lawyer to prevent the escalation of torment?)

A rudimentary but working model of the lungs can be fashioned from a plastic bottle and a balloon (there are demonstrations on YouTube). As a home experiment, it is possible to make the model, add water to the opening to obstruct the "model airway." Then place the artificial lung in the Trendelenburg position, and try and operate the lung. You will find that it is subject to catastrophic functional cyclic failures. This simple demonstration should make one other point clear: waterboarding is reversible and controlled drowning—but drowning nonetheless. The pharynx and larynx will be missing in the model, but the model trachea (windpipe) is present, as is the diaphragm (the experimenter substitutes for the action of the phrenic nerve, which drives the inhalatory and exhalatory function of the diaphragm). Under actual waterboarding, the nasal sinuses, orophayrnx, larynx, trachea, and bronchia fill with water, and the passage of air into the lungs is impossible (it shouldn't be necessary to point this out, but, by definition, when water occludes the upper respiratory tract and prevents air access to the lungs, this is drowning because it simply isn't possible to use the remaining lung fraction to breath *because water is blocking the airways*). Coughing the airways clear, as previously noted, is profoundly problematic, because the presence of the water obstruction will prevent air inhalation, diaphragm expansion, and compression required to generate a deep cough. The diving response will be strongly activated and the frantic and uncontrolled search for air will occur. And then under these conditions of near death, the tortured individual is also expected to engage in a directed search of the cortical networks supporting memory to reveal information that they have previously acquired.

As already mentioned, there is a literature that can be explored focusing on other variables that certainly are relevant to waterboarding. There is a large literature on the effects of facial immersion in cold water and its subsequent effects on breathing. There is also a literature on the effects of whole-body immersion in cold water and its effects on breathing and other variables such as heart rate, cerebral blood flow, and autonomic responsivity. There is also a literature on the effects of chemosensing: the sensing by the body of changes in the concentration of chemicals in the environment. This includes things like variations in the concentration of carbon dioxide and oxygen and the subsequent effect of these variations on breathing. This literature has large and practical implications in areas such as diving and in medicine in areas such as anesthesiology and any of the disorders of lung function. There is even an important literature showing the coupling of oropharyngeal movements during eating, an absolutely vital capacity to ensure that one does not choke while eating. We can use this literature to build up a picture of the effects of waterboarding, first as a stimulus—how it affects reflex and other functions—and second as a stressor, that is, how it causes a variety of reactions that move the body away from homeostasis. At a minimum, waterboarding deliberately interrupts the voluntary control of breathing and imposes a life-threatening stress by directly interrupting the breathing cycle. It will invoke and induce reflexes that are beyond voluntary control. It changes oxygen and carbon dioxide concentrations, inducing hypoxia (decreases in blood oxygen levels) and hypercapnia (increases in blood concentration of carbon dioxide). It induces rapid reflexive changes in breathing that attempt to restore oxygen balance. Furthermore, because waterboarding generally takes place on an inclined plane with the head below the level of the feet, there is an inversion of blood-pressure control. Normal control occurs when the body is upright or is lying horizontal; in waterboarding, the head is below the level of the feet, reversing the normal orthostatic control of blood pressure.

It is sometimes difficult to convey in dry prose just how profoundly these simply manipulations affect one's integrated physiological functioning. I would therefore suggest that you try this simple experiment at home. (Do not do this if you have or suspect you have a heart condition, high blood pressure, respiratory problems, or related complaints.) Take and note your pulse. Now, hold your breath for as long as you can. Take your pulse again. Notice the difference? Now, lie on the floor and place your feet on the seat so that they are above you. Take your pulse again. Now, hold your breath for as long as you can. Now take your pulse again. Notice the difference? Now, repeat this experiment after a few minutes of running on the spot while holding your breath, to simulate the arousal that might be present during a torture session. Notice the difference? A central and recurrent theme of this book is that the imposition of behavioral and physiological stressors affects memory function. Read a few pages of prose or try to learn ten or twenty word pairs or digit strings. Now repeat this little experiment and then try to recall the material you tried to remember a few minutes previously. Not easy, is it? Do you think your recall might be improved by having water poured on your face while lying on the ground? (I do not recommend you try this at home. You might ruin your carpets if you lose autonomic control, and you might drown!) Another way to simulate water-boarding is to place a wet towel (which has been immersed in cold water) over your face while lying supine, covering your mouth, nose, and cheeks. This will induce the diving reflex and will give a sense of how unpleasant breathing under these conditions is, but better still, it will show how it impairs your ability to recall accurately material you have recently encountered. As a final test, while lying in this position, try wet or dry coughing in order to clear your airways— and do this with the wet cloth on your face. Now imaging trying to do this while bound and helpless on a table while being asked questions about your past and future by an interrogator in a language you may not understand.

The diving response occurs from the immersion of the face and body in cold water. It involves peripheral vasoconstriction: the blood vessels in the periphery of the body, the arms and the legs, constrict (or become smaller), concentrating blood in the body trunk, defending the vital organs and, of course, attempting to defend the brain. There is a reduced output from the heart, and the heart rate itself slows (this is known as bradycardia). After immersion, there is also tachycardia—a sudden increase in heart rate. Experienced divers are different from nondivers, as they are not as sensitive to the effects of hypoxia or hypercapnia. They are able to engage in breath holds under normal breathing conditions that are substantially longer than ordinary individuals can. In these highly experienced individuals, muscle oxygenation goes down, or put differently, the relative apportionment of oxygen to the muscles is decreased. There are also relative increases in blood flow through the middle cerebral artery of the brain. This is a major cerebral artery that perfuses much of the brain. In essence, experienced divers have developed a degree of accommodation over time that allows them to engage in an oxygen-conserving response during whole-body immersion in water, where there may be restrictions on oxygen availability.

Physiologists Avijit Datta and Michael Tipton (1985/2006), at the University of Plymouth in the United Kingdom, have investigated respiratory responses to sudden cold-water immersion. They show the cold-shock response of a normal male subject following breath holding during naked-body but head-out immersion in cold water at 11°C. Despite the subject's best efforts to voluntarily maintain apnea (breath holding), maximum breath-hold time was only twenty-three seconds. Furthermore, cold-water immersion induced cardiac arrhythmias, hyperventilation, tachypnea, and hypocapnia following the resumption of breathing. Thus, immersive water shock causes rapid and far-reaching changes in autonomic physiology—changes that have evolved in the attempt to preserve the functions and capacity of central cardiac and neural functions (see Giesbrecht and colleagues 1997, for similar experiments).

Cold-water face immersion (CWFI) is a simple and noninvasive means of inducing the diving response while at rest and also during exercise. As mentioned earlier, this reflex is not under conscious or volitional control. It occurs because there are receptors in the face that detect cold and are coupled to the heart rate and to breathing. (These are cold trigemino-cardiac reflex receptors. We have met the trigeminal nerve previously—it is also involved in the conduction of information about pain from the teeth, among other things.) The overall response to cold water about the face is hyperventilation (increase in the depth and rate of breathing) and bradycardia (slowing of the heart rate), followed by tachycardia (increase in the heart rate) and then finally an increase in blood pressure and a decrease in the relative volume of cerebral blood flow. These changes all are as a result of the cold shock that has occurred. These factors are all associated with increased mortality and may account for some of the sudden and unexpected cases of drowning in cold water of otherwise fit, healthy, and strong individuals.

A series of articles have investigated the effects of body immersion or facial immersion in cold water during breathing. Thomas Kjeld and his colleagues (1985/2009) examined the effect on humans of facial immersion in cold water and found that it enhances cerebral blood velocity while the breath is being held. They investigated very experienced divers. In these experiments, they did not measure functional brain activation, but they did measure blood-flow velocity though the brain, using sonography (which bounces sound waves through different parts of the brain). In the experienced divers group, they found that the velocity of blood flow through the middle cerebral artery is increased during breath holding. This is irrespective of whether they held their breath at rest or during exercise. Hani Al Haddad and his colleagues (2010) examined the influence of cold-water facial immersion on postexercise parasympathetic activation. The parasympathetic nervous system regulates important aspects of heart rate and breathing, among other functions. The researchers hypothesized that cold-water facial immersion would trigger activity in the parasympathetic nervous system after exercise. They had healthy participants cycle an exercise bicycle to the point of exhaustion and then had them place their face in a basin of cold water while wearing a snorkel. They found that cold-water facial immersion triggered parasympathetic activity very strongly in these fit and exercised subjects, including bradycardia. They also found, paradoxically, that there was little effect on breathing.

Teit Mantoni and his colleagues (2008) examined the control of breathing and its effects on blood flow in the brain after iced-water immersion. In their first set of experiments, they instructed subjects on the nature of the response that they would feel when the body is suddenly placed into a tank of 0°C water. The water is fluid, but contains ice, so it is at ice-cold temperature. The participants are lowered into the water to the level of the sternal notch (the meeting point of the bones of the chest) and left there for sixty seconds. Blood flow through the brain was measured using sonography. The researchers found that during descent cerebral blood flow is driven up quickly, and breathing increases dramatically for the first fifteen seconds or so (the gasp response that we experience when suddenly immersed in cold water). Thereafter, subjects can at least partially control their breath under some instruction. In another experiment, subjects were not instructed on their reflexes, and Mantoni and his colleagues measured the effect of sudden immersion in ice-cold water on cerebral blood flow. In this case, they found that there is a sudden drop in cerebral blood flow (measured using sonography). Increases in heart rate were mirrored by decreases in the blood flow through the middle cerebral artery. This in turn can cause disorientation and a possible loss of consciousness. Indeed, during the course of this experiment, two participants exhibited disorientation and clouding of consciousness and so had to be removed quickly from the iced water. The researchers conclude that "cold water immersion associated hyperventilation causes a significant drop in cerebral blood flow velocity to a level which may impair cerebral performance in a situation where it is most needed" (Mantoni and colleagues 2007, 376). To put this in different terms, when you are suddenly placed in cold water, you start to breathe very rapidly and quickly (hyperventilation). This in turn causes a drawing of blood away from the brain, in turn causing decreases in the arterial blood flow to the brain. This drop in blood flow through the brain in turn can cause disorientation, and it can also cause a loss of consciousness. Mantoni and colleagues suggest that this may be the mechanism that underlies drowning or is a possible cause of drowning when people are dropped into cold water, for example, when they are thrown overboard while they are at sea.

A common theme surfaces from these studies (for example, Finnoff 2008; Giesbrecht 2000): sudden exposure to cold water (especially about the torso and the face) causes a redistribution of regional cerebral blood flow. This redistribution favors vital centers principally concerned with survival (typically the brainstem, periaqueductal gray, and amygdala; these play a role in regulating, respectively, breathing and heart rate, panic and pain, and fear and stress). Note that this redistribution can, at the limit, cause a clouding or loss of consciousness too. This redistribution is away from brain areas involved in memory and in the direct recall of information from memory. It is not possible, in humans at least, to easily inspect effects on synaptic function in these areas, but we can conclude with certainty that the loss of blood flow to these rostral areas of the brain will impair function in these areas for many tens of seconds and perhaps minutes or more. Coherent functioning of the brain, such as the processes involved in supporting cognition, might take a substantial period of time to be restored. It is no coincidence that these brain regions are more or less the same ones activated in Dean Mobbs's phobic-stressor studies—a posterior neuraxis mobilizing brain resources toward immediate survival, with blood flow directed away from anterior regions concerned with higher cognitive functions.

The neuropsychological consequences of near drowning are an important topic in their own right. Death by drowning is very common. The brain dies as the result of hypoxia (oxygen restriction). This may result from cardiac arrest, where there is insufficient blood transported with oxygen to the brain; or so-called wet drowning, when water enters the lungs, preventing oxygen uptake; or, occasionally, dry drowning, when the vocal chords and larynx constrict (laryngospasm). Laryngospasm seals the lungs and can prevent water from entering the lungs but in the right circumstances will also prevent the recirculation of air into the lungs when the body is brought back to the surface again. Some estimates suggest that dry drowning occurs in up to 15 percent of drowning cases. This must be a particular risk that is run with repeated waterboarding, especially when it occurs over extended applications. The Torture Memos also state, "If the detainee makes an effort to defeat the technique (e.g., by twisting his head to the side and breathing out of the corner of his mouth), the interrogator may cup his hands around the detainee's nose and mouth to dam the runoff, in which case it would not be possible for the detainee to breathe during the application of the water" (Cole 2009, 168). The danger of accidentally drowning the detainee is here not acknowledged. It takes remarkably little fluid in the lungs to drown a fully grown man. If we take average body weight as eighty kilograms, then the evidence from a case study of a series of drowning and near-drowning cases indicates that it requires only two to four milliliters of water per kilogram to drown a person (that is, a total of 160–320 ml of water—the fluid contents of an average-sized cup and less than a standard-size can of a soft drink) (Oehmichen, Hennig, and Meissner 2008).

There have been many case studies of the effects of near drowning, that is, drowning in which the victim survives. Samuelson and colleagues (2008) discuss case studies of two adult males who suffered near drowning after cardiac arrest, as the result of prolonged submersion in ice-cold water during an accident. In both cases, the core body temperature dropped to the mid-20°C range; the victims became unconscious but were subsequently rescued, were brought to a hospital, and survived the acute near-drowning episode. They were followed up some years later, when they were examined with a full neuropsychological battery: this involved testing memory; attention; visuospatial, visuoperceptual, and visuomotor abilities; and executive functions. A self-assessment of general cognitive problems was also conducted. Both patients had structural MRI scans and showed no visible damage. However, both patients had severe cognitive difficulties across all the test domains. They both showed some limited recovery through time, but of necessity, given the fact that there must have been widespread, if subtle, brain damage, the patients' ultimate cognitive prognosis is poor. An important lesson from a study like this is that anoxia (that is, the loss of oxygen) in the presence of hypothermia (that is, when core body temperatures are lowered to below 35°C/95°F) can be just as dangerous as oxygen restriction that occurs under normal body temperatures, and this may be especially true in adults.

Waterboarding and Carbon Dioxide Narcosis

Inhaling carbon dioxide directly has important physiological consequences also. It can cause feelings of extreme panic and can induce loss of consciousness and perhaps death. Carbon dioxide in the air is not an acid, but when it is dissolved in water or in fluid that is principally water, it becomes mildly acidic. It should not come as a surprise, therefore, that breathing high concentrations of carbon dioxide causes blood pH levels to change in a somewhat more acidic direction. Carbon dioxide becomes dissolved in the bloodstream, making the blood supply more acidic. It has been known for some seventy-five years or more that breathing carbon dioxide concentrations of in excess of 5 percent can induce panic disorder and can cause panic attacks in patients who suffer from panic disorder. Furthermore, Alison Diaper and her colleagues (2012) at Imperial College London have shown that in volunteers, twenty minutes inhaling 7.5 percent carbon dioxide produces a state very similar to that seen in generalized anxiety disorder in psychiatric patients. This carbon dioxide inhalation model has come to be used widely for the screening of drugs for the treatment of generalized anxiety disorder. Valentina Niccolai and colleagues (2008) examined the effect of the inhalation of oxygen mixed with 35 percent carbon dioxide in healthy volunteers. They found that a single inhalation of 35 percent carbon dioxide does not produce a spike in the stress hormone cortisol or in anxiety levels in normal humans, but in patients with panic disorder, there is indeed a stronger anxiety response. We can conclude, therefore, that the effects of inhaling carbon dioxide depend on the extent of the exposure and the concentration to which one is exposed. A single breath of carbon dioxide, even when it constitutes approximately one-third of the air that you breathe, is largely without a physiological effect. However, prolonged inhalation of carbon dioxide, at low concentrations—5 percent or so—can cause a feeling of incipient panic and a feeling of doom. Both feelings of course are strongly associated with the feeling of stress and in particular the exposure to predator stress, the stress of being preyed on and the feeling of imminent death that ensues.

Adam Ziemann and colleagues (2009) provide a mechanistic analysis of the effects of carbon dioxide inhalation. They note that the amygdala expresses acid-sensing ion channels (ASICs), and these ASICs are required for normal fear responses. They pose the question of whether the amygdala might be able to detect changes in brain pH or blood pH. They found that inhaling carbon dioxide reduced brain pH and induced fear behavior in mice. Furthermore, the elimination of the inhibition of ASIC1a reduced this activity dramatically; reexpression of ASIC1a in the amygdala recovered the carbon-dioxide-induced fear deficit in knock-out animals. These data show that the amygdala functions as a chemosensor that detects high concentrations of carbon dioxide, and it can initiate fear-related behavioral responses. These changes are at the basis of how increased carbon dioxide inhalation induces fear and panic responses in both animals and humans. This is most likely the mechanism by which breathing high concentrations of carbon dioxide can induce, in ordinary individuals, feelings of fear and anxiety and, at lower concentrations, can induce similar sorts of feelings in patients suffering from anxiety disorders. There is an emphasis in certain psychotherapies on becoming aware of and maintaining control over respiration, particularly during panic attacks and more generally during fear-evoking situations. I have been unable to find any studies that directly measure the relationship between control of breathing (the instruction to take long, deep breaths), the reduction in blood acidosis, and the reduction in feelings of fear and anxiety, but I would not be at all surprised if there were such a relationship.

We must be clear here that these experiments are not simulating drowning. The induction of the diving response during waterboarding is qualitatively and quantitatively more similar to the experience of drowning than it is to cold-water facial immersion. In the latter case, breathing can proceed normally, because although the diving reflex is triggered, there is no oxygen restriction to the brain. The effects of simulated drowning by waterboarding must cause a very severe and sudden bout of air hunger, which in turn will cause the fight-or-flight panic response. It should be possible—by having subjects voluntarily maintain breath holding (apnea) and to do so repeatedly—to at least simulate some of the effects of waterboarding. Combining such breath holding while performing a concurrent memory task would provide a very effective means of examining the effects of waterboarding on recall from memory. We have been conducting these preliminary experiments at my lab in the Institute of Neuroscience at Trinity College, Dublin; the initial data (which have not yet undergone peer review) suggest that these manipulations negatively impact recall.

Your Mind on Ice: Cooling the Brain and Body

The Torture Memos discuss the use of temperature manipulations very explicitly but entirely without reference to the relevant empirical literature. There is an extended discussion of water dousing, which I quote in part here:

Cold water is poured on the detainee either from a container or a hose without a nozzle. This technique is intended to weaken the detainee's resistance and persuade him to cooperate with interrogators. The water poured on the detainee must be potable, and the interrogators must ensure that water does not enter the detainee's nose, mouth, or eyes. Ambient temperatures must remain above 64°F [17.7°C]. At the conclusion of water dousing session the detainee must be moved to a heated room if necessary to permit his body temperature to return to normal in a safe manner. To ensure an adequate margin of safety, the maximum period of time that a detainee may be permitted to remain wet has been set at two-thirds the time at which, *based on extensive medical literature and experience*, hypothermia could be expected to develop in healthy individuals who are submerged in water of the same temperature. For water temperature of 41°F [5°C], total duration of exposure may not exceed 20 minutes without drying and rewarming. For water temperature of 50°F [10°C], total duration of exposure may not exceed 40 minutes without drying and rewarming. For water temperature of 59°F [15°C], total duration of exposure may not exceed 60 minutes without drying and rewarming (Cole 2009, 164; emphasis added; the medical literature consulted is not cited, nor is the "experience" quantified).

These are remarkable extremes of cold to be exposed to under conditions of imprisonment. Measurements of core body temperature are not reported and may not have been taken. Rewarming and recovery times are not provided, although a U.S. Navy Experimental Diving Unit report from 1990 warns that "it seems to take over 24 hours to recover from even the mildest of hypothermia, after proper hydration, body core temperature and nutritional debts have been paid back" (Storba 1990, 15). One detainee was subjected to "water dousing with 44 degree Fahrenheit water for 18 minutes" (SSCI

2014, 490); other detainees were subjected to ice-water or cold-water baths for variable periods for interrogation purposes or for punishment. Water dousing was also combined with sleep deprivation (SSCI 2014, 104), which likely exacerbated the effects of water dousing, as thermoregulation is impaired during prolonged sleep deprivation. Andrew Young and colleagues summarize their investigations of this issue in a group of Army Rangers in training by noting "chronic exertional fatigue and sleep loss, combined with underfeeding, reduced tissue insulation and blunted metabolic heat production, which compromised maintenance of body temperature. A short period of rest, sleep, and refeeding restored the thermogenic response to cold, but thermal balance in the cold remained compromised until after several weeks of recovery when tissue insulation had been restored" (2001, 774; see also Young and Castellani 2001 for review).

It is not acknowledged in either the Torture Memos or the Senate report just how dangerous immersion in cold water can be. In the memo quoted earlier, it is stated that detainees may be subjected to "water temperature of 41°F [5°C], [and] total duration of exposure may not exceed 20 minutes without drying and rewarming." Boating organizations suggest that humans exposed to water temperatures of between 40°F and 50°F will suffer exhaustion or unconsciousness within 30–60 minutes and death within 60–180 minutes (see chart provided by United States Power Squadrons [2007]). Human ingenuity has therefore given us another way of stressing prisoners by focusing on metabolic and homeostatic drives. Manipulations of temperature—heating and cooling—offer another metabolic tool for the torturer to affect human behavior. As we shall see, however, moving the brain a few degrees outside its normal operating temperature profoundly alters cognition—and for the worse.

Thermal strain is an important and interesting research topic in human physiology and human performance and is especially relevant here. Studies of thermal strain involve imposing heat or cold on people while they perform a task, for example, during exercise (such as cycling a bicycle) or engaging in a cognitive task. It is well known that heat stroke is extremely debilitating. Heat stroke can cause perceptual distortions (somatic and extrasomatic), as well as causing grave distortions of judgment. There is, ironically, a research literature focused directly on these questions and funded by military research programs, as elite soldiers' performance in extreme climactic conditions is a very important variable in the training of armed forces. There is also a relevant literature from sports physiology and sports psychology, as many competitive sports take place in conditions of extreme heat or cold. A focus on this literature is especially important, for it allows us to approach the following issues in a particularly direct way. First, does (prolonged) exposure to thermal strain (hot or cold) enhance or degrade cognition (especially memory and attention), mood, and/or motivation in any way? Second, does such exposure cause other collateral changes in the functioning of other body organs or tissues (I exclude here frostbite, sunburn, or the equivalent) that indirectly impacts cognition, mood, or motivation? In the latter case, there might be enduring inflammatory, endocrine, or autonomic changes that occur because of such thermal strain when it is deliberately used as a stressor. Negative answers to these questions will again support the view that the deliberate attempt to use manipulations of core physiologic functions either to ensure compliance or to adduce information is misguided on its own terms. And, finally, even if compliance or motivation to comply is enhanced, thermal strain manipulations that impact memory will degrade recall independent of motivation. This brings us to a key point to which we have returned time and time again: motivation and compliance are not issues in human volunteers; therefore, any degradation in mood, cognition, and memory is a relatively pure effect of the stressor imposed—and this speaks directly to the issue of whether such stressors degrade recall.

Exposing humans to extremes of heat and cold has always been a simple and cruel technique of torture. Reductions or increases in ambient environmental temperature are easy to achieve with air-conditioning, removal of clothing, waterboarding, and so on. If these techniques are applied as punishments for transgressions, then there may well be a prima facie case under the law for prisoner abuse. Application of these techniques for the purpose of white torture to loosen tongues brings an extra set of issues. The Saltpit at Bagram in Afghanistan is an infamous recent example of where prisoners were subjected to extremes of heat and cold in the Afghan climate. Here, we will examine if manipulating temperature alters cognitive and motivational states in such a way as to facilitate recall, by reviewing the experimental literature to see what effects temperature manipulations have on cognition. Remember: in normal test subjects, intentional deceit or motivated lying is not an issue. So deteriorations or otherwise in cognition resulting from temperature manipulations represent the prime effect of the temperature change, uncontaminated by other factors. A deleterious effect on memory would indicate that these techniques have quite the opposite effect to those intended by their practitioners.

Human beings, in common with all other mammals, are warm-blooded creatures. Our bodies work to maintain a stable core temperature of approximately 38°C. Our receptors are in constant communication with the external environment to provide feedback required in order to ensure that our core body temperature does not move outside a narrow range. If we are too hot, blood flows to the surface of the body (vasodilation), radiating heat away from the body trunk and the brain. We can also discharge heat by means of perspiration. If we are too cold, blood is withdrawn from the periphery of the body (vasoconstriction), and we attempt to keep warm through a variety of involuntary physiological means, including shivering. Humans also are unique because we are able to maintain and regulate our body temperatures by donning or removing clothing to regulate temperature (I exclude molting for obvious reasons). This process is known as temperature homeostasis—the attempt to maintain a more or less constant temperature, despite variations in external temperature. Homeostasis is engaged in by all mammals and is a fundamentally involuntary process. Manipulations of core body temperature have been a target for torture through the years because of the profound effect that body temperature has on our ongoing physiology. Hypothermia is defined as a reduction in core body temperature to below 35°C (95°F; Díaz and Becker 2010).

There is an experimental literature on the effects of hypothermia, that is, extremes of cold, and of hyperthermia, that is, extremes of heat, on cognition. For example, June Pilcher and colleagues (2002) conducted a large-scale retrospective review (or meta-analysis), in which they focused on the effects of cold exposure (defined as exposure to temperatures of equal to or less than 10°C) on variables such as reasoning, learning, and memory. They conclude, unsurprisingly, that all of these cognitive functions are impaired by sustained exposure to extremes of heat or cold (14.88 percent decrement and 13.91 percent decrement, respectively, relative to neutral conditions). Tiina Makinen and colleagues (2006) conducted one of the very few large-scale studies of the effects of repeated exposure to cold on cognitive performance. They were interested in investigating the relationship of repeated exposure to cold to how the body regulates its own temperature, in other words, to thermal regulation. They used young, male volunteers as subjects and tested them in a climactic chamber—an isolated room within which the temperature can be varied independently of the outside environment. The volunteers were exposed to temperatures of 25°C for 90 minutes and in another room at 10°C for 120 minutes, and they did so every day for ten days. This is a remarkable experimental commitment on behalf of these volunteers, who clearly were very motivated to participate. During the course of the experiment, they wore light clothing, consisting of a pair of shorts, socks, and athletic shoes, and they wore monitors that measured their skin temperature at multiple locations; additionally, their oxygen intake was measured, as was their heart rate and blood pressure. The subjects themselves also gave judgments on a scale of how comfortable or uncomfortable they were feeling under the particular environmental conditions.

The researchers analyzed a whole series of broad measures of cognition. These were a series of tasks designed to measure memory, logical reasoning, and reaction times. The measurement of reaction time is straightforward in the laboratory; subjects simply press a key as quickly as possible when presented with a *go* stimulus, that is, a stimulus to which they must respond. Typically, these stimuli are visual (say, a letter or a plus sign) or auditory (say, a beep or a bing). Other tasks involved logical reasoning; subjects were required to compare symbol sequences with pictorial sequences to determine if the one logically represents the other. Memory was assessed using the N-Back task, which requires subjects to view a continuous stream of letters on a computer monitor. Participants must maintain the letter stream in mind for a short time. They press a key if the current letter is the same as the one immediately preceding it. This is a moderately taxing task that is known to involve activation of the frontal lobes. People who have suffered frontal lobe damage typically show catastrophically poor performance on this task. During brain imaging, the frontal lobes are activated on both sides very strongly during this task; the hippocampus, which is concerned with long-term associative memory, is typically suppressed for the duration of the task. The researchers found a very interesting pattern of results. First of all, oxygen consumption, as one might expect, increases. So too does shivering in the cold-exposed group. There were also changes in blood pressure that disappeared gradually over the course of ten days. The overall pattern of effects on cognition is summarized by the authors as follows: "cold exposure was a significant independent predictor of longer response times and decreased efficiency" where cognitive performance was concerned (Makinen and colleagues 2006, 173). They also conclude that "cold exposure had a negative effect on both simple as well as complex cognitive skills requiring sustained attention and concentration, verbal learning, numeric and symbolic facility, reasoning, and operation of the working memory" (174). They did observe one improvement, which "manifested as reduced response times and an increased overall efficiency in the cold" on the logical reasoning task (174). They do not disclose whether the reaction times are correlated with actually poorer performance on the task itself, as opposed to the time taken to respond in the task. Improvements in performance were seen over time, suggesting that there is a cognitive adaptation to the cold, and that takes about five days or so to manifest itself. (Matthew Muller and colleagues conclude similarly that "relative to baseline performance, working memory, choice reaction time, and executive function declined during exposure to 10°C, and these impairments persisted 60 minutes into the recovery period"; 2012, 792.)

Shona Simmons and colleagues (2008) have examined the effect of passive heating and head cooling on perception, cardiovascular function, and cognitive performance. These are a particularly elegant set of experiments, as they separate the effects of increases in skin temperature and increases in core body temperature from each other. Thus, the question of how these increases affect perceptions of heat-related fatigue and how they affect cognitive function can be investigated. In these experiments, ten participants volunteered to visit the laboratory three times. They were administered a battery of cognitive tests, including a simple reaction-time test (you press a button as quickly as possible every time a cue appears, such as the word *press*) and a vigilance task (streams of digits are displayed on a computer screen, and the participants hit a key whenever there is a match to a preagreed target, for example, the number 3). They also engaged in a choice-reaction-time test; whenever the word *yes* or the word *no* was presented, they had to press as quickly as possible the appropriate Y or N key. They also did a rapid visual information-processing task, in which they were presented with digit strings and whenever three odd numbers or three even numbers appeared in a row, they had to press the *yes* key as quickly as possible. They also did a Morse code tapping task in which they had to press a key rapidly for an extended period of time. And then finally they completed a series of mood and alertness self-rating scales so that their own subjective evaluation of how they felt at any particular moment in time could be tapped into.

The clever and elegant part of this experiment is as follows: the volunteers were required to wear a balaclava, which was made of plastic and through which water at 3°C could be perfused. This allowed the head and neck to be cooled easily and effectively (an image of this balaclava is available on the Internet if you conduct a search for "liquid cooled" or "liquid conditioned" balaclava). The researchers also controlled for dehydration; participants were required to drink plenty of warm water, and there was no loss of body mass over the course of the exposure to the experiments. Subjects sat in a climactic chamber, and the temperature was increased to 45°C until core body temperature was increased by 1°C. They completed the battery of cognitive tests several times during the heating process in the climactic chamber. The overall findings were, first, that skin temperature could be increased, as could core body temperature. At normal temperatures (that is, when there was a regular skin temperature and a regular core temperature when the participants sat in the climactic chamber at 25°C), they performed normally on all of the measures. At high body temperatures, high skin temperatures, and high core temperatures (45°C), they showed a huge decrement in performance across all measures. But in the case where the head was cooled but the skin remained warm, thus cooling the core body temperature, they performed identically to normal conditions.

These experiments show that it is possible to tell the difference between the effects of inducing high temperatures in the body periphery and of inducing high temperatures in the body core. And the conclusion? In this case, it is the high temperatures in the body core that cause cognitive impairment. The authors summarize the outcome of the experiment as follows: "raising both skin and core temperature resulted in increases in perception of heat-related fatigue, increased cardiovascular strain, and decrements in cognitive performance" (Simmons and colleagues 2008, 279). They did observe one paradox of heating: simple reaction times decreased a little. However, under conditions of heat, people may respond more quickly, but they do so less accurately. In other words, the speed of response goes up, but accuracy goes down. Now, it is a well-observed phenomenon that nerve conduction velocity is enhanced somewhat under higher temperatures (up to a limit), and increases in simple reaction times may result simply from faster transmission of impulses along the nerves in the periphery. In a parallel set of experiments, Nadia Gaoua and colleagues (2011) also found, using different temperatures (20°C and 50°C), with the head being cooled by cooling packs, that performance decrements in cognitive tasks were reduced but that, in the absence of the cooling packs to take the head temperature down, working memory was impaired, again using a battery of cognitive tests.

One final set of experiments is especially worth mentioning. Mary Beth Spitznagel and colleagues (2009) examined the combination of sleep deprivation and hypothermia on cognitive functioning in a group of six volunteer young, male participants. The particular focus was on measures of attention, reaction time, and executive function, with sleep deprivation (53 hours) and cooling (120 minutes of acute cold exposure in an environmentally controlled chamber at 10°C, while lightly dressed) applied in an additive form. It was predicted that there would be a negative effect of cooling and of sleep deprivation when these conditions were conducted separately and that there would be an additive effect of combining cooling and sleep deprivation. As predicted, both sleep deprivation and cold exposure negatively affected cognitive function across all the domains measured. Furthermore, there was an additive effect of sleep deprivation and cooling when the two treatments were combined. Note here that these experiments were conducted with volunteers under appropriate biomedical supervision and ethical review. All were motivated to participate and compliant with instructions. Nonetheless, their performance degraded across all classes of cognitive task measured. Motivation and compliance are therefore not variables that confound performance, but yet we will still find performance is degraded by this treatment. Combining sleep deprivation with water dousing—for substantially greater and more uncontrolled extremities of experience—can only be expected to have even more degrading effects on cognition (and indeed mood) in prisoners.

The conclusions to be drawn from this review of the evidence of imposing thermal strain on mood, cognition, and motivation are straightforward. First, let us focus on motivation and compliance: volunteers complied easily with the demands of the experiments, and few dropouts from the studies are reported. Thus, thermal strain does not necessarily have a direct effect on motivation—although one might imagine that imposing ever-greater temperature extremes would result in the dropout rate increasing. Second, and crucially, forcing core body temperature away from homeostatic set points causes severe degradations in cognition and mood. In other words, people feel worse and are unable to think easily, fluently, and coherently, and their behavioral performance suffers too. Finally, there is an interesting nuance regarding heat and cold manipulation. The brain is relatively intolerant of minor shifts (of, for example, 2–3°C) upward in its core temperature, presumably because losing heat from the brain in an environment of overall heat gain is difficult to achieve. Downward fluctuations in core brain and body temperature seem somewhat more tolerated, presumably because the body can use a variety of compensatory mechanisms to generate heat (that is, thermogenesis), including motor movements and the burning of any brown adipose tissue that may be available. The overall conclusion is inescapable, though: optimal integrative functioning is best achieved within a reasonable external-temperature thermoneutral zone in which hot and cold fluctuations can be easily and automatically managed by the hypothalamus and related tissues.

There is another issue that is germane (but a little tangential) to the foregoing discussion. The Constitution Project notes that "the guidelines repeatedly call for medical professionals to monitor the severity of harm imposed by interrogators on detainees, rather than preventing any harm. For example, the 2003 guidelines state that '[d]etainees can safely be placed in uncomfortably cool environments for varying lengths of time, ranging from hours to days'" (2013, 213–214). Thus, we have the uncomfortable possibility that medical professionals—who should have the specialist knowledge that these procedures are associated with high potential morbidity and will affect cognition and mood—were either not consulted or were ignored during the writing of these memos, for their advice would have run contrary to the intention of the memos: to impose a regime of surprising cruelty for the ostensible purpose of information retrieval. The identities of the involved medical personnel have not been made public, and they have not gone on the record even in an anonymous fashion; so we have no idea about what their thinking was regarding the imposition of these procedures on the detainees.

Dietary Manipulation of Detainees—Cognitive and Mood Effects

Caloric restriction is a validated method for inducing weight loss in obese individuals (see, for example, Siervo and colleagues 2011). There is now a substantial literature indicating that obesity (defined as a body mass index of greater than 25 or a weight of greater than about 105 kilograms for a five-foot-ten male) can be severely injurious to health (for example, Mokdad and colleagues 2003). Diabetes, cardiovascular problems, cancer, and a wide variety of other metabolic conditions are associated with excess calorie intake and substantial weight gain. Indeed, the animal experimental literature suggests that a calorie-restricted diet in which individual subjects are maintained at approximately 85–90 percent of their free-feeding weight confers considerable benefits, including life extension. Dietary change and restriction has also long been a tool for physiological manipulation during interrogation and for those who are held in captivity. The Torture Memos are explicit in this regard (Cole 2009, 159–160).

This aspect of the manipulation of prisoners has received much less attention than it should have. The normal recommended daily allowance (RDA) for a healthy eighty-kilogram male is approximately two and a half thousand calories of an appropriately balanced diet per day to maintain current weight and to prevent excess weight gain. One Torture Memo states of dietary manipulation, "This technique involves the substitution of commercial liquid meal replacements for normal food, presenting detainees with a bland, unappetizing, but nutritionally complete diet. You have informed us that the CIA believes dietary manipulation makes other techniques, such as sleep deprivation, more effective" (Cole 2009, 177).

To make the situation more explicit, the memos envisage reducing prisoners' daily calorie intake to 1,000 calories per day—which is 40 percent of the average adult intake (2,500 calories for a male of average weight and height; no prisoner is to be provided with a lesser amount of food). The memo goes on to consider the fact that commercially available weight-loss programs (which are for the clinically obese, that is, those individuals who already have a substantial store of body fat from which to derive and support calorific needs) sometimes envisage diets of this type for volunteer dieters. Thus, the sudden reduction in calorific intake to about 40 percent of the normal RDA is regarded as "medically safe" because commercially available diet programs for the obese envisage similar caloric restriction, and so can endure caloric reduction. It is widely known that most weight-loss programs fail; and they fail for many reasons, not the least of which is that the behavior to be engaged in is itself a voluntary behavior, and volunteer dieters find sticking to a regime in which they consume nothing but a liquid diet for days to weeks at a time very difficult to maintain. One reason such diets are very difficult to maintain is the phenomenon of sensory-specific satiety, whereby a food that is repetitively presented and consumed consistently, as a mere result of exposure, causes that food to lose its palatability. Sensory-specific satiety has been explored in some depth, and it is now known that a change in the behavior of neurons in the orbitofrontal cortex (the part of the brain just above the orbits of the eyes) is responsible for this long-term food-intake change. This phenomenon has been noted very widely, including, for example, in refugee camps where nutritionally complete but bland and nonvaried diets have been imposed on the refugees. Despite hunger and privation, refugees may end up refusing their diets, leading to a change in the dietary regimens used in such camps to ensure a greater variety and palatability of the food offered. The memos assert that the food provided to the detainees is nutritionally complete, but this cannot be the case because the food intake envisaged is 40 percent of the normal RDA for an adult. The liquid diet brings one central and simple advantage: if a detainee were to vomit during the course of waterboarding, the lack of solid mass makes the likelihood of his or her asphyxiating as a result of vomiting much lower indeed. The need for medical intervention to ensure removal of particulate matter from the esophagus and the respiratory tract is then obviated.

We have noted that there are positive benefits to caloric restriction in the obese, hence the popularity of weight-loss programs. However, the questions here are twofold in the context of prisoner interrogation. First, what weight loss occurred in the detainees? And second, what is the impact of this weight loss, combined with other stressors, on cognitive function? We have no answer to the first question, as the detainee medical logs have not been released, and we do not know the extent to which they lost body mass as a result of the restricted-calorie-level diet imposed on them. (I am assuming they were of normal or slightly under normal weight to begin with.) The answer to the second question is clear. The imposition of caloric restriction under circumstances of stress exacerbates deficits in cognitive function. We can assert this with reasonable certainty because the studies conducted on military personnel by, for example, Charles Morgan and colleagues conduct studies under simulated combat elite where soldiers undergo dietary restrictions (see Morgan's papers in the further reading section). They may be restricted also in terms of access to liquids, and extreme stressors are imposed on them. Uniformly, there is a decline observed in the soldiers' mood, cognition, and psychomotor function when sleep deprivation is combined with food restriction and other stressors. Furthermore, a study by Celeste Choma and colleagues (1998) examined the effects of rapid weight loss on cognitive function in collegiate wrestlers (a population that is not directly comparable—they are likely younger and healthier than the detainees on average). The study concluded that rapid, precompetition weight loss in wrestlers was accompanied by transient mood reduction and impaired short-term memory. Remember here also that the detainees may show greater-than-normal levels of weight loss because they are also subjected to extended periods of dousing with cold water. The natural response to water dousing is shivering and other attempts by the body to engage in thermogenesis, including a restriction of blood flow to the periphery—including, it is probable, to higher cortical regions so that brainstem regions can maintain homeostasis (or as near to normal physiological levels of functioning as is possible). The *empathy gap* is something we discuss in detail in Chapter 7. It would not have taken much by way of a leap of imagination of either the interrogators or the drafters of these memos to consider how they themselves have felt when they were cold, hungry, and tired simultaneously. The disturbance of mood and clouding of cognition is apparent to anyone who has ever operated (however inadvertently) under these circumstances.

The Senate Torture Report disclosed a further previously undescribed method of food administration, namely, rectal infusion or rectal feeding. Permission was not sought in the original memos for the use of rectal feeding, which involved the administration of pureed food through the rectum into apparently noncompliant prisoners. No meaningful attempt is made to cite gastric physiology to justify the use of this technique, which by any reasonable reading is tantamount to anal rape. The effort can best be likened to filling the combustion chamber of a car engine by forcing fuel in through the exhaust pipe. It is not going to work. The site of digestion and nutritive absorbance through the large and small intestine are so remote from the rectum as to suggest that this technique can only have been engaged in for perhaps retributive or even sadistic purposes. In the case of prisoners who refuse to voluntarily feed themselves, several courses of action are possible. One is to accept that this is what the prisoner wishes to do and to grant him or her that wish, even if that wish eventuates in the person's death. Other possibilities present themselves as well. One is what is an unpleasant but perhaps life-saving procedure, namely, nasogastric infusion, and another is an indwelling venous catheter attached to an appropriate liquid nutritive mix. These latter approaches involve a violation of the integrity of one's body, and there is a substantial ethical, biomedical, and philosophical debate regarding the use of such techniques on captives who refuse food. We will not deal with these ethical issues here as they are outside the purview of this book.

To this point, we have focused largely on the consequences of torture for the individual on whom the torture is visited. We have seen that the theories and predictions presented in the memos fail utterly and predictably. They are not founded on any knowledge of psychology or neuroscience. Rather, they are founded on an evidence base that involves consulting the contents of one's own consciousness. They are also silent on another issue: what are the consequences of administering torture for the torturer? There is no evidence base from film and television to consult for thinking through these policies. After all, a torture regime requires someone to impose it. The Torture Memos are silent regarding the effects of waterboarding on the waterboarders. This is the logic we turn to next—why people might torture someone else and the effects doing so may have on them if they do.

7

Why Does a Torturer Torture?

Interrogator: (silently, to self) This is awful. He's lost control of his bowels again. He screams when he can. He speaks gibberish, any old rubbish he thinks will make it stop. And yet they keep saying, "Squeeze him more. He knows something." I know he doesn't. But all in a good cause. After all, that lawyer said it was okay in that memo.

Interrogator: (years later) I can still see him scream in my dreams. Will it ever stop?

Psychiatrist: Here, take these pills. They'll dull it for you.

To this point, we have discussed torture as something that is done to someone else. We have not paid any attention to the torturer at all. Many, if not most, of us assume that torturing another human being is something that only a minority of people are capable of. Waterboarding requires the use of physical restraints—and perhaps only after a physical struggle—unless the captive willingly submits to the process. Similarly, slapping or hitting another person, imposing extremes of temperature on him or her, electrocuting him or her, or whatever—requires the presence of active others. These others must grapple with, and perhaps subdue, the captive, and impose on him or her levels of physical contact that violate all of the norms of interpersonal interaction of a usual everyday life. Bluntly, for torture to occur, there must be at least two parties present: one who is physically restrained and the other who has considerable freedom to act and is acting at the behest of others in the chain of command. We will discuss in this chapter the famous obedience experiments devised by Stanley Milgram, which showed that ordinary people were capable of apparently electrocuting someone else severely and even to the point of seeming death. One possible conclusion is that there is a torturer inside all of us, waiting to be coaxed out when authority demands it. Torturing someone is not an easy thing to do. In the Milgram experiments, the supposed torturers did in fact suffer distress from the procedures used. What is it like to torture, to subject another person to forces of physical and mental distress? This is not a well-understood or considered subject, and it is to understanding empathy and the infliction of pain, torment, and distress on a defenseless other that we turn to next.

Ian Cobain notes the testimony of one British interrogator from World War II (Griffith-Jones): "The psychological effects on those who administer violence are potentially dangerous; it is essential that they should remain collected, balanced and dispassionate" (2012, 89). The sang froid overlaid here notwithstanding, the underlying truth is recognized—that subjecting a fellow human being to torture is stressful for all but the most psychopathic. The historical literature is replete with accounts of alcohol or drug abuse by torturers. Occasionally, testimony from torturers about the impact that torturing someone else has on them surfaces. Several examples of such testimony are particularly appropriate here. Cobain, in *Cruel Britannia*, interviews a former user of the Five Techniques in Northern Ireland, who says, "The torture continues to leave its mark, of course. Among those unable to escape from the past are the interrogators themselves, some of whom appear traumatised by their memories of what they inflicted upon others. Some have concluded that what they did was a terrible mistake, one that exacerbated the causes of the conflict; others insist they resorted to violence only in desperation, in a bid to vanquish the far more extreme violence that was engulfing their society" (2012, 202–203). Jose Rodriguez states in his book, "Let there be no doubt. The treatment that a small handful of terrorists received at our hands was unpleasant. It was unpleasant for them and, *not insignificantly, unpleasant for us*" (2012, 193; emphasis added). And elsewhere in his book, Rodriguez states, "The EITs were employed by our officers with great reluctance and solemnity" (69). The word "reluctance" is revealing; it suggests that the inner impulses disavowing coercion and torture had to be consciously overcome and subjugated. One of the psychologists involved in the CIA program, Dr. James Mitchell, went on the record after the release of the Senate Torture report, stating, "Those techniques are so harsh that it's emotionally distressing to the people who are administering them. Even though you don't want to do it, you're doing it in order to save lives in the country, and we would just have to man up for lack of a better term" (Mitchell 2014). Note the language employed. These individuals are consciously and with effort setting to one side their reservations about engaging in coercion and torment, ostensibly doing so for the greater good. These actions find a strong echo in the Milgram experiments adverted to above, and discussed in detail below. Many accounts of the effects of torturing on the torturer are recounted in an extraordinary book entitled *None of Us Were Like This Before* by Joshua Phillips. Recounted here are the stories of American soldiers in Iraq who turned to prisoner abuse, torment, and torture for multifarious reasons. Once removed from the theater of war and the supporting camaraderie of the battalion, intense, enduring and disabling guilt, posttraumatic stress disorder, and substance abuse follow. Suicide, sadly and unfortunately, is not uncommon too.

What would it take for an ordinary member of the public to electrocute someone—even to the point of (apparent) death? In what are possibly the most famous experiments in social psychology, the late Stanley Milgram (then at Yale University) investigated the conditions under which ordinary human beings, members of the public, would be willing to obey instructions from an authority figure (a scientist in a white coat) to electrocute another human being. The story of these experiments has often been told, but it is worth describing them again because they continue, more than forty years on and many successful replications later, to retain their capacity to shock the conscience and illustrate how humans will bend to the demands of authority. Milgram invited members of the public by advertisement to come to his laboratory to investigate the effects of punishment on learning and memory. Subjects were brought into the laboratory, introduced to another participant in the experiments who was going to be punished (ostensibly electrocuted) whenever he or she misremembered or misrecalled words from lists that he or she was supposed to learn. This other person who was to be subjected to the electric shocks was an actor and did not actually experience any pain or discomfort. The actor was brought to a room and hooked up to what looked like a set of electric shock pads, and the subject was brought to another room where he or she was in communication via a two-way speaker with the actor. In turn, the subject was seated in front of a large and impressive-looking electric-shock box, which had a dial that could administer electric shocks from 0 to 450 volts. At various points around the dials, differing danger levels associated with particular shock levels were indicated. The experimenter (the authority figure) was a scientist dressed in a white coat, who gave instructions to the unwitting member of the public. The actor was requested to recall items from a list of words that he or she had learned, and for every item that was wrong, the actor was given what appeared to be a single electric shock. At very low levels of intensity, the actor would remain relatively quiet or give minimal sound of discomfort but, at higher levels of intensity, would shout out in pain; and at the highest intensity levels (where it was indicated on the dial that the person who was electric shocked might suffer death), the actor would remain silent. And so the experiment began. The member of the public would ask the actor to recall the words and would turn the dial to administer the supposed electric shock when an error occurred. When the actor did not reply or made an error, the apparent level of the shock was incremented. The subject would apply the electric shock whenever the actor made an error, and the apparent distress of the actor would increase as the shock level increased.

Milgram, at the start of these experiments, had his experimental protocols reviewed. It was generally concluded that the vast majority of people would not go anywhere near the highest levels of shock: that they would desist from shocking the subject (the actor) long before the maximum point on the dial was reached. Milgram asked both Yale University students (Yale was the site of the studies) and forty psychiatrists to predict how far participants would be willing to go, and found a general consensus that few if any participants would go all the way to the extremity of 450 volts. It was suggested that only those of a particularly psychopathic disposition would go all the way to the uppermost shock level. However, Milgram found that about two-thirds of test participants progressed all the way to the maximum shock. Furthermore, few subjects refused to finish the experiment. If the test subject indicated that he or she was worried or distressed by the progress of the experiment, the experimenter would simply say, "The experiment requires that you continue." No coercion was applied, and the subject was actually free to get up and leave the experiment at whatever time he or she pleased. However, simple verbal prompts and the presence of a white-coat-wearing scientist in a laboratory context was sufficient to induce behavior that, if seen in the outside world and actually conducted on an individual there, would be regarded as evidence of extreme psychopathy and lack of empathy. However, the apparent institutional context, the demands of science, the legitimation of conduct because of the presence of a person in a white coat, in a laboratory setting, facilitated obedience on the part of the subjects in the experiment.

Milgram's experiments have been replicated several times since, with a wide number of variations imposed. These range from the actor being present and physically beside the subject to manipulations such as the experimenter not wearing the white coat and not providing any verbal prompts. Under these circumstances, compliance with authority diminishes quite rapidly, but a number of simple manipulations enhance compliance with authority. What is the lesson to be drawn from these experiments? One lesson is simple: human beings have a propensity to obey authority under the right circumstances, and human beings are willing, because an authority gives an apparent go-ahead, to visit what appear to be extremes of pain on another person for what are actually trivial reasons, namely, an apparent inability to recall words from a word list.

On average, during Milgram's experiments, 65 percent of the subjects in the experiments were willing to go all the way to the 450-volt shock limit. Subsequently, cross-cultural analyses have shown that on average, irrespective of place in the world, 66 percent of subjects will go to the limit of 440 volts in shocking the actor. These results are really quite remarkable. People are willing, under certain circumstances, to override their own internal moral imperatives and to subjugate their own behavior to the authority of another. These experiments, unsurprisingly, quickly became controversial and led to an explosion of research within social psychology on the psychology of obedience. Milgram subsequently commented (in what has become a famous and oft-cited quote), "With numbing regularity good people were seen to knuckle under the demands of authority and perform actions that were callous and severe. Men who are in everyday life responsible and decent were seduced by the trappings of authority, by the control of their perceptions, and by the uncritical acceptance of the experimenter's definition of the situation, into performing harsh acts. A substantial proportion of people do what they are told to do, irrespective of the content of the act and without limitations of conscience, so long as they perceive that the command comes from a legitimate authority" (1965, 74).

Thomas Blass notes that there have been some eighteen successful replications of the original study between 1968 and 1985, all with the similar pattern of consistently replicated results (2009, 295). Several more recent replications are worth examining in detail. More recently, Jerry Burger of Santa Clara University conducted a partial replication of Milgram's studies. Burger used a cut-off of 150 volts—the point at which about 80 percent of Milgram's subjects continued to the 450-volt maximum. As Burger puts it, "the 150-volt switch is something of a point of no return" (2009, 2)—if you go through this behavioral threshold, you are most likely to continue all the way to the maximum point of punishment. Burger therefore decided to stop the study at 150 volts—after participants indicated that they were willing (or not) to continue escalating the shock levels. Burger found (similar to Milgram) that 70 percent of subjects would continue beyond 150 volts. He found no sex differences or age-related differences. There was only a small relationship between subjects' measured levels of empathic concern for others and their need for control affected participants' responses. In other words, the situational demands are more important than individual differences. The idea of a threshold of obedience or disobedience is one that receives support from a meta-analytic review of Milgram's data using techniques unavailable in 1963. Dominic Packer (2008), then of Ohio State University, reanalyzed data from eight of Milgram's original experiments. He concludes two things: that disobedience to instructions was most likely to occur at the 150-volt threshold and that those who disobeyed saw that they could help strengthen or vindicate the voluntary participant learner's right to leave or terminate the experiment whenever they chose. This 150 volt point could be therefore characterized as an inflection point, where intervention can prevent further escalation into more brutal forms of torture.

A major barrier to deepening our understanding of the extremities of human behavior that the obedience experiments reveal (and that the facts of human history disclose) is the ethical one. It is difficult, if not almost impossible, to obtain permission to replicate the experiments as originally conceived and executed, as they involve subjecting participants to both deception, stress, and some degree of moderate compulsion (in the form of direct verbal points). Jerry Burger has shown one possible route; Mel Slater and his colleagues in London and Barcelona have shown another. In their experiments, they use an immersible virtual-reality approach with a female avatar as the learner. Participants here gave the avatar electric shocks as part of the word-learning regime; simultaneously, behavioral and electrodermal measures of stress were assayed. Remarkably, participants experienced a considerable degree of stress when electrocuting the large-scale but not terribly life-like avatar (Slater and colleagues 2006; see also Cheetham and colleagues 2009). There have been at least two replications of this result, one of which is especially interesting. The promise of Slater's approach is that it might allow an unraveling of the underlying psychological and prevailing social mechanisms that generate such obedience to authority. Using an independently originated immersive video environment with an actor rather than an avatar, the psychologists Michaël Dambrun and Elise Vatiné (2010) explored individual differences that predict obedience. Here, there was no deception: participants were told that the learner was an actor feigning being shocked. Several results stand out from this study: participants reported less anxiety and distress when the learner was of North African origin. Participants who exhibited higher levels of right-wing authoritarianism and who showed higher levels of state anger were more likely to show high levels of obedience (both variables measured by psychometrically valid questionnaires).

A further replication and extension of Milgram's work has been undertaken in France by Laurent Bègue and his colleagues (2014). This study transposes the Milgram paradigm to a television game-show setting. Here, the participants perform teacher-learner roles for a mocked-up television production. The general aspects of the

Milgram paradigm were reproduced: variable-intensity electric shocks to motivate learning, the presence of an authority figure (the host), the incrementing of the punishment until there is silence from the learner. Three conditions were tested: the "standard Milgram" condition (the voice of authority); a "social support" condition (in which an accomplice intervenes to say that the show must be stopped because it is immoral); and a "host-withdrawal" condition (in which the host departs, leaving participants to decide for themselves whether to continue). There was 81 percent obedience in the standard condition, whereas there was only 28 percent obedience in the host-withdrawal condition. Follow-up work focused on personality variables using the Big Five MiniMarkers questionnaire. Data were collected some months after the study by telephone interview. Two personality constructs were associated (moderately) with obedience: agreeableness and conscientiousness. These are dispositions that might indeed be necessary for wiling or unwilling participation in a program of coercive interrogation or torture. Interestingly, individuals of a more rebellious disposition (as evidenced by going on strike) tended to administer lower-intensity shocks. Of course, rebels are not usually selected by institutions to operate sensitive programs: Edward Snowden is the exception, not the rule.

In the United States, in the early 1970s, Philip Zimbardo conducted a different but also extremely important set of experiments on obedience. In a set of experiments that became known as the Stanford Prison experiment, Zimbardo (1971) investigated a very simple question: what would happen if you took people—in this case, psychology students—randomly, from an original group of seventy-five, divided them into two groups, prisoners and prison guards, and then put them to live in a mock prison in the basement of the psychology department at Stanford University? Again, similar to the Milgram experiments, remarkable effects on behavior were observed. The prison guards became, in many cases, very authoritarian, and the prisoners became passive and adapted themselves very quickly and adopted the role of prisoners. The experiment, which was supposed to last two weeks, had to be terminated after six days, given what happened. The prison guards became abusive in certain instances, and they adopted the use of wooden batons as symbols of status. They adopted mirrored sunglasses and clothing that simulated the clothes of a prison guard. The prisoners, by contrast, were fitted in prison clothing or very similar clothes, were referred to by their numbers rather than by their names, and wore ankle chains. Guards became sadistic in about one-third of cases. They harassed the prisoners, imposed protracted exercise as punishments on the prisoners, refused to allow prisoners access to toilets, and would remove prisoners' mattresses. These prisoners were, until a few days previously, fellow students and certainly not guilty of any criminal offense. Zimbardo himself, who role-played as a warden, subsequently came to believe that he also became too identified with his role and overidentified with the prison setup that he had created. The scenario that Zimbardo created gave rise to what he and others subsequently referred to as deindividualization or deindividuation, in which under certain circumstances, people define themselves with respect to their roles and not with respect to themselves or their ethical standards as persons. These experiments again emphasize the importance of institutional context as a driver for individual behavior and the extent to which an institutional context can cause a person to override his or her individual and normal predispositions.

The combined story that emerges from Milgram's obedience experiments and Zimbardo's prison experiments is quite disturbing for naive psychological views of human nature. Such views might suggest that people have an internal moral compass and a set of moral attitudes and that these will drive behavior, almost irrespective of circumstance. The emerging position, however, is much more complex. Individuals, while having a moral compass of their own, are capable of overriding that moral compass and inflicting severe punishments on other individuals when an authority figure is present and institutional circumstances demand it. Moreover, when individuals are placed in certain situations in which they lose their own personal identities, they become deindividuated. They can disregard their own internal moral sentiments and impose on fellow human beings punishments that are out of all proportion to the transgressions that have been perceived to have occurred.

There are some parallels and some differences between these experiments and the subjects' willingness to engage in torture. In the first instance, the obedience experiments were conducted under controlled laboratory conditions, and they had undergone some form of ethical review and were conducted by professionals. But the results, nonetheless, are really striking: 66 percent of a randomly chosen sample of participants would push the dial all the way to 450 volts on another human being. Similarly, 100 percent of participants in a randomly chosen sample in the prison experiments were capable, when suitably inducted into a particular role, of engaging in abusive behavior toward another human being. It is likely, therefore, that under the very different circumstances that are found in prisons and other situationally or contextually remote places, individuals will be capable of engaging in much greater extremes of behavior than have been seen in these laboratory settings. However, while people are capable of engaging in extremes at particular moments in time, this does not mean that there is not a psychological cost to engaging in behavior of this type. Anecdotally, it is clear that many, but not all, individuals who have engaged in behavior of this type come to have regrets about what they have done; they evince great degrees of distress over what they have done, and some indeed pay a high psychological price themselves. Why should this be the case? Humans are empathic beings. We, with certain exceptions, are capable of mentalizing or simulating the internal states that other human beings experience; imposing pain or stress on another human being comes with a psychological cost to ourselves.

Regarding Distress in Others

Humans—those of use that are not psychopaths or those who have not been deindividuated or who are acting on the instructions of a higher authority—do have a substantial capacity for sharing the experiences of another person, in other words, empathy. The roots of prosocial or empathic behavior have deep neural and psychological roots in humans. Over the past fifteen to twenty years, neuroscientists have made substantial strides in understanding the brain systems that are involved in empathy—in our capacity to engage in intersubjective analysis and to understand the thoughts and feelings of others. It is now possible to experimentally investigate questions that formerly were at best difficult to explore. What is the difference, for example, between experiencing pain yourself and watching pain being visited on another human being? In other words, do we experience empathy when we regard the pain of others? What happens in our brains when we see another person in pain or distress, especially somebody with whom we have a close relationship? Many of these experiments revolve around a profound but straightforward paradigm. Participants compare their own internal subjective states while experiencing pain or watching another person experience pain, and fMRI brain-imaging techniques and rating scales are used to estimate participants' own rating of the feelings that the other person is undergoing. Many particularly clever experiments have been conducted in which the experience of one's own pain has been compared with the experience of seeing another person in pain. As previously discussed, pain has sensory, affective, cognitive/evaluative, and motoric components. The site of interpretation for these differing components is in the pain matrix (the core set of cortical and thalamic structures involved in pain processing). In what has to be one of the most remarkable findings in brain imaging, it has now been shown repeatedly that when we see another person in pain, we experience activations in our pain matrix that correspond to the activations that would occur if we were experiencing the same painful stimuli, *absent the sensory input and motor output* because we have not directly experienced a noxious insult to the surface of the body. This core response accounts for the sudden wincing shock and stress we feel when we see someone sustain an injury. The collective intake of breath and shared distress at the collective witnessing of a sudden, severe, and unexpected sports injury is a good example, but there are many more prosaic ones. Why do you feel pain when you see your child bang his or her head accidentally? Or someone stub a toe? Or even something as trivial as a paper cut? It is because we experience the cognitive/evaluative and affective components of the pain, without the noxious nociceptive input. And this experience is stressful, unlearned, and reflexive. We will now examine a series of experiments supporting this contention and will then examine it in the context of what the torturer experiences during a torture session.

Tania Singer and colleagues (2004), for example, have conducted an especially revealing experiment analyzing how we understand the pain of others and our own pain. They asked couples to come to the laboratory for a simple but far-reaching experiment. Subjects were asked to lie in an MRI scanner, and then, through an arrangement with mirrors, they saw the back of their own hand or the back of the hand of a significant other, their partner. Then a number of different conditions were tested randomly, in which the subjects themselves experienced electric shocks to the back of the hand (a painful and somewhat noxious stimulus). Participants showed activation in the periphery of the body (reflecting the sensory components of pain), but activation also occurred in the brain networks concerned with affective and cognitive components of pain. The researchers also studied what happened if subjects saw electric shocks being visited on someone with whom they had a close social relationship. They found that the same network is activated in the brain; in other words, the parts of the brain associated with the affective and cognitive components of pain are activated, but the sensory and motor activity usually accompanying pain are not activated. What the researchers found is very straightforward and telling. Empathy for pain involves the affective and cognitive components of the experience of pain but does not include the sensory components.

Kevin Ochsner and colleagues (2008), in an article titled "Your Pain or Mine?," also examined whether there were distinct brain systems involved in perceiving one's own pain and someone else's. They asked participants to view videos of seventeen events with injuries (such as leg breaks or ankle twists from a soccer match). They then induced pain in the participants using a heat pad while they watched others enduring injuries. They found that during both tasks the anterior cingulate cortex and the anterior insula were activated, but during pain inflicted on the self there were additional activations in the pain matrix, including other parts of the insula, parietal cortex, and the amygdala. Thus, there were common areas of activation when experiencing pain through a heat pad and watching somebody else suffer pain. They also measured, using a "fear of pain" questionnaire, the extent to which subjects were worried about experiencing pain. They found that the results of the questionnaire—in other words, how relatively impervious one might be to the experience of pain—predicted the degree of activation found in the anterior cingulate cortex, but only for pain anticipated by the self, not pain that might be experienced by another. Such experiments directly examine what might happen when you see pain visited on another person or when injuries occur to another person and the source of pain is seen as the kind that might occur in everyday life.

Thomas Tölle and colleagues (1999) investigated the extent to which there is region-specific encoding of sensory and affective components of pain, using positron emission tomography (PET). They applied a thermode (a device that induces heat pain) to the forearm of subjects and measured the intensity of the pain induced by stepping up the heat intensity using a visual analogue scale (VAS), where participants simply indicate on a line how intense the pain might be. The line might be ten centimeters long, with 0 indicating no pain at all and 10 indicating the maximum pain possible. They also had the participants use a set of verbal descriptors, in order to rank a stimulus from not painful at all to the most unpleasant pain imaginable. They found that the intensity of pain and the unpleasantness of the pain (at least for heat pain) are not necessarily the same thing. As has been found in many other experiments, the anterior cingulate cortex is involved in pain perception. Further, the greater the level of activity in the cingulate cortex, the greater the level of pain experienced by the participants in the study. Finally, they also found that there are variations in pain sensitivity between individuals, and this variation is predicted by the level of activation found in a key component of the pain matrix, namely, the sensory thalamus. The sensory thalamus is hypothesized to act as a pain gate, and the positioning of this gate determines a person's experience of pain and how sensitive he or she is to pain.

Claus Lamm and colleagues (2007) have used functional brain imaging to assess the sensory and affective responses occurring during possible empathy for pain. They examine the extent to which activation in the pain matrix, when we witness pain experienced by another, is driven automatically—in other words, the extent to which we do not have control over the empathic pain response. They conducted three separate experiments. In the first set of experiments, subjects rated the extent to which a needle injecting various parts of the hand was more or less painful. They used 127 color photos with varying injection sites that would be more or less pain provoking: for example, seeing a needle directly inserted into the bed of the finger nail or a needle injecting directly into the joint. They also used images of the needle in nonpainful situations, such as the needle with a cap on it placed adjacent to the hand. Each of these images was then rated by the subjects for the extent to which they were perceived to be painful. Subjects also filled out questionnaires assessing their sensitivity to pain. The researchers also conducted two separate brain-imaging experiments. In the first experiment, subjects observed the needle being inserted in painful and nonpainful sites. There was strong activity in the pain matrix when the needle was placed in the painful sites. This confirms that not only did subjects respond to the pain experienced by another person, but the pain they perceived to be present in another person activated regions concerned with processing pain in themselves.

In an especially novel manipulation, subjects were informed that the hand that was being injected was anaesthetized. In other words, the hand was seemingly numbed and thus could not experience pain. However, even in this case, the researchers found that participants still had a more or less automatic response to the images. In other words, when you see another person being subjected to potentially painful stimuli, even though those stimuli are occurring to an anaesthetized hand, which by definition cannot feel pain, there is nonetheless an automatic response, an emotional or affective response that is not under volitional control. Under conditions of torture, as has been discussed previously, this automatic response would have to be actively inhibited unless other steps are taken. Other steps might involve the interrogated person being deindividuated by forcing him or her to wear clothing that covers the face and that reduces the apparent personal impact of the stimulus. However, in this case, there are two issues. First, masking the person who is being interrogated muffles the most important channel of communication—voice and facial expressions. Second, masking removes the connections that might form between individuals and that might act to resist escalation of brutality. In any event, the essence of interrogation involves prompted recall of information from memory, which in turn necessarily involves social interaction. Seeing someone with whom you have a close social relationship being subjected to pain and stress will cause you to have a similar experience of pain; the pain matrix is activated for both self and for other, even without the somatasensory stimulation of the self.

Philip Jackson and colleagues (2006) examined the mechanisms underlying how one feels one's own pain versus how one feels about the pain of another person. They start from the observation that pain in others often provokes prosocial behavior, which is something that is required in everyday life. The kinds of prosocial behavior that can be elicited include the comforting and helping of another. These kinds of prosocial tendencies occur naturally and, of course, in a situation of torture would have to be actively inhibited. The researchers compared the experience that people had when viewing digital images of right hands and right feet in painful and nonpainful situation. The painful situations were familiar events (such as a finger being caught in a door—something that most of us have experienced in our everyday lives), and these situations were then compared to similar pictures of artificial limbs being trapped in doors hinges (or comparable situations). The subjects were asked to imagine experiencing these situations from the point of view of the self, from the point of view of another person, or from the point of view of an artificial limb. The researchers found that the pain matrix is activated both for self-oriented imagination where pain is concerned and for other-oriented imagining. But certain areas were activated that discriminated between self and others, in particular, the secondary somatasensory cortex, the anterior cingulate cortex, and the insula (bilaterally).

Other experiments have focused on the issue of compassion and how we understand the intensity of pain in another person. Miia-maaria Saarela and colleagues (2007) examined subjects' judgments about the intensity of suffering that occurs in chronic pain patients. These patients suffer from the continual presence of pain and thus are qualitatively different from actors who are simulating the experience of pain. These brave patients also volunteered to have the pain provoked so that the momentary intensity of the chronic pain that they experience was enhanced. The subjects in these experiments were asked to estimate the intensity of pain that the patients experienced and to fill out questionnaires focused on the measurement of their empathy with others and their ability to adopt the perspective of another person. The researchers found that the activation in one's own brain is dependent on the estimate of the intensity of the pain in another's face and that this activation in the brain is very highly correlated with one's own self-rated empathy. This activity is correlated with activity in the bilateral anterior insula and the left inferior frontal gyrus.

Thus, what we can conclude from these experiments is that humans have a very strong capacity for empathy (as is obvious). Humans also engage in prosocial behavior—this is again something that we know. But we also see that at least two networks are activated in the brain on witnessing suffering in others. One involves elements of the pain matrix, which allows one to simulate the intensity of the pain that another person is experiencing; the second is a brain network concerned with discriminating between suffering or distress in oneself versus suffering or distress in another. Studies of this type show something that is very important, that people are very capable, first, of engaging in empathy for the pain of another; that the mechanisms by which they do so revolve around brain mechanisms that are activated when one experiences pain oneself; but that additional brain systems are recruited to discriminate between the experience of one's own pain and the experience of seeing another's pain. In other words, people, during states of empathy, do not experience a merging of the self with the psychological state of another. We continue to experience a boundary between self and other, while simultaneously being able to qualitatively and quantitatively share in the experiences of another.

Torture involves one person imposing an extreme stressor state on another person. In a normal person, the brain networks involved in recognizing the intensity of suffering in another person need to be actively inhibited, and other brain networks need to be invoked that allow one to actively impose the stressor state on another person. Doing so must come with some considerable psychological costs. As we have seen, torturers themselves can and do experience distress at what they are doing to another human being. There is a large anecdotal literature that presses the same point. The Constitution Project states,

> An often-overlooked problem, perhaps because of the dearth of empirical studies, is the impact of detainee abuse on the U.S. forces involved. As explained by Jennifer Bryson, a former Guantánamo interrogator, "Engaging in torture damages the torturer. The starting point for torture is the dehumanization of a detainee. Those who dehumanize others corrupt themselves in the process; dehumanization of other is a paradigm shift in how two people relate to each other, and as such it has an impact on both sides of the relationship. Once the detainee's human status no longer matters in the mind of the torturer, he or she can unleash personal, even national, aggression. The detainee is subjected to suffering and the torturer lets go of reason, one of the marks of humanity, and descends into rage."
>
> Psychologists Mark Costanzo and Ellen Gerrity point out that studies examining the effects of torture on the torturers extend back to post–World War II: "It may be only later, outside of that specific environment, that the torturer may question his or her behavior, and begin to experience psychological damage resulting from involvement in torture and trauma. In these cases, the resulting psychological symptoms are very similar to those of victims, including anxiety, intrusive traumatic memories, and impaired cognitive and social functioning."

There is abundant anecdotal evidence of psychological trauma affecting U.S. forces who engaged in abuse of detainees.

Damien Corsetti, a notorious former interrogator, was respon-sible for the death of the detainee named Dilawar and the al-leged abuse of then-teenager Omar Khadr. He is now a disabled veteran of two wars, suffering from post-traumatic stress dis-order (PTSD). (2013, 276–277)

The Constitution Project provides many more such individual case studies. Ian Cobain also documents a few similar cases in *Cruel Bri-tannia*. One former torturer states, in the context of making a case for what he did, "We are where we are—and we're left popping our Prozac and taking our pills at night" (2012, 203). Jane Mayer, in her book *The Dark Side,* provides similar testimony: "The officer was deeply concerned about the impact that these methods had on his colleagues who inflicted them. . . . The former officer said that during the 'enhanced' interrogations, officers worked in teams, watching each other behind two-way mirrors. Even with this group support, he said, a friend of his who had helped waterboard Khalid Sheikh Mohammed 'has horrible nightmares.' He went on, 'When you cross over that line of darkness, it's hard to come back. You lose your soul. You can do your best to justify it, but its well outside the norm. You can't go to that dark a place without it changing you.' He said of his friend, 'He's a good guy. It really haunts him. You are inflicting something really evil and horrible on somebody' " (2008, 174).

More recent sources of evidence have become available. James Risen, a *New York Times* correspondent, in his important book *Pay Any Price* (2014), discusses at length the personal price that torturers have paid. He describes the case of Damien Corsetti, the interrogator already mentioned. Corsetti is beset by posttraumatic stress disorder and is "an emotional cripple" (164), requiring ongoing antidepres-sant medication and drugs to assist in sleeping. According to Risen, Corsetti claims that virtually every interrogator who served in Iraq and Afghanistan is suffering from some form of PTSD and is doing so mostly in silence. Risen analyzes the situation as an informal

experiment—which has been disastrous in outcomes for the participating personnel: they are "shell-shocked, dehumanized. They are
covered in shame and guilt. . . . They are suffering moral injury"
(166). Comprehensive neuropsychiatric research studies should be
conducted that quantify precisely what variables predict such disturbing and terrible outcomes and that try to isolate variables that
may predict recovery. One thing does seem certain, though: no such
psychiatric price seems to have been paid by people further up and
further away from the actual imposition of torture. The units of psychological distance here can be measured down the chain of command, from the decision to torture being a "no-brainer" for the those
at the apex to its being one where "you lose your soul" for the ones
implementing it.

Another important source of evidence is the testimony provided
within the Senate Torture Report, which details some of the responses of those who attended and perhaps actively participated
in (it is not especially clear) some of the waterboarding sessions on
one captive:

> August 5, 2002: "want to caution [medical officer] that this is
> almost certainly not a place he's ever been before in his medical
> career . . . It is visually and psychologically very uncomfortable."
>
> August 8, 2002: "Today's first session . . . had a profound
> effect on all staff members present . . . it seems the collective
> opinion that we should not go much further . . . everyone seems
> strong for now but if the group has to continue . . . we cannot
> guarantee how much longer."
>
> August 8, 2002: "Several on the team profoundly affected . . .
> some to the point of tears and choking up.
>
> August 9, 2002: "two, perhaps three [personnel] likely to
> elect transfer" away from the detention site if the decision
> is made to continue with the CIA's enhanced interrogation
> techniques.

August 11, 2002: Viewing the pressures on Abu Zubaydah on video "has produced strong feelings of futility (and legality) of escalating or even maintaining the pressure." Per viewing the tapes, "prepare for something not seen previously." (SSCI 2014, 44–45)

These are the normal empathic responses to be expected of humans witnessing something for which their training and experience has ill prepared them. No detail is provided on the long-term effects on the individuals involved of witnessing such coercion or participating in such coercion. Risen's account suggests that the long-term outcomes for such personnel are profoundly difficult to bear on an ongoing basis. We also know from the testimony and evidence gathered by Joshua Phillips (2010) that soldiers who served in Iraq who engaged in abuse and torture have suffered ongoing and profound psychic injuries because of their own actions. These actions generally occurred in a group context, with group support present and fidelity to a greater cause providing transient mitigation which buffers the individual from the consequences of their own actions. However, the long-term consequences are present, insidious, and initially hidden, even to the perpetrator. In the long days and nights that follow away from the group and the context, the depth of psychopathology induced becomes apparent; humans in general are profoundly social beings, with a depth of empathic relations toward others that is difficult to violate. Empathic ruptures are not consequence-free. A natural question is why this moral and psychic injury arises in soldiers who are, after all, charged with the job of killing others. One response might be that the training, ethos, and honor code of the solider is to kill others who might kill him too: in others, to kill others who are capable of engaging in self-defense, and to do so according to the laws and conventions of war, in which they are steeped and trained. A deliberate and focal assault upon the defenseless (as occurs during torture), by contrast, violates at its core everything that a soldier is ordinarily called upon to do. And during military training, there is a strong emphasis on concepts such as honor, courage, the call to greatness, self-sacrifice, duty, valor, and the like—concepts that are very far indeed from the reality of stress positions, beatings, electrocution, and waterboarding. This desire for a fair fight manifests itself in many ways. Somewhat analogous situations arise in combat and contact sports: great efforts are made to ensure through competition and selection that opponents are as evenly matched as possible. Egregious violations of these implicit and explicit rules and expectations give rise to expressions of disgust and annoyance by fans, who want and expect to see a fair and evenly matched contest. This might explain why, when torture is institutionalized, the practice of torture becomes the possession and practice of a self- regarding, -supporting, -perpetuating, and -selecting group, housed within secret ministries and secret police forces (Arrigo 2004; Rejali 2007). Under these conditions, social supports and rewards are available to buffer the extremes of behavior that emerge, and the acts that are perpetrated are done so away from public view.

How Does an Empathy Gap Arise?

The ability to understand how others feel provides us with essential information about our fellow human beings and with a basis for acting on what we believe their intentions are likely to be. However, the primacy of the experienced emotion, particularly under conditions of duress or stress, leads us badly astray when we consider the ability of others to reveal information when they are under duress. We experience activity in our own pain matrix, but this activity occurs in the absence of sensory input or motor output. In other words, the sensory and motoric components of the experience are missing. This leaves us with the cognitive space for the rational evaluation of alternatives that are not possible when one is experiencing the actual stressor. The reason for this arises simply because of what is known as the empathy gap. No matter how great our capacity to engage in intersubjective identification, no matter how great our ability to simulate the likely thoughts and feelings of another person, there are elements missing because we are not directly experiencing the sensory and motor components of a stressor. We lack the capacity to fully feel our way into the state of another person who is being subjected to predator stress and experiencing an extreme loss of control over his or her own bodily integrity.

The empathy gap has been explored in a brilliant set of experiments by Loran Nordgren and colleagues in an article titled "What Constitutes Torture? Psychological Impediments to an Objective Evaluation of Enhanced Interrogation Tactics" (2011). They conducted four experiments that we will discuss in detail here. They start by commenting, "Because policymakers do not subject themselves to interrogation before assessing its permissibility, in evaluating interrogation policies they must predominantly rely on their subjective intuitions about how painful the experience seems. This ambiguity in judging torture policy has become particularly acute with the increased use of 'enhanced interrogation techniques,' such as prolonged sleep deprivation, social isolation, and exposure to cold temperatures, that are intended to induce physical and psychological distress without inflicting enduring harm. . . . Because such a tactic produces no physical trace, judging the severity of suffering becomes purely a matter of judging what is going on in the mind of the person on whom the act is performed" (689). They also comment in passing that there is a simple assumption predominating among policymakers that inducing psychological and physical distress is sufficient to induce compliance during interrogation. Their reasoning proceeds from the following position. Persons who are not experiencing particular states such as fear, pain, anxiety, or distress will underestimate both the intensity and the motivational force of that state as compared with somebody who is actually experiencing it: the empathy gap. The empathy gap is seen, for example, when physicians systematically underestimate the severity of the pain that their patients experience. Nordgren and colleagues therefore examine the effect on subjects of a small dose of pain or a particular interrogation tactic in order to see whether this experience leads them to a greater understanding of the tactic and therefore affects their judgments about the use of that tactic. The point is not to replicate the effects of an interrogation technique exactly but rather to provoke or engage the likely brain systems that would be engaged by the tactic itself and to ask how this engagement affects subjects' judgment about the use of the tactic during interrogation. The researchers investigated the effects of mild solitary confinement, sleep deprivation, exposure to cold temperatures, and real versus simulated pain. We will describe each of their experiments in detail in order to understand how these variables can be manipulated and how they subsequently affect judgment.

The first experiment concerned the effects of solitary confinement. The researchers induced social pain—the pain felt by individuals when they are excluded in some way from participating fully in a social activity or when their capacity to engage in natural social affiliation is blunted by others. They used an online ball-toss game that was ostensibly with two other players but that in reality was entirely preprogrammed. Participants were enrolled in one of three conditions. In the no-pain condition, the ball was tossed to them on one-third of the occasions—in other words, corresponding to full engagement and full equality in the game. In the social-exclusion or social-pain condition, the ball was tossed to the participants on only 10 percent of occasions. In other words, participants were ostensibly excluded from full participation in the game by what they believed to be the other two players and thus would have experienced a modicum of social rejection and the provocation of the social pain that is caused by social rejection. Control subjects did not play the online game at all. Then the researchers led subjects through a second study that was apparently unrelated to the first. Subjects were given a description of solitary confinement practices in U.S. jails and asked to estimate the severity of pain that these practices induce. The extent of the pain was measured using a very common estimation tool: the Face Pain Scale (revised form), or FPSR. This scale presents you with a series of faces of people in pain, and your task is to judge the relative severity of the pain that they are experiencing. Subjects were then also asked if they would support the use of solitary confinement in U.S. jails. As predicted by the authors, the social-pain group perceived solitary confinement to be more severe than the no-pain and control groups did, and the social pain group was nearly twice as likely to oppose extended solitary confinement in U.S. jails.

The second experiment examined the acceptability of sleep deprivation, using participants' own state of fatigue to see whether it impacted their judgments about sleep deprivation as a tactic during interrogations. Participants were a group of part-time MBA students. These students were holding down full-time employment and were required to attend classes from six to nine p.m. A group of this type offers a great advantage. You can manipulate, within the one group, the extent of people's fatigue by having them measure their own level at the start of the three-hour class and then again at the end of the class. As you would expect, subjects are very tired at the end of a long day in which they have worked a full day and then attended evening school in what would be a demanding class—namely, the study for an MBA. The researchers also measured the subjects' mood to ensure that there was no confound (or problem) caused by changes in mood as a result of fatigue. Again, they found that there was no effect of mood on fatigue. Half the students were asked to judge the severity of sleep deprivation as a tool for interrogation at the start of the class (that is, prior to heavy fatigue setting in). The other half were asked to judge it at the end of the class (that is, after their own self-judged fatigue was at very high levels). The researchers found that the fatigued group regarded sleep deprivation as a much more painful technique than the nonfatigued group did. But the two groups did not differ in their judgments of the pain of temperature manipulations on interrogation. They also judged sleep deprivation to be a more unethical tactic than did the nonfatigued group but did not judge temperature manipulation to be more unethical than did the nonfatigued group.

What Nordgren and colleagues provide here is very powerful evidence that the specific state that people are feeling profoundly affects the judgment of the severity of a tactic and also of the ethics of the use of a particular tactic. In a third experiment, they examined the effects of temperature manipulations on the judgments of participants as to whether temperature manipulations are ethical and/or painful in interrogations. The cold condition involved the cold pressor test, in which participants place their nondominant arm in iced water while completing a questionnaire regarding the severity of the pain and the ethics of the use of cold manipulation. Control subjects placed their arm in room-temperature water while they completed the questionnaire. A third group, the prior-cold group, placed their arm in water for ten minutes while completing an irrelevant task and then completed the questionnaire without having their arm in water. There was a striking effect of the presence of actual cold on subjects' judgment of the painfulness of cold and its use as a tactic. The researchers stated their key conclusion this way: "A particularly striking finding of this study is that an empathy gap emerged between the cold and prior-cold conditions. Experiencing cold temperature just 10 min prior to answering the pain and ethicality questions did not affect participants' evaluations, a finding that underscores the point that people need to actively experience pain in order to appreciate torture's severity. This finding also challenges the notion that people who have experienced the pain produced by interrogation tactics in the past—for example, interrogators who have experienced enhanced interrogation during training or people who have experienced cold in their daily lives—

are in a better position than others to assess the ethicality of using such tactics" (2011, 692). A striking implication of this experiment is that humans do not remember prior states of pain that they have experienced especially well and, as a consequence, do not have a memory that they can use to make a judgment as to the severity of that particular powerful stimulus.

The fourth and final experiment conducted by Nordgren and colleagues examined the difference between real and simulated pain. They tested the hypothesis that "the discrepancy between judgements of interrogation tactics by people who are and are not experiencing pain results from underestimations on the part of those not in pain" (2011, 692). Three groups of participants were involved. The first group was placed in a cold-weather condition, in which they had to stand outside without their jacket on for three minutes, at just above 0°C. A second group was a warm-water group, who submersed a hand in warm water. The third group was a cold-water group, who submersed a hand in ice-cold water. Each group was then required to judge a vignette about cold punishment at a private school. The researchers found that the cold-weather and iced-water groups gave higher estimates of the pain and were much less likely to support cold manipulations as a form of punishment. Pain estimates were more or less the same in the cold-water and outside groups and were substantially higher than in the warm-water group. The researchers conclude, "Our findings suggest that empathy gaps for physical and psychological pain undermine people's ability to objectively evaluate interrogation practices. . . . Small doses of pain bridge the empathy gap and provide a more realistic and complete understanding of how torture is experienced by people who are tortured" (693).

In many respects, these experiments address a central issue. Proponents of coercive interrogation do not have personal experience of torture. University professors who provide arguments in favor of torture have not advised the use of the rack to enhance students' examination performance in eliciting forgotten details of lectures. They are working from what they believe to be true (from media accounts, perhaps televisual fiction) to make recommendations for action in the real world. Those who talk about torture do not have the responsibility for conducting the torture itself. Judges will not leave the safe confines of their court to personally waterboard a captive. Politicians will not leave the safe confines of their legislative offices to keep a captive awake for days at a time. However, the responsibility for imposing the torture will fall to another human being or group of human beings.

We have deliberately discussed the empathy gap at some length. An important question is whether the empathy gap has any real or meaningful consequences for the framing of policy. I would submit that it does, and I give the following example. In the Torture Memos, there is, as we have already seen, an extended discussion of water-boarding (Cole 2009, 109). This discussion is really remarkable, for it shows the effect of distancing on any empathy that might be felt toward the victim of this procedure. It is noted that the waterboard produces the involuntary perception of drowning and that the procedure may be repeated (the memos do not make clear how many times), but it is to be limited to twenty minutes in any one application. One can do all sorts of basic arithmetic to calculate how much water, at what flow rate, needs to be applied to the face of a person to induce the experience of drowning. The water might be applied from a hose; it might be applied from a jug; it might be applied from a bottle—many possibilities are available, given human ingenuity and the lack of response that might occur during these intermittent periods of the "misperception of drowning," as the Torture Memos so delicately put it. However, the implication is not drawn out in the memos: that the detainee is being subjected to the sensation of being drowned for a prolonged period of time—for twenty minutes. There is a literature on near-death experience from drowning, from which we know that drowning happens quickly, and the person loses consciousness and then either dies or is rescued and recovered. Here, no such relief is possible. A person is subjected for twenty minutes to an extended, reflexive near-death experience, one over which they have no control and in the course of which they are expected also to engage in the guided retrieval of specific items of information from their long-term memories. I have belabored this point because we subsequently read in the memos that "even if one were to parse the statute more finely to treat 'suffering' as a distinct concept, the waterboard could not be said to inflict severe suffering. The waterboard is simply a controlled acute episode, lacking the connotation of a protracted period of time generally given to suffering" (118). There is a profound failure of imagination and empathy here. To be subjected to a reflexive near-death experience for twenty minutes in one session, knowing that multiple sessions will occur, is, by any reasonable person's standards, a prolonged period of suffering. I would note here that the U.S. courts have found this to be the case in the context of both war crimes tribunals and waterboarding by Texas police officers (Wallach 2007 provides details of both cases).

There is a further confusion in thinking here: the position that is being adopted is entirely one of a third party focused on their own actions. In this context, waterboarding is clearly a "controlled acute episode" in terms of its procedural imposition by the person who is doing the waterboarding. However, to be suffocated or asphyxiated without the possibility of blackout or death for twenty minutes will, for the person on whom it is being imposed, not be a "controlled acute episode"; it will be a near-death experience. There is a (deliberate?) confusion here of what the person who is engaged in the imposition of waterboarding feels with what the person who is being waterboarded actually feels. (The memos themselves do agree that the use of the waterboard "is a threat of imminent death"; Cole 2009, 123.) We do not have the videos of waterboarding available, as they were destroyed in contravention of the law, but we do have at least some written evidence of the effect of waterboarding from the emails quoted in the Senate Torture Report. For example, "Waterboarding technique was physically harmful, inducing convulsions and vomiting. Abu Zubaydah, for example, became 'completely unresponsive, with bubbles rising through his open, full mouth'" (SSCI 2014, 3). Internal CIA records describe the waterboarding of Khalid Shaykh Mohammad as evolving into a "series of near drownings." Another suspect, Abu Zubaydah, "coughed, vomited, and had 'involuntary spasms of the torso and extremities' during waterboarding" (ibid., 46). I doubt that repeated involuntary emesis and the repeated induction of near-death experiences are conducive to complete and accurate recall of multiple items of episodic and semantic information from long-term memory. One unnamed "medical officer" reported after the waterboarding session as follows: "NO useful information so far. . . . He did vomit a couple of times during the water board with some beans and rice. It's been 10 hours since he ate so this is surprising and disturbing" (41–42).

The Compassionate Brain in Action

Video games have proven to be a great boon to experimental cognitive neuroscience. They allow the imposition of three-dimensional immersible contexts with a real feel. Subjects can be fully engaged in the game they are playing, and there is minimal or no risk as a result of their playing the game. John King and colleagues (2006) used a three-dimensional video game in which participants either shot a humanoid alien assailant (reminiscent of the alien beings in the *Predator* movie series), gave aid to a human in the form of a bandage, shot the wounded human, or gave aid to the attacking alien. The researchers examined whether there was a distinctive neural signature associated with appropriate compassionate behavior toward a fellow human being, versus the shooting of an attacking nonhuman. Additionally, they examined whether there was a distinctive neural signature associated with inappropriate behavior toward a fellow wounded human, that is, shooting the human or offering aid to the attacking alien assailant. They used a virtual three-dimensional environment consisting of 120 identical square rooms. Each of these rooms contained either a casualty or the assailant. The instruction given to the participant was to pick up the tool at the door and use it appropriately. This tool consisted either of a bandage to give aid or of a gun that could be used to shoot whoever was in the room. Participants rated the shooting of the casualty as relatively disturbing but shooting the assailant as not disturbing. However, assisting the wounded human was seen as approximately as disturbing as shooting the alien assailant was. The overall pattern of the data was surprising: the same neural circuit (amygdala: medial prefrontal cortex) was activated during context-appropriate behavior (that is, helping the wounded human) and when shooting the alien assailant. This suggests that, for the brain at least, there is a common origin for the expression of appropriate behavior, depending on the context—that is, shooting the assailant and assisting the wounded.

This finding leads to a more subtle view than might originally have been suspected: that we have a system in the brain with the specific role of understanding the behavioral context within which we find ourselves and behaving appropriately according to that context. Here, the context is simple: to give aid to a conspecific and to defend oneself against the aggressive attack of a nonhuman assailant. Unsurprisingly, it has been shown that humans with damage to the prefrontal cortex (think Phineas Gage, whom we met in Chapter 2) and also to the amygdala do not behave appropriately in the contexts within which they find themselves. They are not able to generate behaviors that are appropriate to the social settings within which they are acting. This in turn can of course have serious consequences for one's ability to integrate oneself into social networks. Acting inappropriately can of course lead to social exclusion. And recruiting individuals with these deficits to engage in the questioning of suspects does not seem like a very smart idea (although such individuals may well have few internal psychological barriers to torturing another human being). Such individuals will not have the capacity to accurately represent what the other person is thinking, and they will spend inordinate amounts of time trying to interpret what are simple social cues. And of course, they may misinterpret these cues (with perhaps grievous consequences). We are left to consider one last possibility on which to base prisoner interrogations: the use of the basis of our social life, language; our innate need for affiliation and respect; our need to have warm human relations and our need to be part of a group, sharing warm human relations. We will consider all of these possibilities in Chapter 8.

The data and experiments on empathy that have been reviewed in this chapter are significant, as they point in a particular direction, which is that humans respond automatically and naturally when they see another person in distress. It appears, for example, that damping down one's own autonomic response, even when you know that the other person cannot feel pain (because of the presence of anesthetic), does not reduce the automatic activation of the pain matrix in oneself. This does not mean, however, that there are not questions that remain unanswered or that there are not variations between individuals in their response to the sight of pain in another person. One remarkable study is titled "When You Dislike Patients, Pain Is Taken Less Seriously." In this study, Lies De Ruddere and colleagues (2011) examined how much a physician's liking of a patient influences his or her estimations of the pain that the patient suffers. They found that where severe pain was concerned, as rated in the patient, the pain ratings for those patients who were less likeable were significantly lower than were the pain ratings for patients who were relatively more likeable. One reason given by the authors is that physicians, as observers, might be more suspicious of patients whom they do not like, and they thus attribute these patients' pain to malingering or exaggeration. Many studies have found that there are ethnic differences in pain attribution and pain management. Kimberley Kaseweter and colleagues (2012) found a prowhite bias in a sample of white, male and female Canadian students who watched videos of black and white patients exhibiting facial expressions of pain and were then asked to provide pain-treatment decisions and report their feelings of empathy for each patient. The subjects prescribed more pain treatment for white patients and described feeling more empathy for white patients (for similar results, see Drwecki and colleagues 2011, and Burgess and colleagues 2006; for a review, see Cintron and Morrison 2006).

How generally applicable this phenomenon is, is open to question, but it does raise the possibility that the pain matrix may be less activated when we see people whom we do not like being subjected to pain. However, it is inevitable that some form of relationship will develop over time between the interrogator and the person being interrogated. The question is the extent to which this relationship is desirable or undesirable. It could be prevented by potentially using interrogators who have low empathic abilities or by constantly rotating interrogators, so that they do not build up a relationship with the person who is being interrogated. The problem here, of course, is that this strategy misses what is vital about human interaction, namely, the enduring predisposition that humans have for affiliation to each other and our capacity to engage with others as human beings and to like them as individuals. And this in turn will diminish the effectiveness of the interrogation. It will even make it easier for the person being interrogated to game the interviewer, for example, giving lots of differing stories and answers to the questions. In turn, this makes detecting reliable information much harder.

What Should a Former Torturer Do Now?

We have argued at length in this chapter that seeing another human being in distress, or imposing such distress on another human being, is itself psychologically traumatic. Multiple lines of evidence have indicated that this is so. Testimonies from former torturers have been cited, case studies of psychiatric treatment of former torturers argue that this is so, and evidence collected under controlled conditions and by clinical psychiatrists also indicate that this is so. A moment's pause for reflection on our own inner turmoil when we see duress being visited on another human being should also be sufficient grounds to know that this is so. (I ignore for present purposes people of a sadistic-psychopathic disposition who would take active pleasure in the torture of another human being.) This sense must have been apparent to Jose Rodriguez, who ordered the destruction of videotapes of coercive interrogations by the CIA on a variety of not-too-clearly-articulated grounds. We can surmise, though, that the content of these tapes must have been quite shocking, given his willingness to have the tapes destroyed. He did go so far as to say in his own book, "I was just getting rid of some *ugly visuals* that could put the lives of my people at risk" (2012, 184; emphasis added), concurring with the testimony of others who have been in his position that material of this nature would have been visibly shocking and distressing. He has not accounted for his actions in a court of law, where a verbal description of the contents of the tapes could be elicited and read into the public record and the secrecy regarding their contents lifted.

Regrettably, a veil of secrecy continues to be present over what torture was imposed on CIA detainees, under what conditions, and by whom. One way to pierce the veil of secrecy would be for servicepersons and others who have been required under orders from their governments to engage in coercive interrogations and who have been traumatized by what they have done to sue their own governments for restitution for requiring them to engage in such acts. These acts would have been represented to them as part of their duty, and they would have been told that they were serving a higher purpose; but we now know that these acts were of no use or benefit, and there was or is no meaningful legal cover. Servicepersons, contractors, civilian staffers, and others who were required to torture, who believed that in so doing that they were acting under the cover of law and who have been left psychiatrically damaged, with their sense of subjective well-being substantially and enduringly impaired as a result of their experiences, would seem to have a very substantial case to make against their own governments in general and named individuals and officials in particular. In common-law jurisdictions, there are substantial bodies of employment laws regulating the dangers to which employees may be exposed. Requiring individuals to torture another human being as part of their employment would seem to present a real and meaningful danger to the long-term well-being of employees, and redress could and should be sought through the courts. The point here is that if senior members of government and of the deep state will not hold themselves, their colleagues, or their predecessors to account, then a more permanent reckoning can be made via multiple simultaneous civil actions for substantial damages for enduring psychiatric distress caused by the requirement that coercive interrogation be conducted under the force of seemingly legitimate orders provided by more senior authority figures. The ultimate message here is that interrogation of this type is not cost-free, either monetarily or psychologically, either for the interrogator or for the person being interrogated. And if the interrogator suffers substantially because of what he or she has been required to do, then an avenue of redress may be available.

8

Why Torture? Why Not Talk?

Interrogator: I propose we use something intrinsic to our humanity and our sense of self to get them to talk: words and language, appropriately conveyed and deployed.

Worried politician: You mean words and language are important? That words and language can change people? Get them to reveal things to you? Mere words? Mere talk? Mere conversation?

Every voter: But isn't that what you trade in? What do you do all the time? Talk? Or do you just sit there with nothing to say?

Humans start to acquire language soon after birth. They learn to orient to specific sounds in their environment, and they learn words at a reasonably constant rate thereafter. The basis of this capacity has long been debated, and we do not need to worry about this debate here. If we focus on the brain for a moment, we find a network of brain areas have been implicated in language comprehension (that is, the understanding of language) and in language generation (that is, the ability to speak language). Paul Broca (1824–1880) was a French neurologist active during the various Napoleonic campaigns. He described, in a series of patients, how damage in a right-handed male to an area at about the level of the left temple resulted in the loss of the ability to generate language. Soldiers during the Napoleonic wars often did not die from head wounds. Musket balls were often of low velocity, and instead of a bullet passing through the brain (as would happen with even a relatively low-caliber bullet of today), the musket ball would merely break through the skull and cause a shallow-penetrating head injury, restricted to a smallish area of the surface of the brain. Broca described a patient who has subsequently become known as "Tan" because the word *tan* was all that he was able to say. Tan suffered such a musket ball wound and lost the ability to utter words as a result. He could generate this word repetitively but no other words. Patient Tan did not lose the ability to understand language; rather, he lost the ability to generate language. He could follow verbal commands with ease. This implies that the parts of the brain concerned with understanding language at best only partially overlap with the parts of the brain concerned with generating speech (the motor parts of the brain responsible for making speech happen). Similar studies were conducted on another patient group by the German neurologist Karl Wernicke (1848–1905). He showed that damage to a separate brain area could cause patients to be unable to comprehend what was said to them, despite their being able to continue to speak. Thus, we can conclude that the network of brain areas responsible for language generation and comprehension have subcomponents that may be separate from each other. These respective brain areas have been named after their discoverers. The phrase *Broca's area* now refers to a well-described area on the lateral (that is, on the side) surface of the left frontal lobe of right-handed humans. *Wernicke's area* similarly refers to an area at about the level of the peak of the left ear in right-handed humans. Language is therefore something inscribed deeply into the brains of humans. Note, however, that while one can speak of language centers in the brain, it is certainly more appropriate to speak of language networks of the brain (see Kolb and Whishaw 2008, for a textbook discussion of the foregoing).

During the interrogation of suspects, language is the primary means by which information is to be elicited. Interrogators question suspects about events in the past. The questions may or may not elicit responses, and the responses in turn are used to determine the truth, or otherwise, of what the suspect says. Here we have an interaction between directed free recall, in which the subject is primed or probed with questions, and memory, mediated by the use of language. The interaction, however, goes much further than that. Humans have an innate need for affiliation; that is, humans bond with each other relatively easily and come to like each other, even when one of them has committed an appalling atrocity. This natural affiliative process can be prevented by deindividualizing both the interrogator and the person being interrogated. We have already seen how, by stripping individuals of their individuality and their identity, as in the Stanford Prison experiment, or by applying pressure from authority figures, as in the Milgram obedience experiments, humans are capable, in a laboratory setting, of violating social norms. The consequences of violating these social norms, though, for other psychological processes are profound. Humans, under these circumstances, slip into culturally determined roles, and the effect of the roles that they are adopting and the stressors that they encounter during these roles change everyday cognition. They alter cognition in ways that militate against the very psychological operations that are being engaged. Humans also display an innate desire to punish a transgressor. The regulation of individual behavior in the large and small social networks within which we find ourselves, from families to large institutional settings, requires that behavior is tightly regulated, and it is tightly regulated using a combination of incentives to shape positive behavior and punishments to suppress unwanted behavior. The key point here, though, is that during an interrogation the desire to punish the detainee conflicts very directly with the signal importance of extracting information from the memory systems of the individual who is being interrogated.

A few years ago, I wrote an article that suggested the basis for this book. It caused some degree of controversy (O'Mara 2009). It ended up being cited in many newspapers, in a wide variety of languages, and featured in a great many blog posts. I did many interviews based on the article. By and large, the response to it was very positive. The CIA even issued a press release regarding it. However, I also received a few interesting emails from individuals who were somewhat unhappy with the analysis presented in the article. One such email read as follows: "I saw your recent report on interrogation techniques used by the US on suspected terrorists. Maybe you would prefer it that we give them a mocha latte and ask them to play nice with others. Frankly, I think you're as crazy as the terrorists." In some senses, this email cuts to the core of the problem. The assumption that the terrorists are crazy and not rational actors and that coercive methods are most appropriate for interrogating them leads policy desperately astray, however nicely it might be dressed up in the aseptic language of the Torture Memos. On the other hand, if we are interested in maximizing the information we take from individuals, then coercive, kinetic techniques that violate norms of social interaction, that disrupt the normal expectations and bases on which social relations should be conducted, should be utterly foresworn. Furthermore, terrorist suspects may expect to be treated in a rough fashion. Confounding their expectations by treating them in quite different fashion, which engages with what they have to say and the story that they wish to tell, is much more likely to be successful.

Should we be worried that under these circumstances people will simply refuse to talk? The evidence is to the contrary. One study, by Stephen Moston and Terry Engelberg (1993), found that of 1,067 audiotaped police interviews, only 5 percent of subjects refused to talk. One of the motivations for imposing torture is to loosen tongues: to get detainees to speak and to speak freely about their own past, their motivations, their memories, and their experiences. Moston and Engelberg show that in police custody upward of 95 percent of people will answer questions during the course of their custody. The percentage may actually be even higher—we simply do not know because of the lack of quality studies in this area. Further, we do not know the extent to which we can motivate, prompt, or shape the behaviors of individuals in custody to get them to speak freely about their past experiences.

Suppressing disclosure about the self is remarkably difficult, and this phenomenon has deep roots in our own neurobiology. Talk about the self (self-disclosure) constitutes a remarkably high fraction of our daily speech. Estimates from Robin Dunbar and colleagues (1997) show that approximately 40 percent of what we say to other people involves disclosing information about ourselves. In other words, nearly half of what we have to say to other people is describing ourselves. In narcissistic, egotistic, and high-self-esteem populations, we might expect this fraction to go up even more. Multiple surveys show that social media such as Facebook and Twitter have rates of description of personal states that run even higher than this 40 percent estimate (some estimates suggest as high as 80 percent). Would you have guessed that this estimate of speech acts being about the self was so high? You probably would not have, for the simple reason that self-disclosure comes so effortlessly and so easily that we do not notice we are doing it. It would require an abnormally high degree of monitoring of one's own behavior through time to know what fraction of one's own speech acts consist of self-disclosure. Any prolonged and sustained effort at self-monitoring would be very tiresome and require enormous levels of concentration. This effort alone impinges on other processes, such as being able to control, understand, suppress, and regulate your own emotional state.

Furthermore, recent experiments have shown that self-disclosure activates reward circuits in the human brain and does so to an unexpectedly high degree. The psychologists Diana Tamir and Jason Mitchell (2012) at Harvard University have shown, in a series of behavioral and brain-imaging studies, that humans value highly the opportunity to talk to others and to tell others about what they are thinking and feeling. Tamir and Mitchell show that people are willing to pay a monetary price (in that they will forgo monetary rewards in order to do so) and that in the course of personal disclosures, the nucleus accumbens (a nucleus involved in the brain's reward circuitry) is activated. Here again I am not attempting to claim that there is an easy path to ensuring that captives who are being interrogated will voluntarily self-disclose. We, at this moment, simply do not know enough about the circumstances under which this type of self-disclosure is rewarding; we do not know if suppression of self-disclosure in the service of a greater cause than the self is, in turn, a source of reward. In other words, we do not know enough. The consequence of the failure to support research in the experimental psychology and the experimental cognitive neuroscience is palpable.

The Psychology of Compliance

One of the strongest stated rationales for the application of coercive interrogation is to make reluctant prisoners comply with the questioning regime. The assumption here is that coercion, especially coercion that violates norms regarding bodily integrity and social interaction, is the appropriate vehicle to ensure compliance with the demands of questioning. We have already noted that most prisoners and most suspects will comply with questioning—in other words, they will not resort to silence. The question still remains though: are there noncoercive means to ensuring compliance from suspects who are being questioned? There is a small experimental literature available on the group processes that are involved in compliance, as well as on the individual social processes involved. There is no doubt that certain detainees will be extremely difficult, perhaps to the point of never being willing to answer questions. However, we must look at the motivations of these individuals, as well as the context they find themselves in. We need to try to understand the drivers of their behavior. If we adopt the working assumption that there are interindividual differences between people who are interrogated (that is, they differ from one another) and also intraindividual differences within them (in other words, their state of motivation varies from time to time), we may have a basis on which interrogation can proceed and on which effective probes for both past behaviors and future intentions can be divined. Here, the temptation may be to say that coercive techniques will work more quickly. The empirical evidence is quite to the contrary. Jose Rodriguez states unequivocally that the expectation he was given was that coercive techniques would take thirty days to "work"—which was soon doubled to sixty days, as coercive techniques did not "work" within the original thirty-day time frame (2012, 62).

Interrogations conducted using only language and associated social skills will require extreme skill on the part of questioners. Questioners will have to engage in real rapport building with suspects. They may have to spend time building trust and providing the necessary safety signals to suspects, signals that will allow suspects to eventually start to reveal information. There are many possible clues from the literature about how a process like this may be engaged in. Psychologists and psychiatrists have, for generations, been trained in the processes that are involved in a psychological or psychiatric interview, especially with clients who may not be compliant or who may not be motivated, for a wide variety of reasons. Similarly, within neuropsychology and specifically in reference to medical-legal work, there is a long history of techniques that have been adopted for use with so-called malingerers, that is, individuals who claim to be suffering from a brain injury in order to sustain some form of financial claim against a third party. We have shown exhaustively in this book that the imposition of extreme stressors (whether in the form of dietary manipulations, extremes of hot and cold, dehydration, or directly aggressive techniques such as waterboarding) have a deleterious effect on the very fabric of the organ within which memory is inscribed, that is, the brain. We also know that mild levels of stress hormone, such as might be present as a result of the experience of capture, transport, and jailing, may actually facilitate recall. The task is to overcome these issues in order to initiate and maintain directed free recall by the captive. Providing captives with an appropriate external environment, with proper food and water, appropriate clothing, and some degree of control over their own circumstances, and not engaging in coercion may seem to some people to be insufficiently tough—but so what? To individuals of a certain disposition, engaging in kinetic techniques, in which subjects are actively physically and psychologically manipulated, coerced, and tormented, seems obviously the correct way to go. However, the obviousness of this method as the appropriate way to engage in interrogation is based solely on intuitions about the relationship between the imposition of extreme stressors and motivation and the subsequent retrieval of information from memory—intuitions that, of course, are utterly false.

Interrogation

I argue in this book that preexisting notions, intuitions, and heuristics regarding psychological and brain function are profoundly unhelpful as a guide to understanding how to proceed in the questioning of suspects in captivity. I also argue that the techniques that are supposed to "enhance" interrogation do precisely the opposite—they impair interrogation. I also argue that there is a large empirical literature demonstrating why this is so. The imposition of severe stressor states, while it may have the effect of subduing suspects and making them easier to manage behaviorally, has the unintended and unwanted consequence of also affecting the very fabric of mood, memory, and thought in their brains. It also violates our innate sense of social relations and social interactions with each other. This is not to advance a naive position that one should be holding hands with terrorist suspects or others who are undergoing interrogation, but it is to emphasize the fact that, once the decision to impose torture is reached, the consequences are that it will be ineffective, pointless, morally appalling, and unpredictable in its outcomes. We are still left, though, with the problem of how to proceed with interrogations. This, regrettably, is a problem for which there is little guidance in the literature. There is a small literature on the psychology of false confessions, which are easy to induce, and there is a relatively small literature on how interrogations themselves should proceed.

It is disturbing and surprising that a central behavioral-science question (that is, how to question suspects in a safe, reliable, reasonable, replicable, humane, and ethical fashion) has received little attention in the experimental social psychological literature. Given the stresses and strains that police and security forces operate under, it is little less than a dereliction of duty that the major government agencies concerned with funding research in these areas have not initiated large-scale experimental or quasi-experimental programs in how to conduct interrogations with a whole variety of individuals who might end up in custody. One small-scale program was announced by the FBI in 2012, limited to examining the interrogation practices and techniques in the Army Field Manual. The program includes the daft proviso that all "contractor personnel working on this contract may be required, at the Government's discretion, to undergo *counterintelligence focused polygraph examinations*" (FBI 2012, 17; emphasis added), the equivalent of NASA requiring its astronauts to have their astrological charts read prior to space flight, or the FDA requiring pharmacologists to provide homeopathic data for their latest anticancer agents. The fight to extirpate pseudoscience clearly has some way to go.

There is an adjacent literature that may be of some use, as mentioned previously. In clinical psychology and psychiatry, the SCID (Structured Clinical Interview for the *Diagnostic and Statistical*

Manual) has been and continues to be in widespread use. The SCID is designed to map to the psychiatric diagnostic axes of the *DSM*. It has not been adapted for police or security-force interrogation, but given the form that the interview takes and the types of individuals who might be interviewed, it is surprising to find that it has not been considered in these contexts as a set of tools to be adapted to the questioning of suspects.

At the core of psychotherapeutic or psychiatric engagement is the interaction between the client and the psychologist or psychiatrist. By definition, patients with mental health problems who are engaged with clinical psychologists or psychiatrists are patients who, for a variety of reasons, may be either personally incapable of engaging with the psychotherapeutic process or resistant to it. This leads to the central problem of how to engage difficult clients of this type for their own benefit. An important and useful pair of articles by Holdsworth and colleagues (2014a, 2014b) analyze and discuss peer-reviewed empirical studies examining the process of client engagement during therapy, extending this analysis to offender engagement in therapy. The offenders were convicted of a wide range of serious criminal offenses; the reviews were solely of relevant research with adult offenders. The researchers first review seventy-nine studies, showing that there are inconsistent definitions and assessments of what constitutes engagement. This is problematic because psychotherapeutic outcomes are positively affected by an appropriate level of engagement. One factor the researchers do note is the capacity of clients to address their problems—in other words, their ability to state what their problems are is positively associated with engagement. The other component of engagement is of course the therapy provider, and the researchers here find, unsurprisingly, that therapists' interpersonal skills are at the heart of the capacity of the therapeutic relationship to generate positive change in clients. One variable they do note as useful as a proxy measure for engagement is the client's willingness to engage in homework (clients' willingness to perform tasks provided by the therapist within the therapeutic context is predictive of engagement also). In the offender group, the researchers note that demographics were poor predictors of engagement, whereas individual psychological variables (poor impulse control and high hostility) predicted a low level of engagement. Other psychological variables (such as anger and anxiety) were unrelated to engagement in therapy.

Holdsworth and colleagues did find some relationship between engagement and variables related to the overall treatment program and its therapeutic objectives. In psychotherapy, engagement with the client is treated with the utmost seriousness. On the other hand, the interrogator's engagement with a suspect may not be treated seriously, despite the fact that it is at the heart of many investigative processes, including those involving terrorists. I say this because of the profound limitations on training and the lack of serious research expenditure in this area and because of the dismissive and gung-ho attitude taken by interrogators from whom we have public statements. Many such statements could be cited here. Kirk Hubbard (a former CIA psychologist) is cited in the Constitution Project report as follows: "Are we to think the terrorist has the following thoughts: 'You know, nobody has ever been as nice to me as these people—I'm going to turn my back on my God and my life's work and tell them what they want to know.' Alternatively, maybe the terrorist will think 'What a clever way of asking that question. Now that they put it that way, I have no choice but to tell them what they need to know to disrupt my plans.' Unfortunately, it is difficult to envision scenarios where useful information will be forthcoming. . . . For terrorists who do not care if they live or die and have no fear of prison, there is little or no incentive to work with interrogators" (2013, 263). Rather than assuming, as is the case, that there is great variability in human behavior within and between subjects and variability also in behavior depending on context and time, there is an assumption of an out-group homogeneity of the people they are interrogating. We need to move beyond macho posturing and assume that interrogation is a process that will take, in the most difficult of cases, from days to weeks. We already have evidence that, for waterboarding, estimates of the time within which it is expected to work were doubled from thirty to sixty days, and the number of waterboarding sessions used ran into the range of 100 to 200 occasions. Thus, there is plenty of time available to engage in what will be, for all parties involved, a protracted interrogation. The fantasies about time constraints derived from ticking time bombs need to be set aside. After all, if you have every piece of information but the bomb itself to know with certainty that there is a bomb, then you will be able to get the bomb too, if you engage in proper forensic work.

The Interview: Context and Consequences

Interviewing and interrogation in a forensic context has distinct needs that require articulation. There is a distinction to be drawn between, on the one hand, acquiring intelligence and information that is actionable and that provides the context, motivation, and information on the individual and on the individual's social networks and, on the other hand, acquiring the kinds of information or confession that can be used to support or secure a conviction in a court of law. These are definitively not the same things, although it may well be the case that the information acquired under the first scenario (that is, intelligence gathering) might support a conviction in a court of law. I am inclined to suggest that an oblique approach should always be chosen in both circumstances: that a confession should never be the object either of intelligence gathering or of the securing or supporting of a conviction. If a confession is provided and is believable, is credible, and can be supported by other forms of noncontaminable information, then that is very useful information and a great achievement on behalf of the interrogator. The real object, though, is to maximize the diverse forms of information yield that are possible, whether or not they happen to be self-incriminating. The danger with seeking a direct confession is that, as we have seen repeatedly in the laboratory and disturbingly in police forces across the world, confessions from the innocent are very easy to elicit. Once the investigation or interrogation proceeds with a confession bias in mind, its focus will be subject to a variety of cognitive biases, especially (but not exclusively) those revolving around confirmation bias and motivated reasoning. In the former case, evidence appropriate to the preexisting theory will be collected, and countervailing evidence will be disregarded or unweighted; and in the latter case, a narrative that is appropriate to a particular interpretation will be imposed on the data that are derived or elicited, irrespective of the coherence of that narrative.

The persistent human problem with respect to evidence is that there is a will to believe your own pet hypothesis (this is known formally in psychology as a confirmation bias or myside bias). There is probably no better comment on this tendency than that of the Nobel Prize winner Peter Medawar, who warned bluntly against being "deeply in love" with your own hypothesis, and not being willing to expose it to a "cruelly critical test," in order to discard it as wrong as quickly as possible (Medawar 1979, 39). Medawar also warned that "the intensity of the conviction that a hypothesis is true has no bearing on whether it is true or not" (ibid, 39), a key point to be always borne in mind during interrogation. In any event, what the interviewee says at any particular time during the interrogation should be treated as easily contaminable trace evidence, evidence that is subject to change because cognitive state, motivation, access to memory, tiredness, and a whole variety of other factors impinge on memory, especially when these memories are repeatedly elicited. I have suggested previously that indirect approaches to information elicitation might be the most appropriate and most effective for gaining reliable and veridical information. I argue in the final paragraphs of this book that it is a sad fact that there is no appropriate experimental social psychology available regarding interview techniques and how they should proceed. Here, I therefore present suggestions based on my own reading and reflection on the literature. Some may appear outlandish; some are, without any doubt, completely incorrect or will be inappropriate in a given set of circumstances or will fail to discriminate adequately information that is true from statements that are false. I believe that in the current context, nonetheless, making something of a laundry list of suggestions is appropriate, for in the absence of any serious funded and directed effort in this area and without a good theoretical and experimental base, the best we can offer are surmises and suggestions based on a reading of the literature.

Approaches to Interrogation

Virtual-Reality-Based Approaches

Virtual reality, which has been discussed as a methodological tool for the exploration of brain function, has also shown itself useful for the exploration of the willingness to punish using a Milgram-style paradigm (Slater and colleagues 2006). Here, I simply note that there may be an unwillingness on the part of interviewees to provide information in the guise of their own actual present self, for this may involve betrayal of individuals and of belief systems in which they are more or less completely invested. However, it may well be the case that allowing individuals, in a safe environment, to adopt a persona who is really, in their eyes, a different person to the person that they are might allow them to overcome barriers that inhibit their willingness to engage in free expression about themselves and significant others. In other words, it will allow them to step outside their own real daily self and act as if they were another person. This approach is not necessarily as outlandish as it might appear. There are now reliable virtual-reality-based methodologies for inducing out-of-body experiences and for inducing extreme plasticity in the representation of one's own body, even to the point of feeling like one is occupying two bodies (for example, see Blanke 2012; and Heydrich and colleagues 2013). Extending this kind of methodology to a virtual-reality-based interrogation should be a reasonably trivial task, and it should be easily determinable whether it proves effective.

Role-Playing and Narrative Scripting

The givens of the interrogation are straightforward: one person asks questions; the other provides answers. The individuals are distinguished by their clothing, their relative position of freedom, their legal situation, and a whole host of other variables. What would happen if captives were allowed to drive or apparently drive the narrative or questioning, according to some preprovided set of protocols? Suppose they were given questions to use and notes to make and required to provide essays or other extended written materials describing the interview? Will they find themselves inevitably struggling with the lack of information that the actual interviewer possesses and inadvertently providing information to facilitate responses on the behalf of the interviewer? Again, we do not know—but it would be good to know.

Third-Party Observation

A very indirect approach is to focus simply on observation of individuals in third-party contexts. During World War II, for example, the British High Command sequestered and captured senior Nazi officers together in two locations—Trent Park House in North London and Latimer House in Buckinghamshire, which were bugged throughout (for an account, see Neitzel 2007). This allowed intelligence officers to listen in to conversations between the captured individuals and provided invaluable information on the individuals and of the group dynamics operating between them. It also provided a valuable database for generating further questions during interrogation regimes, and differences between what was said during questioning and what was said by the officers to each other could be quickly and easily determined. The basis for these differences, of course, then became an important focus of further questioning. A wide variety of questions could then be asked. Do the individuals talk to each other? Do they have a position of primacy or leadership within the group, even one that is hidden from the interviewer? If so, why? Do they have characteristic strategies in their discussions? Do they give directions by means of nonverbal communication? Do they allow silences at appropriate moments to speak for them, or do they engage in boastful statements and conduct themselves at length with others? What is the quality of their interaction with others? Do they show respect? Do they elicit respect? Do they elicit contempt? Are they respected, or are they hated? These variables all can go into the mix in determining the quality of the statements elicited and the inferences that may be drawn therefrom, as well as the conclusions that can be evidentially supported and those that cannot.

It is a characteristic of certain regimes to put prisoners into long periods of isolation. Is such isolation useful? A first guess based on the literature has to be that it is not; extended periods of psychological and physical isolation from others are psychiatrically disabling to isolated individuals and may cause them to become hallucinatory under certain circumstances and cause grave and crippling deficits in managing social interactions, because they have become deskilled at managing these interactions. Language use may become impoverished, and mood and cognition may be impacted in very negative ways. The maintenance of such regimes has to be subject to an evidence test, and except in cases of extreme violence or aggression on the part of the individual, the use of such regimes for behavioral management must be discouraged on psychological and psychiatric grounds, as well as on simple principles of humanitarianism.

Big-Data Approaches

The amount of data harvested from regimes such as the ones I have described will be vast in storage terms and multimodal in form. The data will consist of verbal protocols and characteristic behaviors elicited during dyadic, triadic, and other social interactions, and so on. It will need to be coded, and it will need to be analyzed. To the greatest extent possible, biases deriving from badly trained human interrogators will need to be removed from the interpretation of the data elicited. Here, analytic tools derived from big-data approaches could potentially be applied fruitfully. Programs such as this would enable prediction and validation of data structures elicited from individuals and would provide to the appropriately trained interrogator a huge database of potential routes for questioning.

Challenging Behavior and Applied Behavior Analysis

Another approach that might be adapted is the approach to understanding challenging behavior from the behavior analysis tradition. Applied behavioral analysis (ABA) approaches have been used with learning-disabled individuals who manifest a wide variety of behavioral problems, including extremes of aggression directed toward the self (self-injurious behavior) and toward others. The ABA approach is sometimes characterized as focusing on the "ABC" of the situation, that is, the antecedents of any particular behavior or behaviors, the behavior itself, and the consequences that result from those behaviors. This means, where behavioral management is concerned, focusing on understanding how the suspect is situated within the context of the interrogation and his or her relation with guards, interrogators, and others. Behavioral management regimes for individuals of this type could, in principle, be used at least to analyze the structure of the behaviors manifested by more dangerous and aggressive individuals in captivity. Behavioral analysis grew out of the experimental tradition of B. F. Skinner of Harvard University. Skinner had little interest in understanding what went on in what he derided as the "conceptual nervous system" (Skinner 1988, 469). He did, however, provide a focus on behavior itself and in particular on asking the question of what it was that behavior of any type generated—its consequences in an environment.

The ABA tradition in psychology has found a particular utility in understanding and controlling what is referred to as challenging behavior. These are the kinds of behaviors that are often manifested in psychiatric populations, in which extremes of other-directed aggression or self-directed injurious behavior occur. Initially, a functional behavioral assessment is conducted. This involves discussing with caregivers the triggers in the environment for particular behaviors. An analysis of the conditions that are present when the behavior occurs is performed using checklists, particularly by third-party observers. The purpose of the sorts of questions that are asked, for example, with regard to self-injury, is to discover whether the behavior occurs across differing environmental contexts and to ask in particular what the sensory function of the behavior is and whether there is a contingent relationship between the behavior and the presence of particular environmental stimuli or behaviors engaged in by others. Repetitive behaviors, by this analysis, may arise as the result of the lack of a sensory input (as might occur under conditions of sensory deprivation). In this case, the person is self-generating the sensory input that the brain requires. Similar analyses may be conducted with respect to extreme other-directed aggression. Does the aggression arise as the result of a particular pattern of treatment? Exposure to particular food, or events? Does it occur in one room but not in another? Does it occur after small but random acts of cruelty (for example, purposefully tying shackles too tight, in order that the prisoner be made uncomfortable)?

Here, again, I am not attempting to suggest that there is a ready-made technology that can be transferred to prisoner or captive management, and then all will be well. What I am suggesting is that there is a long tradition in psychology and psychiatry of working with and dealing with difficult, challenging, or problematic individuals and that some of the methodologies that demonstrably have worked might, under certain circumstances, be capable of being transferred to this new context. Certainly, this has to be seen to be a better option than relying on individual intuition and the consequent disregarding of knowledge that has been hard won in other domains.

While it seems obvious that simple restraint-based approaches are the best way to manage behavior, this may in fact not be the case. As we have seen, restraint causes the release of large quantities of stress hormones into the bloodstream. These, in turn, elicit offensive and defensive behaviors and also cause deficits in learning and memory. Other alternatives can and should be explored. One very useful alternative may be barrier or partial-barrier approaches, in which the captive is not restrained but is physically isolated from the interrogator. Partial-barrier approaches would use dividers placed in part of the room, which impede physical movement and allow the use of restraint stress by appropriately positioned guards, if the circumstances warrant it. The key thing in using the ABA approach, though, is to know the characteristics of the individuals (not to focus on what you think they are or what you would like them to be). Having access to structured third-party observations with checklist evidence is absolutely vital.

Cutting across these kinds of suggestions is another countervailing emotion—the desire to punish captives for crimes they are perceived to have committed. One has to be very clear thinking about what it is that any interrogation regime is attempting to achieve. In the case of captive prisoners who have not yet been convicted, it is wise to focus on behavioral management regimes that allow the maximum amount of information to be obtained from the prisoners. Punishment is a separate issue and should be adjudicated by a court of law. So-called coercive or enhancement techniques may actually act as a proxy for the imposition of extrajudicial punishment—a perfectly foreseeable outcome.

A Socio-Cognitive Framework for Interrogation

The theories and data presented here do not add up to comprehensive theory and practice of interrogation. We are some way from that point, although there is a useful and substantial literature starting to build. However, there are useful pointers that can be brought to bear at this point. The conditions of capture, holding, and interaction need to be framed with the end goal ever present: that of directly or indirectly eliciting the maximum amount of reliable and veridical information from the detainee. There are several components to the interrogation: its prehistory (the conditions of detention and transport); the current conditions of detention; the interaction between the detainee and the questioner; the interaction between these actors and their peer groups (which need not be present: loyalty transcends captivity); and the larger institutional cultural context and the greater political context within which all of this activity is embedded. Approaches must focus not alone on the prisoner or prisoners but on the relationship between the prisoner and other prisoners; the relationship between the prisoner and the captors; and the relationship between the prisoner and the interrogators. This is a complex social network, and how this social network is to be managed really forms the key component of any process by which information, memories, and the like are to be recovered from suspects.

Thus, as a matter of normal, good practice, detainees should be treated with the maximum amount of respect, not exposed to deliberate or degrading treatment, and permitted, within the demands of security, to exercise some degree of choice or control over the conditions of their captivity with respect to nourishment, freedom of association, exercise, and cognitive stimulation (including access to reading and writing materials). Coercive methods of interrogation need to be explicitly repudiated as a matter of culture, action, ethics, and policy. The regime should not be designed as one that deliberately engages in punishment—that is solely a judicial and court-prescribed function. Neither is the purpose of the interrogation to elicit a confession. It is the maximum amount of information gathering that is the object here—about detainees, their social network, their activities in space and time, and so on. In other words, the setting conditions or contextual conditions must be focused on these ends and do in so in a maximally humane, ethical, and moral fashion.

The conditions for the interview or interrogation itself should be systematized to the greatest extent possible, with structured questioning formats that can be repeatedly administered to get an estimate of the stability and reliability of responses across differing occasions. The interviews can and should be recorded. Detainees should be provided with multiple opportunities to tell their stories. These stories need to parsed and analyzed; detainees should be allowed multiple methods to tell their stories—in conversation, in written statements they make, as part of joint narratives constructed between them and their questioner (and in other forms too, perhaps instant messaging via computer or mediated interrogation via telephone). The statements themselves should be expected to be variable and somewhat inconsistent. The linear narrative should be tested both backward and forward in time. The narratives should be used to generate further questions and prompts. Questions should not be leading but should be facilitative. Interrogators will need substantial training to overcome prepotent biases about the wellsprings of human conduct (for example, gaze aversion as a reliable sign of lying). The cultural practices surrounding interrogation should become one of shared problem solving—changing the expectations of the detainees so that they become participants in the process, rather than attempting to resist the process. Experimental methodologies need to be developed to allow the questioner to establish a reliable relationship. The case-study literature is replete with stories about the marked effect of calming fears and providing something as simple as a coffee or a drink on detainees' expectations.

To summarize, there are the initial antecedent conditions of capture and the current conditions of interviewing and questioning. These should be separated to the greatest extent possible, with the clear end goal of eliciting information in mind. The thoughts here suffer from one severe limitation: they apply under the controlled conditions of security and captivity. Under other conditions—the battlefield, the airport, or wherever—the setting conditions and context are different, although the goal is the same. Theory and experiment need to reach these areas too.

Empirical Work on Interrogation Practices

An important issue of the journal *Applied Cognitive Psychology* (December 2014) is devoted entirely to the issue of interrogation. This issue should and must be required reading for anyone who pretends to have a serious opinion on the topics being discussed in this book. Two articles stand out in the present context: the first by Melissa Russano and colleagues and the other by Jane Goodman-Delahunty and colleagues. Russano and colleagues conducted structured interviews with forty-two highly experienced military and intelligence interrogators. Each interrogator concurred (each and every one of them) that noncoercive methodologies are always superior to coercive methodologies. The interrogators also point to something else, in marked contradistinction to the standard interrogators who were used by the CIA and others: that "older, better-educated, more experienced" individuals with a curiosity about people are best capable of building a relationship and of generating rapport with the captive (851). None suggested that torture was in any way useful. They all concur on the idea that confrontational or aggressive approaches are the least reliable, especially those that rely on extreme physical or mental coercion. Primary evidence in favor of these contentions derives from the work of Jacqueline Evans and colleagues in the same issue, who found that positive approaches to interrogation increased information yield and reduced anxiety, increased the perception of a friendly and facilitative atmosphere, and enhanced the strength of the information given. Goodman-Delahunty and colleagues found that detainees were more likely to disclose information under conditions of rapport building. The researchers invite the consideration of the prime features of a good interview and suggest that interviews can be classified into physical, cognitive, and social (interpersonal) variables. The researchers conducted extensive interviews with interrogators of high-value detainees; all of the interrogators suggest that strategies focused on information gathering are superior.

Two other recent articles by Laurence Alison and colleagues (2014a, 2014b) complement this work. These are important and rare articles because they are empirical investigations of interrogations of a field sample of terrorists. They focus on two related issues: individual differences in the counterinterrogation techniques that may be employed and whether rapport-based techniques are efficacious at minimizing counterinterrogation techniques. The form that counterinterrogation techniques may take is a central issue. If they can be reliably predicted, they can be studied, analyzed, and perhaps countered, neutralized, or even prevented from emerging in the first place. Alison and colleagues analyzed 181 interviews with suspects, using the statistical technique of principal component analysis, and suggest that there are five major counterinterrogation techniques. These are *passivity,* in which suspects refuse to look at interviewers and/or remain silent; *verbal passivity,* with limited monosyllabic responses and/or claiming lack of memory; *verbal deflections,* in which suspects talk about unrelated topics, provide information about something that was already well-known, or provide a previously scripted response; and two other categories, the *retraction* of previously made statement statements and a *no comment tactic.* Interestingly, differing terrorist groups used differing tactics. Paramilitary suspects were more likely to use passive, verbal, and no comment tactics, whereas international terrorists were more likely to use retraction tactics.

The question of course arises of how to neutralize such counter-interrogation techniques. The Senate Torture Report provides an interesting clue: one captive (Khalid Sheikh Mohammed) "generally only provided information when 'boxed in' by information already known to CIA debriefers" (SSCI 2014, 186). This seems an important point of leverage: having the appearance or actuality of possessing information that the captive may be surprised by or will use to surmise what the interrogator already knows will markedly temper the quality of the conversation or interrogation. The former FBI interrogator Ali Soufan makes similar points in his book. Thus, the interrogation should be reconceptualized as an iterative attempt to estimate what it is that one thinks the other knows. Framed this way, the interrogation becomes a metacognitive exercise: "What do you know that I know you know?" Preparation therefore should involve role-play sessions of discussion and disclosure, reviewing the provision of leading information and making guesses based on the review; then review again and repeat the process. This suggests that interrogation sessions should also be carefully monitored by external observers who have the specific role of suggesting either on the fly or afterward conversational tactics that may be adopted during current or subsequent interrogation phases.

Laurence Alison and colleagues focus in their second article on understanding the deployment of rapport-based interrogator skills. They assessed motivational interviewing skills and interpersonal competence in interrogators who conducted 181 interviews with 49 suspects who were convicted of terrorism. These skills are translated into two dimensions: the use of adaptive interviewing behaviors and the absence of maladaptive interviewing behaviors. Overall, the researchers report that an adaptive rapport-based interrogation style in which suspects are treated with respect, dignity, and integrity is an effective approach for reducing suspects' use of counterinterrogation techniques. There are complexities, however. Rapport-based interviewing was directly associated with decreases in passive counterinterrogation techniques (averted eye gazing and/or silence), but it did increase the likelihood of passive verbal responding. Clearly, there are further nuances to be teased out here, and the development of appropriate neutralizing techniques is awaited (such as the boxing-in technique already mentioned).

It is clear that the science here is in a very young state and that the gap between what is known from the science and from what has happened in real-world circumstances is truly substantial. It will require a huge degree of effort on behalf of all of the institutions involved to ensure that reality-based, evidence-based, and ethically sound methodologies are adopted in the future. In particular, practices that are designed to elicit confessions will need to be discarded for two reasons. The first is that torture is the methodology par excellence for extracting a confession (and this has been historically and contemporaneously one of its prime uses). Second, the ease with which false confessions can be extracted in the real world and under laboratory circumstances is absolutely remarkable. An important and telling article by Julia Shaw and Stephen Porter shows that straightforward manipulations (information provided by a caregiver to a target participant) could lead the participants to believe, in the context of episodic memory recall, that they had committed a criminal offense in the past. Shaw and Porter summarize, "We explored whether complete false memories of committing crimes involving police contact could be generated in a controlled experimental setting. If so, we wanted to explore how prevalent they would be and how their features would compare with those of both false memories of other emotional events and true memories. If supposed corroboration by caregivers informs young adults that they committed a crime during adolescence, can they generate such false memories, or do they reject the notion?" (2015, 2). Disturbingly but probably not too surprisingly, 70 percent of subjects allocated to the criminal manipulation condition admitted to a crime they did not in fact commit. Confessions should be treated as extremely suspect and contaminable trace evidence. It is little wonder that the Innocence Project has had so many false confessions and convictions overturned when forensic evidence is brought to bear on crimes. The worry with the use of confessions as evidence, of course, is that members of the general public and police forces alike regard confessions as probative, when they are nothing of the sort.

A Menu of Some Interrogation Possibilities

I will not pretend that there is an easy solution available for eliciting reliable, truthful information from captives. Rather, I am making the obvious point that this is an area that experimental social psychology can address quickly and readily and that research funding in this area would be valuable and would pay dividends quickly and easily. Throughout this book, we have examined studies that have involved a wide variety of human participants. These range from people who have had, for surgical or accidental reasons, portions of their brains removed; people who have volunteered to participate in brain-imaging scans; individuals who are enlisted in the armed forces and who undergo interrogation as part of their training; individuals who willingly allow themselves to be whole-body immersed in ice-cold water; and the old standby, undergraduate students. There have even been extensive studies of psychopaths and individuals in psychiatric and prison settings who manifest extreme aggression and manipulative behavior. Participation of such differing groups of individuals really should not be a problem, assuming that the studies undergo the appropriate ethical review.

Committing time and funding to the experimental analysis of how interrogations should proceed is quite a different matter. It requires a great degree of commitment of political will and leadership; it requires a willingness to ignore the media networks where such programs may be misrepresented for partisan purposes (after all, these networks have an audience with a confirmation bias, subscription fees, and advertising revenue to serve); and it requires a commitment on the behalf of people involved in behavioral and parabehavioral sciences to conduct these studies. If substantial, meaningful funds become available to support research in this area, then it is a certainty that a great many individuals working in our most respected research institutions worldwide will indeed participate in or lead such programs. What would research programs in this area look like? These can be envisioned in a number of different ways. Experiments on interrogation that fall back on the old reliable, the undergraduate student, may not be the most appropriate. It may actually be the case that the population to be focused on should be people who will themselves be expected to perform interrogations in the future, that is, police and other law-enforcement officers and the like. This component of their training has to involve participation in a variety of structured experimental programs that will allow the probing of the best methods to elicit information. This may involve giving suspects role-playing tasks; it may involve off-site isolation; it may involve the planting of stooges in work groups or role groups. The way these programs could be conducted really should only be bounded by the limits of our current knowledge and our imaginations.

There are lots of obvious and nonobvious variables to focus on. For example, people stop in doorways or just after they walk through doorways to check a mobile phone, to think, to do a variety of things.

Doorways are a ubiquitous component of environments and, in the jargon, are regarded as event boundaries. Recent clever experiments have shown that the learning of material in one room and the mere act of walking from that room to another room can cause deficits in memory (for example, Swallow and colleagues 2008; see Kurby and Zacks 2008, for review). This is surprising, perhaps, but nonetheless important. If we monitor our own behavior, walking into meeting rooms, walking into concert venues, walking onto stages (or whatever it happens to be), doorways signal events that are about to occur and a transition from something that has previously occurred. George Orwell understood this. From his novel, *1984*, Room 101, the door behind which there was "the worst thing in the world," has become a symbol for the terrors that may lie behind a door. Therefore, the design of the events that occur when suspects progress from initial conditions of captivity to the place where they are to be questioned may be a variable of great importance (or it may not be: we simply have not got the data).

The layout of the interrogation room may also be very important. The layout of interrogation rooms seems absolutely stereotypical across the whole world. It involves a couple of chairs, a table, and complete and total environmental sterility. Further, it involves some form of confrontation or interrogation across a table. Why are other layouts not considered? I am not suggesting here a Freudian couch, but why not comfortable chairs? Why have a table? Why not have other props and facilities available? Why not have a pleasant view, so that the interrogation room becomes somewhere that the captive looks forward to being? Why set up the interrogation so that the conditions for mutual gaze occur and staring contests and other macho but irrelevant behaviors might be elicited? In some cultures, gaze aversion is the appropriate response, and a hard stare may be simply something that elicits defensive responses, freezing, surges in stress hormones, and the like. But bringing these faulty assumptions into the interrogation is a profound problem: the Senate Torture

Report notes that "several interrogators . . . insisted on conducting interrogations in English *to demonstrate their dominance over the detainee*" (SSCI 2014, 122n723; emphasis added). At play here is the base assumption of a primitive dominance hierarchy constructed around power and its use. Humans are primates and do have hierarchies as a natural form of social coexistence, but humans are also well equipped to engage in deception during power-plays by the seeming or nominal alpha male in transiently formed dominance hierarchies. Such behaviors are commonly seen in nonhuman primate groups as well, where acts of submission, deflective behaviors, gaze aversion, and actions that conceal deceptive intent are a common part of the behavioral panoply in the attempt to survive and adapt within dominance hierarchies. There is a large research literature available on such phenomena.

There is no particular reason other than historical precedent for why interrogations need to occur under these stereotypical conditions. Breaking the stereotype will break the preformed script. It might be possible to try two interrogation rooms, slightly different in design and features—one that provides writing material and access to other stimulating or enriching materials, another that is perhaps less stimulating but that provides views of an extended environment or whatever it happens to be. A walking interrogation might be possible too—it would have the advantage of directing attention forward in the environment and not toward each of the participants in the interrogation dyad. We know from nearly a century of experimental psychological studies of memory that the context within which memories are retrieved is vitally important and that varying the context can vary the contents retrieved. Again, the design of interrogation spaces needs to be alive to these kinds of possibilities. More recently, a generation of immersible virtual-reality devices have become available. Why not use these to create safe mental spaces within which avatars can interact and information can be elicited easily? Prisoners may be more willing to provide information if they can easily role-play someone, for example. These devices may have a deleterious effect on memory, or they may enhance memory, or they may enhance surface behavioral compliance or deep psychological compliance. Prisoners may reasonably refuse them—or they may not. We simply do not know because the appropriate research and experimentation has not been conducted. This is a very grave failing, given the circumstances that governments are attempting to deal with worldwide.

Interrogations, therefore, may simply fall back on a combination of rudimentary training, intuitions, and what interrogators teach each other and how they respond to those who are being questioned. There are other approaches. Maybe difficult suspects should be group housed with two or three properly trained captors and a social network allowed to develop between them. Affiliative bonds are difficult to prevent forming, and perhaps confinement under circumstances in which some form of affiliation and trust that cuts across the affiliation and trust that captives have in their own preexisting networks is desirable. Again, we have no good guides from the experimental literature. This is a terrible failing, but recruitment of individuals to participate in these kinds of experiments, the training of these participants, and the training of their interrogators is something, in principle, that can be done. There are vast institutional memories available for the ethical conduct of these kinds of investigations; knowing what to measure and how to measure it are issues that, again, while not straightforward, can be dealt with, using appropriate experimental designs. The important point to focus on here is that we simply do not know, and it is because the literature does not exist. A commitment to this kind of experimental work will pay huge and unexpected dividends. What is clear, though, is that naive intuitions about how to proceed have led us very badly astray and that policymakers have a duty to go outside their comfort zones to access the appropriate legal, moral, ethical, and evidence-based advice. The trajectory of the past decade would have been considerably different had that occurred.

The Training and Role of the Interrogator

The average interrogator for a U.S. police force has between ten and fifteen hours of training in total to provide him or her with a basis for a career that revolves around criminal investigation (Simon 2012). The situation in other investigational regimes is not much better. Interrogators may receive some limited training in techniques such as the cognitive interview or other interview techniques (there are several). The problem of course is that the evidence base on which these other techniques rely is poor—it is remarkable how few peer-reviewed articles are available in the literature that test the major tenets of these differing interview methodologies. I have been unable to find any properly statistically powered, substantial randomized-controlled trials on the differing methodologies—a significant empirical lacuna. By contrast, for clinical psychiatry and clinical psychology, hundreds of hours are invested in training for interviews during the four or five years that are required to qualify as a clinical psychologist or psychiatrist.

Given that in many cases the investigating officer is also the same individual that will attempt to create a case file, assemble evidence, and in general provide the evidence required to show that individual A was involved in events B, I recommend that interrogation should be taken entirely out of the hands of such individuals. They may be involved in question setting, prompting, reviewing, and so on but otherwise should be at a remove from questioning. Interrogations or interviews in the current context should be conducted only by forensic psychologists who have at least an M.Sc. and preferably Ph.D.-level training in clinical, forensic, and interviewing techniques for normal, neuropsychological, and neuropsychiatric populations as well as criminal or terrorist populations. In addition, there should be a period of apprenticeship and certification after the M.Sc. or Ph.D. and ongoing, continuing professional development to ensure that advances in the experimental literature are incorporated into interviewing practice. This is clearly a major professional and institutional step and one that, given tight budgets and preexisting and entrenched institutional resistance, would be hard to roll out easily in the short term. Therefore, over the immediate time horizon, it is vital that appropriately trained forensic psychologists with a genuine footing in the relevant research literature be drafted in as part of interviewing teams. These forensic psychologists should be subject to monitoring and review and must not be allowed to become personally invested in any particular methodology. Rather, they must be professionally invested in evidence-based approaches. Furthermore, they must be required to be members of the relevant professional associations and must subject themselves to regular ethical review and clearance by those associations.

The Senate Torture Report notes, "The CIA did not employ adequately trained and vetted personnel. The CIA deployed individuals without relevant training or experience. CIA also deployed officers who had documented personal and professional problems of a serious nature—including histories of violence and abusive treatment of others—that should have called into question their employment, let alone their suitability to participate in the sensitive CIA program" (SSCI 2014, Findings and Conclusions, Point 3, p. 3). It is astounding that an agency tasked with such a sensitive mission would think it appropriate to undertake an activity at the purported evidential core of what they are doing—the acquisition of reliable and truthful information—by deploying such ill-trained and personally ill-equipped individuals. The report goes further, citing the email of a CIA chief of base, who laments "the production of mediocre or, I dare say, useless intelligence" resulting from poor-quality interrogation (144). The chief then goes on to state the obvious: "If this program truly does represent one of the agency's most secret activities then it defies logic why inexperienced, marginal, underperforming and/or officers with potentially significant [counterintelligence] problems are permitted to deploy to this site" (144). The necessary conclusion is that interrogators need to be highly valued, high-prestige, high-competence, and highly trained individuals. However, the evidence suggests that inexperienced, badly trained, and badly briefed individuals conducted the interrogations. This underlines another key point: the United States in this instance, and other nations in similar instances, will state publicly that this kind of program is vital for securing national security. But such statements are not to be taken seriously because the evidence suggests that, rather than using properly trained and valued interrogators, interrogation regimes are implemented by inexperienced officers with little or no training in interrogation at all. In other words, despite the apparent seriousness of intent and mission, the reality is that once the decision was made to engage in coercive techniques, no meaningful further oversight was ever engaged in because this would have demonstrated the pointlessness and brutality of the methods chosen for interrogation.

If the suggestions presented here are acted on, then a cadre of highly trained, ethically aware, and valuable professionals will be available to conduct interrogations, not rank amateurs. However, stress-related burnout among mental health professionals is a profound and serious professional challenge. Again, in the present context, training needs also to focus on the issue of self-awareness, especially awareness of the limitations of one's own capacities and abilities, and also to focus on the issue of resilience and mental hygiene to ensure that interviewers or interrogators do not suffer excessive occupational-related stress, negating the investment in their training and disabling them as individuals. A capacity for some degree of psychological distancing or some other appropriate techniques (for example, mindfulness training) might be required to ensure that burnout does not occur.

I hope that at this point it has become clear that neuroscience, experimental psychology, and the brain and behavioral sciences more generally have made great strides in understanding the wellsprings of human behavior over the past few decades. It should also be clear that policymakers, left to rely on their own impoverished thinking, experience, and imagination, really have simply been making it up as they go along. Many do not have the appropriate internal legal or moral constraints in place, nor are they appropriately informed by the evidence-based sciences that are available to them. In fact, I suspect that it should also be clear that we still, as scientists, do not sufficiently understand the very psychological processes at the core of these issues: how to change behavior ethically and effectively, how to understand the mechanisms that underpin behavior, and how to adequately institutionalize decision-making supports and procedures to prevent the horrors of torture from ever being practiced by democracies again. It should also be clear that driving policy on the basis of intuitions or heuristics derived from fiction is simply not good enough. That a character from fiction such as Jack Bauer is thought of as an appropriate model for action would be hilarious if it were not so ridiculous and appalling. We are, it seems, in a situation similar to what might be found in medicine if doctors were allowed to freely ignore everything that we have learned from biology, physiology, and pharmacology over the past 100 years, instead relying on their hunches. It is the rough equivalent of evolving a cure for leukemia out of your own inner consciousness. Given what we know, given the stakes, given what we could discover, that is simply not good enough.

References

Aggleton, J. P., S. M. O'Mara, S. D. Vann, N. F. Wright, M. Tsanov, and J. T. Erichsen. (2010). "Hippocampal-Anterior Thalamic Pathways for Memory: Uncovering a Network of Direct and Indirect Actions." *European Journal of Neuroscience* 31 (12): 2292–2307. doi: 10.1111/j.1460-9568.2010.07251.x. http://onlinelibrary.wiley.com/doi/10.1111/j.1460-9568.2010.07251.x/abstract.

Al Haddad, H., P. B. Laursen, S. Ahmaidi, and M. Buchheit. (2010). "Influence of Cold Water Face Immersion on Post-exercise Parasympathetic Reactivation." *European Journal of Applied Physiology* 108:599–606. doi: 10.1007/s00421-009-1253-9. http://link.springer.com/article/10.1007%2Fs00421-009-1253-9.

Alison, L., E. Alison, G. Noone, S. Elntib, S. Waring, and P. Christiansen. (2014a). "The Efficacy of Rapport-Based Techniques for Minimizing Counter-interrogation Tactics amongst a Field Sample of Terrorists." *Psychology, Public Policy, and Law* 20:421–430. http://dx.doi.org/10.1037/law0000021.

———. (2014b). "Whatever You Say, Say Nothing: Individual Differences in Counter Interrogation Tactics amongst a Field Sample of Right Wing, AQ Inspired and Paramilitary Terrorists." *Personality and Individual Differences* 68:170–175.

American Psychological Association. (2004). Workshop entitled "Science of Deception: Integration of Practice and Theory." http://web.archive

.org/web/20030802090354/http:/www.apa.org/ppo/issues/decept scenarios.html.

———. (2008). By the Numbers: A Psychologically Healthy Workplace Fact Sheet. http://www.apaexcellence.org/resources/goodcompany /newsletter/article/44.

Arrigo, J. M. (2004). "A Utilitarian Argument against Torture Interrogation of Terrorists." *Science and Engineering Ethics* 10:543–572.

Baddeley, A., and B. Wilson. (1988). "Frontal Amnesia and the Dysexecutive Syndrome." *Brain and Cognition* 7:212–230.

Bain, A. (1855). *The Senses and the Intellect*. London: John W. Parker. https://archive.org/details/sensesintellectb00bain.

Begin, M. (1979). *White Nights: The Story of a Prisoner in Russia*. New York: Harper and Row.

Bègue, L., J.-L. Beauvois, D. Courbet, D. Oberlé, J. Lepage, and A. A. Duke. (2014). "Personality Predicts Obedience in a Milgram Paradigm." *Journal of Personality*. doi: 10.1111/jopy.12104. http://onlinelibrary .wiley.com/doi/10.1111/jopy.12104/abstract.

Bennett, D. A., et al. (2006). "Social Network Effects on the Relation between Alzheimer's Disease Pathology and Level of Cognitive Function in Old People: A Longitudinal Cohort Study." *Lancet Neurology* 5:406–412.

Blanke, O. (2012). "Multisensory Brain Mechanisms of Bodily Self-Consciousness." *Nature Reviews Neuroscience* 13:556–571.

Blass, T. (2009). *The Man Who Shocked the World: The Life and Legacy of Stanley Milgram*. New York: Basic Books.

Bonaparte, N. (1798). On the subject of torture, in a letter to Louis Alexandre Berthier (11 November 1798), published in "Correspondence Napoleon" edited by Henri Plon (1861), Vol. V, No. 3606, p. 128.

Bridges, N. and A. A. Jarquin-Valdivia. (2005). "Use of the Trendelenburg Position as the Resuscitation Position: To T or Not to T?" *American Journal of Critical Care* 14:364–368.

Brown, R. (2007). "Alfred McCoy, Hebb, the CIA, and torture." *Journal of the History of the Behavioral Sciences* 43 (2): 205–213. doi: 10.1002/jhbs.20225.

Brügger, M., D. A. Ettlin, M. Meier, T. Keller, R. Luechinger, A. Barlow, S. Palla, L. Jäncke, and K. Lutz. (2011). "Taking Sides with Pain— Lateralization Aspects Related to Cerebral Processing of Dental Pain." *Frontiers in Human Neuroscience* 5:12. doi: 10.3389/

fnhum.2011.00012. http://journal.frontiersin.org/Journal/10.3389/fnhum.2011.00012/abstract.

Burger, J. M. (2009). "Replicating Milgram: Would People Still Obey Today?" *American Psychologist* 64:1–11. http://www.apa.org/pubs/journals/releases/amp-64-1-1.pdf.

Burgess, D., M. van Ryn, M. Crowley-Matoka, and J. Malat. (2006). "Understanding the Provider Contribution to Race/Ethnicity Disparities in Pain Treatment: Insights from Dual Process Models of Stereotyping." *Pain Medicine* 7:119–134.

Burke, R. E. (2007). "Sir Charles Sherrington's 'the integrative action of the nervous system': a centenary appreciation." *Brain* 130:887–894.

Bush, G. W. (2010). *Decision Points*. New York: Random House.

Button, K. S., J. P. Ioannidis, C. Mokrysz, B. A. Nosek, J. Flint, E. S. Robinson, and M. R. Munafò. (2013). "Power Failure: Why Small Sample Size Undermines the Reliability of Neuroscience." *Nature Reviews Neuroscience* 14 (5): 365–376. doi: 10.1038/nrn3475. http://www.nature.com/nrn/journal/v14/n5/abs/nrn3475.html.

Campbell, T. A. (2007). "Psychological Assessment, Diagnosis, and Treatment of Torture Survivors: A Review." *Clinical Psychology Review* 27:628–641.

Carskadon, M. A., and W. C. Dement. (2011). "Monitoring and Staging Human Sleep." In *Principles and Practice of Sleep Medicine*, 5th ed., ed. M. H. Kryger, T. Roth, and W. C. Dement, 16–26. St. Louis: Elsevier Saunders. http://apsychoserver.psych.arizona.edu/jjbareprints/psyc501a/readings/Carskadon%20Dement%202011.pdf.

Catani, C., M. Kohiladevy, M. Ruf, E. Schauer, T. Elbert, and F. Neuner. (2009). "Treating Children Traumatized by War and Tsunami: A Comparison between Exposure Therapy and Meditation-Relaxation in North-East Sri Lanka." *BMC Psychiatry* 9:22. doi: 10.1186/1471-244X-9-22. http://www.biomedcentral.com/1471-244X/9/22.

Cheetham, M., A. F. Pedroni, A. Antley, M. Slater, and L. Jäncke. (2009). "Virtual Milgram: Empathic Concern or Personal Distress? Evidence from Functional MRI and Dispositional Measures." *Frontiers in Human Neuroscience* 3:29. doi: 10.3389/neuro.09.029.2009. http://journal.frontiersin.org/Journal/10.3389/neuro.09.029.2009/full.

Choma, C. W., G. A. Sforzo, B. A. Keller. (1998). "Impact of Rapid Weight Loss on Cognitive Function in Collegiate Wrestlers." *Medicine and Science in Sports and Exercise* 30:746–749.

Cintron, A., and R. Morrison. (2006). "Pain and Ethnicity in the United States: A Systematic Review." *Journal of Palliative Medicine* 9:1454–1473.

Clark, C. (2015). "Is Torture as Ineffective as It Is Abhorrent?" *Brian Blogger,* January 16. http://brainblogger.com/2015/01/16/is-torture-as -ineffective-as-it-is-abhorrent/.

Cobain, I. (2012). *Cruel Britannia: A Secret History of Torture.* London: Portobello Books.

Colavito, V., P. F. Fabene, G. Grassi-Zucconi, F. Pifferi, Y. Lamberty, M. Bentivoglio, and G. Bertini. (2013). "Experimental Sleep Deprivation as a Tool to Test Memory Deficits in Rodents." *Frontiers in Systems Neuroscience* 7:06. doi: 10.3389/fnsys.2013.00106. http:// journal.frontiersin.org/Journal/10.3389/fnsys.2013.00106/full.

Cole, D. D., ed. (2009). *The Torture Memos: Rationalizing the Unthinkable.* New York: New Press.

Colquhoun, D. (2014a). "An Investigation of the False Discovery Rate and the Misinterpretation of *p*-Values." *Royal Society Open Science,* November 19. doi: 10.1098/rsos.140216. http://rsos .royalsocietypublishing.org/content/1/3/140216.

———. (2014b). "On the Hazards of Significance Testing. Part 1: The Screening Problem." *DC's Improbably Science* (blog), March 10. http://www.dcscience.net/?p=6473.

Constitution Project, Task Force on Detainee Treatment. (2013). *The Report of the Constitution Project's Task Force on Detainee Treatment.* Washington, DC: Constitution Project. http://detaineetaskforce .org/read/.

Corkin, S. (2013). *Permanent Present Tense: The Man with No Memory, and What He Taught The World.* London: Penguin.

Dambrun, M., and E. Vatiné. (2010). "Reopening the Study of Extreme Social Behaviors: Obedience to Authority within an Immersive Video Environment." *European Journal of Social Psychology* 40:760–773. doi: 10.1002/ejsp.646. http://onlinelibrary.wiley.com/doi/10.1002 /ejsp.646/abstract.

Datta, A., and M. Tipton. (2006). "Respiratory Responses to Cold Water Immersion: Neural Pathways, Interactions, and Clinical Consequences Awake and Asleep." *Journal of Applied Physiology* 100 (6): 2057–2064.

Dawson, D., and K. Reid. (1997). "Fatigue, Alcohol and Performance Impairment." *Nature* 388:235.

Defrin, R., K. Ginzburg, M. Mikulincer, and Z. Solomon. (2014). "The Long-Term Impact of Tissue Injury on Pain Processing and Modulation: A Study on Ex-Prisoners of War Who Underwent Torture." *European Journal of Pain* 18:548–558. doi: 10.1002/j.1532-2149 .2013.00394.x. http://onlinelibrary.wiley.com/doi/10.1002/j.1532 -2149.2013.00394.x/full.

Dershowitz, A. M. (2002). "Torture of Terrorists: Is It Necessary to Do and to Lie about It?" In *Shouting Fire: Civil Liberties in a Turbulent Age*. New York: Little, Brown.

De Ruddere, L., L. Goubert, K. Prkachin, M. Stevens, D. Van Ryckeghem, and G. Crombez. (2011). "When You Dislike Patients, Pain Is Taken Less Seriously." *Pain* 152:2342–2347.

D'Hooge, R., and P. P. De Deyn. (2001). "Applications of the Morris Water Maze in the Study of Learning and Memory." *Brain Research Reviews* 36:60–90. doi:10.1016/S0165-0173(01)00067-4.

Diaper, A., D. J. Nutt, M. R. Munafò, J. L. White, E. W. Farmer, and J. E. Bailey. (2012). "The Effects of 7.5% Carbon Dioxide Inhalation on Task Performance in Healthy Volunteers." *Journal of Psychopharmacology* 26:487–496. doi: 10.1177/0269881111415729.

Díaz, M., and D. E. Becker. (2010). "Thermoregulation: Physiological and Clinical Considerations during Sedation and General Anesthesia." *Anesthesia Progress* 57:25–33. doi: 10.2344/0003-3006-57.1.25. http://www.ncbi.nlm.nih.gov/pmc/articles/PMC2844235/?report=classic.

Drwecki, B. B., C. F. Moore, S. E. Ward, and K. M. Prkachin. (2011). "Reducing Racial Disparities in Pain Treatment: The Role of Empathy and Perspective-Taking." *Pain* 152:1001–1006. doi: 10.1016/j. pain.2010.12.005.

Dunbar, R. I. M., A. Marriott, and N. D. C. Duncan. (1997). "Human Conversational Behavior." *Human Nature* 8:231–246.

Edelson, M., T. Sharot, R. J. Dolan, and Y. Dudai. (2011). "Following the Crowd: Brain Substrates of Long-Term Memory Conformity." *Science* 333 (6038): 108–111. http://www.weizmann.ac.il /neurobiology/labs/dudai/uploads/files/Science-2011-Edelson-108 -11.pdf.

el Gorani, M. (2011). "Diary." *London Review of Books* 33 (24):33–35. http://www.lrb.co.uk/v33/n24/mohammed-elgorani/diary.

European Agency for Safety and Health at Work. (2014). "Calculating the Cost of Work-Related Stress and Psychosocial Risks: European Risk

Observatory Literature Review." https://osha.europa.eu/en/publications /literature_reviews/calculating-the-cost-of-work-related-stress-and -psychosocial-risks.

European Commission. (1999). "Guidance on Work-Related Stress." http://www.av.se/dokument/inenglish/European_Work/Slic_2012 /Guidance_workrelated_stress.pdf.

Evans, J. R., K. A. Houston, C. A. Meissner, A. B. Ross, J. R. LaBianca, S. A. Woestehoff, and S. M. Kleinman. (2014). "An Empirical Evaluation of Intelligence-Gathering Interrogation Techniques from the United States Army Field Manual." *Applied Cognitive Psychology* 28:867–875. doi: 10.1002/acp.3065.

Evans, K. C., S. A. Shea, and A. J. Saykin. (1999). "Functional MRI Localisation of Central Nervous System Regions Associated with Volitional Inspiration in Humans." *Journal of Physiology* 520:383– 392. doi: 10.1111/j.1469-7793.1999.00383.x.

Farah, M. J., J. B. Hutchinson, E. A. Phelps, and A. D. Wagner. (2014). "Functional MRI-Based Lie Detection: Scientific and Societal Challenges." *Nature Reviews Neuroscience* 15:123–131. doi: 10.1038/nrn3665.

FBI (Federal Bureau of Investigation). (2012). "Intelligence Interviewing and Interrogation Research Solicitation Number: BAA-202200." https://www.fbo.gov/index?s=opportunity&mode=form&id=0f11cc9 ef04f799f3998e054af57f3ce&tab=core&tabmode=list&=.

Finnoff, J. T. (2008). "Environmental Effects on Brain Function." *Current Sports Medicine Reports* 7:28–32.

Ganis, G., S. M. Kosslyn, S. Stose, W. L. Thompson, and D. A. Yurgelun-Todd. (2003). "Neural Correlates of Different Types of Deception: An fMRI Investigation." *Cerebral Cortex* 13:830–836.

Gaoua, N., S. Racinais, J. Grantham, and F. E. Massioui. (2011). "Alterations in Cognitive Performance during Passive Hyperthermia are Task Dependent." *International Journal of Hyperthermia* 27:1–9. doi:10.3 109/02656736.2010.516305.

Giesbrecht, G. G. (2000). "Cold Stress, Near Drowning and Accidental Hypothermia: A Review." *Aviation, Space, and Environmental Medicine* 71:733–752.

Giesbrecht, G. G., M. S. L. Goheen, C. E. Johnston, G. P. Kenny, G. K. Bristow, and J. S. Hayward. (1997). "Inhibition of Shivering Increases Core Temperature Afterdrop and Attenuates Rewarming in Hypothermic Humans." *Journal of Applied Physiology* 83:1630–1634.

Goodman-Delahunty, J., N. Martschuk, and M. K. Dhami. (2014). "Interviewing High Value Detainees: Securing Cooperation and Disclosures." *Applied Cognitive Psychology* 28:883–897. doi: 10.1002/acp.3087.

Greely, H., and J. Illes. (2007). "Neuroscience-Based Lie Detection: The Urgent Need for Regulation." *American Journal of Law and Medicine* 33:377–431.

Greenberg, D. L. (2004). "President Bush's False 'Flashbulb' Memory of 9/11/01." *Applied Cognitive Psychology* 18:363–370. doi: 10.1002/acp.1016.

Haidt, J. (2012). *The Righteous Mind: Why Good People Are Divided by Politics and Religion.* New York: Pantheon.

Hall, L., T. Strandberg, P. Pärnamets, A. Lind, B. Tärning, and P. Johansson. (2013). "How the Polls Can Be Both Spot On and Dead Wrong: Using Choice Blindness to Shift Political Attitudes and Voter Intentions." *PLoS ONE,* April 10. doi: 10.1371/journal.pone.0060554. http:// journals.plos.org/plosone/article?id=10.1371/journal.pone .0060554.

"Hard Measures: Ex-CIA Head Defends Post-9/11 Tactics." (2012). Jose Rodriguez, interview by Leslie Stahl. CBS News, April 29. http://www .cbsnews.com/news/hard-measures-ex-cia-head-defends-post-9-11 -tactics/.

Harlow, J. M. (1848). "Passage of an Iron Rod through the Head." *Boston Medical and Surgical Journal* 39:389–393. doi: 10.1056/ NEJM184812130392001. http://www.nejm.org/doi/full/10.1056 /NEJM184812130392001.

Harris, C., A. Barnier, J. Sutton, and P. Keil. (2014). "Couples as Socially Distributed Cognitive Systems: Remembering in Everyday Social and Material Contexts." *Memory Studies* 7:285–297. doi: 10.1177 /1750698014530619.

Harris, S. (2011). "In Defense of Torture." *Huffington Post,* May 25. http://www.huffingtonpost.com/sam-harris/in-defense-of-torture_b _8993.html.

Harrison, Y., and J. A. Horne. (2000). "The Impact of Sleep Deprivation on Decision Making: A Review." *Journal of Experimental Psychology: Applied* 6:236–249.

Hartwig, M., and C. F. Bond. (2011). "Why Do Lie-Catchers Fail? A Lens Model Meta-Analysis of Human Lie Judgments." *Psychological Bulletin* 137 (4): 643–659. doi: 10.1037/a0023589.

Hebb, D. O. (1949). *The Organisation of Behavior.* New York: Wiley.

Hebb, D. O., and W. Heron. (1955). "Effects of Radical Isolation upon Intellectual Function and the Manipulation of Attitudes." In "Terminal Report on Conditions of Attitude Change in Individuals." Ottawa: Defense Research Board.

Hebb, D. O., W. Heron, and W. H. Bexton. (1952). "The Effect of Isolation upon Attitude, Motivation, and Thought." In *Fourth Symposium, Military Medicine I*, in cooperation with McGill University. Ottawa: Defense Research Board.

Heydrich, L., T. J. Dodds, J. E. Aspell, et al. (2013). "Visual Capture and the Experience of Having Two Bodies—Evidence from Two Different Virtual Reality Techniques." *Frontiers in Psychology* 4:946. doi: 10.3389/fpsyg.2013.00946. http://journal.frontiersin.org/Journal/10.3389/fpsyg.2013.00946/full.

Hirst, W., E. A. Phelps, R. L. Buckner, A. E. Budson, A. Cuc, J. D. Gabrieli, M. K. Johnson, C. Lustig, K. B. Lyle, M. Mather, R. Meksin, K. J. Mitchell, K. N. Ochsner, D. L. Schacter, J. S. Simons, and C. J. Vaidya. (2009). "Long-Term Memory for the Terrorist Attack of September 11: Flashbulb Memories, Event Memories, and the Factors That Influence Their Retention." *Journal of Experimental Psychology: General* 138 (2): 161–176. doi: 10.1037/a0015527.

Hitchens, C. (2008). "Believe Me, It's Torture." *Vanity Fair,* August. http://www.vanityfair.com/news/2008/08/hitchens200808.

Holdsworth, E., E. Bowen, S. Brown, and D. Howat. (2014a). "Client Engagement in Psychotherapeutic Treatment and Associations with Client Characteristics, Therapist Characteristics, and Treatment Factors." *Clinical Psychology Review* 34 (5): 428–450.

———. (2014b). "Offender Engagement in Group Programs and Associations with Offender Characteristics and Treatment Factors: A Review." *Aggression and Violent Behavior* 19:102–121.

Horne, J. (1988). *Why We Sleep: The Functions of Sleep in Humans and Other Mammals.* New York: Oxford University Press.

Horne, J., and L. Reyner. (1999). "Vehicle Accidents Related to Sleep: A Review." *Occupational and Environmental Medicine* 56:289–294. doi: 10.1136/oem.56.5.289.

Hosenball, M. (2014). "CIA Chief Admits Agency Used 'Abhorrent' Methods on Detainees." Reuters, December 11. http://www.reuters .com/article/2014/12/11/us-usa-cia-torture-brennan-idUSKBN0JP 29F20141211.

ICRC (International Committee of the Red Cross). (2007). *ICRC Report on the Treatment of Fourteen "High Value Detainees" in CIA Custody.* http://assets.nybooks.com/media/doc/2010/04/22/icrc-report .pdf.

Irwin, M., A. Mascovich, J. C. Gillin, R. Willoughby, J. Pike, and T. L. Smith. (1994). "Partial Sleep Deprivation Reduces Natural Killer Cell Activity in Humans." *Psychosomatic Medicine* 56:479–578.

Irwin, M., J. McClintick, C. Costlow, M. Fortner, J. White, and J. C. Gillin. (1996). "Partial Night Sleep Deprivation Reduces Natural Killer and Cellular Immune Responses in Humans." *FASEB Journal* 10 (5): 643–653.

Jackson, P. L., E. Brunet, A. N. Meltzoff, and J. Decety. (2006). "Empathy Examined through the Neural Mechanisms Involved in Imagining How I Feel versus How You Feel Pain." *Neuropsychologia* 44:752–761. http://www.sciencedirect.com/science/article/pii/S0028393 205002666.

Johnson, H., and A. Thompson. (2008). "The Development and Maintenance of Post-Traumatic Stress Disorder (PTSD) in Civilian Adult Survivors of War Trauma and Torture: A Review." *Clinical Psychology Review* 28:36–47.

Jones, K., and Y. Harrison. (2001). "Frontal Lobe Function, Sleep Loss and Fragmented Sleep." *Sleep Medicine Reviews* 5 (6): 463–475.

Kahan, D. M. (2013). "Ideology, Motivated Reasoning, and Cognitive Reflection: An Experimental Study." *Judgment and Decision Making* 8:407–424. http://papers.ssrn.com/sol3/papers.cfm?abstract_id =2182588.

Kahneman, D. (2011). *Thinking, Fast and Slow.* New York: Farrar, Straus and Giroux.

Kaseweter, K. A., B. B. Drwecki, and K. M. Prkachin. (2012). "Racial Differences in Pain Treatment and Empathy in a Canadian Sample." *Pain Research & Management: The Journal of the Canadian Pain Society* 17:381–384. http://www.ncbi.nlm.nih.gov/pmc/articles/PMC3659010/.

Kassin, S. M., and K. L. Kiechel. (1996). "The Social Psychology of False Confessions: Compliance, Internalization, and Confabulation."

Psychological Science 7:125–128. doi: 10.1111/j.1467-9280.1996.
tb00344.x. http://web.williams.edu/Psychology/Faculty/Kassin/files
/kassin_kiechel_1996.pdf.

Kato, M., B. G. Phillips, G. Sigurdsson, K. Narkiewicz, C. A. Pesek,
and V. K. Somers. (2000). "Effects of Sleep Deprivation on Neural
Circulatory Control." *Hypertension* 35:1173–1175.

Kiel, P. (2008). "Senate Investigation Reveals Frank 2002 Discussion of
Gitmo Interrogation." *ProPublica,* June 17. http://www.propublica
.org/article/senate-investigation-reveals-frank-2002-discussion-of
-interrogation617.

Kim, J. J., and D. M. Diamond. (2002). "The Stressed Hippocampus,
Synaptic Plasticity and Lost Memories." *Nature Reviews Neuroscience* 3:453–462.

King, J. A., R. J. Blair, D. G. Mitchell, R. J. Dolan, and N. Burgess. (2006).
"Doing the Right Thing: A Common Neural Circuit for Appropriate
Violent or Compassionate Behavior." *Neuroimage* 15:1069–1076.
http://www.icn.ucl.ac.uk/nburgess/papers/king05_app_behav
_neuroimage.pdf.

Kjeld, T., F. C. Pott, and N. H. Secher. (1985/2009). "Facial Immersion in
Cold Water Enhances Cerebral Blood Velocity during Breath-Hold
Exercise in Humans." *Journal of Applied Physiology* 106 (4):
1243–1248. doi: 10.1152/japplphysiol.90370.2008. http://jap
.physiology.org/content/106/4/1243.

Kolassa, I.-T., C. Wienbruch, F. Neuner, M. Schauer, M. Ruf, M. Odenwald, and T. Elbert. (2007). "Altered Oscillatory Brain Dynamics
after Repeated Traumatic Stress." *BMC Psychiatry* 7:56. http://www
.biomedcentral.com/1471-244X/7/56.

Kolb, B., and I. Q. Whishaw. (2013). *An Introduction to Brain and
Behavior.* 4th ed. New York: Worth.

Kozel, F. A., K. A. Johnson, E. L. Grenesko, S. J. Laken, S. Kose, X. Lu,
D. Pollina, A. Ryan, and M. S. George. (2009). "Functional MRI
Detection of Deception after Committing a Mock Sabotage Crime."
Journal of Forensic Science 54 (1): 220–231. doi:
10.1111/j.1556-4029.2008.00927.x

Krauthammer, C. (2005). "The Truth about Torture: It's Time to be Honest
about Doing Terrible Things." *The Weekly Standard,* 5 December,
Vols. 11, 12. http://www-rohan.sdsu.edu/~digger/305/torture
.htm#A13.

Kurby, C. A, and J. M. Zacks. (2008). "Segmentation in the Perception and Memory of Events." *Trends in Cognitive Sciences* 12:72–79. doi:10.1016/j.tics.2007.11.004.

Lakshminarasimhan, H., and S. Chattarji. (2012). "Stress Leads to Contrasting Effects on the Levels of Brain Derived Neurotrophic Factor in the Hippocampus and Amygdala." *PloS ONE* 7(1): e30481.

Lamm, C., H. C. Nusbaum, A. N. Meltzoff, and J. Decety. (2007). "What Are You Feeling? Using Functional Magnetic Resonance Imaging to Assess the Modulation of Sensory and Affective Responses during Empathy for Pain." *PLoS ONE* 2 (12): e1292. http://journals.plos .org/plosone/article?id=10.1371/journal.pone.0001292.

Leal, S., A. Vrij, S. Mann, and R. P. Fisher. (2010). "Detecting True and False Opinions: The Devil's Advocate Approach as a Lie Detection Aid." *Acta Psychologica* 134:323–329. doi: 10.1016/j.actpsy.2010.03.005. http://eprints.port.ac.uk/6688/1/Devils_advocate.pdf.

Leung, L., and C. E. Becker. (1992). "Sleep Deprivation and House Staff Performance: Update 1984–1991." *Journal of Occupational Medicine* 34 (12): 1139–1225.

Lieberman, H. R., G. P. Bathalon, C. M. Falco, F. M. Kramer, C. A. Morgan III, and P. Niro. (2005). "Severe Decrements in Cognition Function and Mood Induced by Sleep Loss, Heat, Dehydration, and Undernutrition during Simulated Combat." *Biological Psychiatry* 57 (4): 422–429.

Lieberman, H. R., C. M. Caruso, P. J. Niro, and G. P. Bathalon. (2006). "Acute Effects of Battlefield-Like Stress on Cognitive and Endocrine Function of Officers from an Elite Army Unit." In *Human Dimensions in Military Operations—Military Leaders' Strategies for Addressing Stress and Psychological Support,* 33-1–33-14. Meeting Proceedings RTO-MP-HFM-134, Paper 33. Neuilly-sur-Seine, France: RTO. http://www.rto.nato.int/abstracts.asp.

Lim, J., and D. F. Dinges. (2010). "A Meta-Analysis of the Impact of Short-Term Sleep Deprivation on Cognitive Variables." *Psychological Bulletin* 136:375–389.

Loftus, E. F. (2013). "How Reliable Is Your Memory?" TEDGlobal, June. http://www.ted.com/talks/elizabeth_loftus_the_fiction_of_memory ?language=en#t-324905.

Loftus, E. F., and J. M. Doyle. (1997). *Eyewitness Testimony: Civil and Criminal.* 3rd ed. Charlottesville, VA: Lexis Law.

Lopez, N., F. H. Previc, J. Fischer, R. P. Heitz, and R. W. Engle. (2012). "Effects of Sleep Deprivation on Cognitive Performance by United States Air Force Pilots." *Journal of Applied Research in Memory and Cognition* 1:27–33.

Lupien, S. J., F. Maheu, M. Tu, A. Fiocco, and T. E. Schramek. (2007). "The Effects of Stress and Stress Hormones on Human Cognition: Implications for the Field of Brain and Cognition." *Brain and Cognition* 65 (3): 209–237.

Makinen, T. M., L. A. Palinkas, D. L. Reeves, T. Paakkonen, H. Rinta-maki, J. Leppaluoto, et al. (2006). "Effect of Repeated Exposures to Cold on Cognitive Performance in Humans." *Physiology & Behavior* 87:166–176.

Mantoni, T., J. H. Rasmussen, B. Belhage, and F. C. Pott. (2007). "Reduced Cerebral Perfusion on Sudden Immersion in Ice Water: A Possible Cause of Drowning." *Aviation, Space, and Environmental Medicine* 78:374–376

———. (2008). "Voluntary Respiratory Control and Cerebral Blood Flow Velocity upon Ice-Water Immersion." *Aviation, Space, and Environmental Medicine* 79:765–768.

Marin, M. F., C. Lord, J. Andrews, R. P. Juster, S. Sindi, G. Arsenault-Lapierre, A. J. Fiocco, and S. J. Lupien. (2011). "Chronic Stress, Cognitive Functioning and Mental Health." *Neurobiology of Learning and Memory* 96:583–595. doi: 10.1016/j.nlm.2011.02.016.

Markus, G. B. (1986). "Stability and Change in Political Attitudes: Observed, Recalled, and 'Explained.' " *Political Behavior* 8:21–44. http://deepblue.lib.umich.edu/bitstream/handle/2027.42/45497/11109_2004_Article_BF00987591.pdf.

Masicampo, E. J., and R. F. Baumeister. (2013). "Conscious Thought Does Not Guide Moment-to-Moment Actions—It Serves Social and Cultural Functions." *Frontiers in Psychology* 4:478. doi: 10.3389/fpsyg.2013.00478. http://journal.frontiersin.org/article/10.3389/fpsyg.2013.00478/abstract.

May, K. T. (2013). "The Fiction of Memory: Elizabeth Loftus at TED-Global 2013." *TEDBlog,* June 11. http://blog.ted.com/2013/06/11/tk-elizabeth-loftus-at-tedglobal-2013/.

Mayer, J. (2008). *The Dark Side: The Inside Story of How the War on Terror Turned into a War on American Ideals.* New York: Doubleday.

McCain, J. (2011). "Bin Laden's Death and the Debate over Torture." *Washington Post,* May 11. http://www.washingtonpost.com/opinions /bin-ladens-death-and-the-debate-over-torture/2011/05/11/AFd1mdsG _story.html.

McCann, C., and T. Pointing. (1995). "The Effect of Alerting Drugs on Planning Performance during Sustained Operations." *Proceedings of the 37th Annual Conference of the International Military Testing Association,* 91–96. http://cradpdf.drdc-rddc.gc.ca/PDFS/zbb55 /p506693.pdf.

McCoy, A. W. (2007). "Science in Dachau's Shadow: HEBB, Beecher, and the Development of CIA Psychological Torture and Modern Medical Ethics." *Journal of the History of the Behavioral Sciences* 43:401–417. doi: 10.1002/jhbs.20271.

McEwen, B. S. (2006). "Sleep Deprivation as a Neurobiologic and Physiologic Stressor: Allostasis and Allostatic Load." *Metabolism* 55 (10 Suppl. 2): S20–23.

McIlwaine, M. (2007). "Chest Physical Therapy, Breathing Techniques and Exercise in Children with CF." *Paediatric Respiration Reviews* 8: 8–16.

McLellan, T. M., D. G. Bell, H. R. Lieberman, and G. H. Kamimori. (2003–2004). "The Impact of Caffeine on Cognitive and Physical Performance and Marksmanship during Sustained Operations." *Canadian Military Journal—Military Medicine,* Winter, 47–54. http://www.journal.forces.gc.ca/vo4/no4/doc/military-meds-eng.pdf.

Medawar, P. B. (1979). *Advice to a Young Scientist.* New York: Basic Books.

Merback, M. (1999). *The Thief, the Cross and the Wheel: Pain and the Spectacle of Punishment in Medieval Europe.* Chicago: University of Chicago Press.

Milgram, S. (1965). "Some Conditions of Obedience and Disobedience to Authority." *Human Relations* 18:57–76. http://psyc604.stasson.org /Milgram2.pdf.

Milner, B., S. Corkin, and H. L. Teuber. (1968). "Further Analysis of the Hippocampal Amnesic Syndrome: 14-Year Follow-Up Study of H.M." *Neuropsychologia* 6 (3): 215–234. http://dx.doi.org/10 .1016/0028-3932(68)90021-3.

Mitchell, J. (2014). "Man Who Interrogated Khalid Sheikh Mohammed Speaks Out." http://insider.foxnews.com/2014/12/15/exclusive-james

-mitchell-man-who-interrogated-khalid-sheikh-mohammed-speaks
-out-kelly.

Mobbs, D., P. Petrovic, J. Marchant, D. Hassabis, B. Seymour, N. Weis-
kopf, R. J. Dolan, and C. D. Frith. (2007). "When Fear Is Near:
Threat Imminence Elicits Prefrontal-Periaqueductal Grey Shifts in
Humans." *Science* 317:1079–1083. http://www.gatsby.ucl.ac.uk
/~demis/DistanceFear(SCI07).pdf.

Mobbs, D., R. Yu, J. Rowe, O. Feldman-Hall, and T. Dalgleish. (2010).
"Neural Activity Associated with Monitoring the Oscillating Threat
Value of a Tarantula." *Proceedings of the National Academy of
Sciences* 107:20582–20586. http://www.pnas.org/content/107/47
/20582.abstract.

"Mohammed el Gharani." *Reprieve*, n.d. http://www.reprieve.org.uk/case
-study/mohammed-el-gharani/.

Mokdad, A. H., E. S. Ford, B. A. Bowman, et al. (2003). "Prevalence of
Obesity, Diabetes, and Obesity-Related Health Risk Factors, 2001."
Journal of the American Medical Association 289:76–79.

Mollica, R. F., I. Lyoo, M. C. Chernoff, et al. (2009). "Brain Structural
Abnormalities and Mental Health Sequelae in South Vietnamese
Ex–Political Detainees Who Survived Traumatic Head Injury and
Torture." *Archives of General Psychiatry* 66:1221–1232. doi: 10.1001/
archgenpsychiatry.2009.127. http://archpsyc.jamanetwork.com
/article.aspx?articleid=210410.

Morgan, C. A, III, A. Doran, G. Steffian, G. Hazlett, and S. M. Southwick.
(2006). "Stress-Induced Deficits in Working Memory and Visuo-
Constructive Abilities in Special Operations Soldiers." *Biological
Psychiatry* 60:722–729. doi: http://dx.doi.org/10.1016/j.biopsych
.2006.04.021.

Morgan, C. A., III, G. Hazlett, A. Doran, S. Garrett, G. Hoyt, P.
Thomas, M. Baranoski, and S. M. Southwick. (2004). "Accuracy of
Eyewitness Memory for Persons Encountered during Exposure to
Highly Intense Stress." *International Journal of Law and Psychiatry*
27 (3): 265–279.

Morgan, C. A., III, A. Rasmusson, R. H. Pietrzak, V. Coric, and S. M.
Southwick. (2009). "Relationships among Plasma Dehydroepiandros-
terone and Dehydroepiandrosterone Sulfate, Cortisol, Symptoms of
Dissociation, and Objective Performance in Humans Exposed to

Underwater Navigation Stress." *Biological Psychiatry* 66 (4): 334–340. doi: 10.1016/j.biopsych.2009.04.004.

Morgan, C. A., III, S. Wang, A. Rasmusson, G. Hazlett, G. Anderson, and D. S. Charney. (2001). "Relationship among Plasma Cortisol, Catecholamines, Neuropeptide Y, and Human Performance during Exposure to Uncontrollable Stress." *Psychosomatic Medicine* 63 (3): 412–422.

Morgan, C. A., III, S. Wang, S. M. Southwick, A. Rasmusson, G. Hazlett, R. L. Hauger, and D. S. Charney. (2000). "Plasma Neuropeptide-Y Concentrations in Humans Exposed to Military Survival Training." *Biological Psychiatry* 47 (10): 902–909.

Moriarty, O., and D. P. Finn. (2014). "Cognition and Pain." *Current Opinion in Supportive and Palliative Care* 8:130–136. doi: 10.1097/SPC.0000000000000054. http://journals.lww.com/co-supportiveandpalliativecare/pages/articleviewer.aspx?year=2014&issue=06000&article=00008&type=abstract.

Moriarty, O., B. E. McGuire, and D. P. Finn. (2011). "The Effect of Pain on Cognitive Function: A Review of Clinical and Preclinical Research." *Progress in Neurobiology* 93:385–404. doi: 10.1016/j.pneurobio.2011.01.002. http://www.sciencedirect.com/science/article/pii/S0301008211000037.

Morris, R. G. M. (1981). "Spatial Localization Does Not Require the Presence of Local Cues." *Learning and Motivation* 2 (2): 239–260. doi:10.1016/0023-9690(81)90020-5.

Moston, S., and T. Engelberg. (1993). "Police Questioning Techniques in Tape-Recorded Interviews with Criminal Suspects." *Policing and Society* 6:61–75.

Muller, M. D., J. Gunstad, M. L. Alosco, L. A. Miller, J. Updegraff, M. B. Spitznagel, and E. L. Glickman. (2012). "Acute Cold Exposure and Cognitive Function: Evidence for Sustained Impairment." *Ergonomics* 55:792–798. doi: 10.1080/00140139.2012.665497. http://www.ncbi.nlm.nih.gov/pmc/articles/PMC3375336/.

Naitoh, P., T. L. Kelly, and C. Englund. (1990). "Health Effects of Sleep Deprivation." U.S. Naval Health Research Center, San Diego, CA. http://www.dtic.mil/cgi-bin/GetTRDoc?AD=ADA249653.

Nance, M. (2007). "Waterboarding Is Torture . . . Period (Links Updated #9)." *Small Wars Journal Blog,* October 31. http://smallwarsjournal.com/blog/waterboarding-is-torture-period-links-updated-9.

Neitzel, S., ed. (2007). *Tapping Hitler's Generals: Transcripts of Secret Conversations, 1942–45.* London: Greenhill Books.

Niccolai, V., M. A. van Duinen, and E. J. Griez. (2008). "Objective and Subjective Measures in Recovery from a 35% Carbon Dioxide Challenge." *Canadian Journal of Psychiatry* 53:737–744.

Nordgren, L. F., M. H. McDonnell, and G. Loewenstein. (2011). "What Constitutes Torture? Psychological Impediments to an Objective Evaluation of Enhanced Interrogation Tactics." *Psychological Science* 22:689–694. doi: 10.1177/0956797611405679.

Ochsner, K. N., J. Zaki, J. Hanelin, et al. (2008). "Your Pain or Mine? Common and Distinct Neural Systems Supporting the Perception of Pain in Self and Other." *Social Cognitive and Affective Neuroscience* 3:144–160. doi: 10.1093/scan/nsn006. http://www.ncbi.nlm.nih.gov /pmc/articles/PMC2555461/.

Oehmichen, M., R. Hennig, and C. Meissner. (2008). "Near-Drowning and Clinical Laboratory Changes." *Legal Medicine* 10:1–5.

Office of the Inspector General. (2004). "Special Review, Counterterrorism Detention and Interrogation Activities." Retrieved from: http:// documents.nytimes.com/c-i-a-reports-on-interrogation-methods#p=1.

O'Mara, S. M. (2009). "Torturing the Brain: On the Folk Psychology and Folk Neurobiology Motivating 'Enhanced and Coercive Interrogation Techniques.'" *Trends in Cognitive Science* 13:497–500. http://www .sciencedirect.com/science/article/pii/S1364661309001995.

Osadnik, C. R., C. F. McDonald, A. P. Jones, and A. E. Holland. (2012). "Airway clearance techniques for chronic obstructive pulmonary disease." *Cochrane Database Systematic Reviews* 14 (3): CD008328. doi: 10.1002/14651858.CD008328.pub2.

Packer, D. J. (2008). "Identifying Systematic Disobedience in Milgram's Obedience Experiments: A Meta-Analytic Review." *Perspectives on Psychological Science* 4:301–304. http://www.michaelinzlicht.com /Packer_Perspectives.pdf.

Payne, J. D., M. A. Tucker, J. M. Ellenbogen, M. P. Walker, D. L. Schacter, and R. Stickgold. (2012). "Memory for Semantically Related and Unrelated Declarative Information: The Benefit of Sleep, the Cost of Wake." *PLoS ONE* 7 (3): e33079. http://journals.plos.org/plosone /article?id=10.1371/journal.pone.0033079.

Phillips, J. E. S. (2010). *None of Us Were Like This Before: American Soldiers and Torture.* London: Verso Books.

Pilcher, J. J., and A. J. Huffcutt. (1996). "Effects of Sleep Deprivation on Performance: A Meta-Analysis." *Sleep: Journal of Sleep Research & Sleep Medicine* 19:318–326.

Pilcher, J. J., E. Nadler, and C. Busch. (2002). "Effects of Hot and Cold Temperature Exposure on Performance: A Meta-Analytic Review." *Ergonomics* 15:682–698.

"Pope Must Answer People without Any Reservations." (2010). *Independent.ie,* January 24. http://www.independent.ie/opinion/analysis/pope-must-answer-people-without-any-reservations-26625453.html.

Qin, J., K. J. Mitchell, M. K. Johnson, J. H. Krystal, S. M. Southwick, A. M. Rasmusson, and E. S. Allen. (2003). "Reactions to and Memories for the September 11, 2001 Terrorist Attacks in Adults with Posttraumatic Stress Disorder." *Applied Cognitive Psychology* 17:1081–1097. doi: 10.1002/acp.987. http://memlab.yale.edu/sites/default/files/files/2003_Qin_Mitchell_Johnson_ACP.pdf.

Ray, W. J., M. Odenwald, F. Neuner, M. Schauer, M. Ruf, C. Wienbruch, B. Rockstroh, and T. Elbert. (2006). "Decoupling Neural Networks from Reality: Dissociative Experiences in Torture Victims Are Reflected in Abnormal Brain Waves in Left Frontal Cortex." *Psychological Science* 17:825–829. http://kops.uni-konstanz.de/bitstream/handle/123456789/11194/Ray_PsyScience06.pdf?sequence=1.

Rayfield, D. (2004). *Stalin and His Hangmen: An Authoritative Portrait of a Tyrant and Those Who Served Him.* London: Viking.

Reinhardt, V., C. Liss, and C. Stevens. (1995). "Restraint Methods of Laboratory Non-human Primates: A Critical Review." *Animal Welfare* 4:221–238. http://www.awionline.org/lab_animals/biblio/aw6metho.htm.

Rejali, D. (2007). *Torture and Democracy.* Princeton, NJ: Princeton University Press.

Reynolds, A. C., and S. Banks. (2010). "Total Sleep Deprivation, Chronic Sleep Restriction and Sleep Disruption." *Progress in Brain Research* 185:91–103. doi: 10.1016/B978-0-444-53702-7.00006-3.

Reynolds, A. C., J. Dorrian, P. Y. Liu, H. P. A. Van Dongen, G. A. Wittert, et al. (2012). "Impact of Five Nights of Sleep Restriction on Glucose Metabolism, Leptin and Testosterone in Young Adult Men." *PLoS ONE* 7 (7): e41218. doi: 10.1371/journal.pone.0041218. http://journals.plos.org/plosone/article?id=10.1371/journal.pone.0041218.

Riemann, D., U. Voderholzer, K. Spiegelhalder, M. Hornyak, D. J. Buysse, C. Nissen, J. Hennig, M. L. Perlis, L. T. van Elst, and B. Feige. (2007). "Chronic insomnia and MRI-measured hippocampal volumes: a pilot study." *Sleep* 30:955–958.

Risen, J. (2014). *Pay Any Price: Greed, Power, and Endless War.* New York: Houghton Mifflin Harcourt.

Rodriguez, J. (2012). *Hard Measures: How Aggressive CIA Actions after 9/11 Saved American Lives.* New York: Simon and Schuster.

Roozendaal, B., B. S. McEwen, and S. Chattarji. (2009). "Stress, Memory and the Amygdala." *Nature Reviews Neuroscience* 10 (6): 423–433. doi: 10.1038/nrn2651. http://www.nature.com/nrn/journal/v10/n6/full/nrn2651.html.

Rosch, P. J., ed. (2001). "The Quandary of Job Stress Compensation." *Health and Stress* 3: 1–4.

Rubini, A., and E. L. Carniel. (2014). "A Review of Recent Findings about Stress-Relaxation in the Respiratory System Tissues." *Lung* 192:833–839. doi: 10.1007/s00408-014-9630-5.

Russano, M. B., F. M. Narchet, S. M. Kleinman, and C. A. Meissner. (2014). "Structured Interviews of Experienced HUMINT Interrogators." *Applied Cognitive Psychology* 28:847–859. doi: 10.1002/acp.3069. http://onlinelibrary.wiley.com/doi/10.1002/acp.3069/abstract.

Saarela, M. V., Y. Hlushchuk, A. C. Williams, M. Schürmann, E. Kalso, and R. Hari. (2007). "The Compassionate Brain: Humans Detect Intensity of Pain from Another's Face." *Cerebral Cortex* 17:230–237. http://cercor.oxfordjournals.org/content/17/1/230.long.

Samuelson, H., M. Nekludov, and M. Levander. (2008). "Neuropsychological Outcome Following Near-Drowning in Ice Water: Two Adult Case Studies." *Journal of the International Neuropsychological Society* 14:660–666.

Sands, P. (2008). *Torture Team: Deception, Cruelty and the Compromise of Law.* London: Allen Lane.

Sapolsky, R. M., L. C. Krey, and B. S. McEwen. (1986). "The Neuroendocrinology of Stress and Aging: The Glucocorticoid Cascade Hypothesis." *Endocrine Reviews* 7:284–301.

Schacter, D. (1999). "The Seven Sins of Memory: Insights from Psychology and Cognitive Neuroscience." *American Psychologist* 54 (3): 182–203. http://scholar.harvard.edu/files/schacterlab/files/schacter_american_psychologist_1999.pdf.

———. (2001). *The Seven Sins of Memory*. New York: Houghton Mifflin.

Scott, J. P., L. R. McNaughton, and R. C. Polman. (2006). "Effects of Sleep Deprivation and Exercise on Cognitive, Motor Performance and Mood." *Physiology & Behavior* 87:396–408. http://mres.gmu.edu/pmwiki/uploads/Main/rmanova.pdf.

Seligman, M. E. P. (1975). *Helplessness: On Depression, Development, and Death*. New York: W. H. Freeman.

Shallice, T. (1972). "The Ulster Depth Interrogation Techniques and Their Relation to Sensory Deprivation Research." *Cognition* 1: 385–405.

Shaw, J., and S. Porter. (2015). "Constructing Rich False Memories of Committing Crime." *Psychological Science* 26 (3): 291–301. doi: 10.1177/0956797614562862.

Shepherd, G. M. (1991). *Foundations of the Neuron Doctrine*. Oxford: Oxford University Press.

Siervo, M., R. Arnold, J. C. K. Wells, A. Tagliabue, A. Colantuoni, E. Albanese, C. Brayne, and B. C. M. Stephan. (2011). "Intentional Weight Loss in Overweight and Obese Individuals and Cognitive Function: A Systematic Review and Meta-Analysis." *Obesity Reviews* 12:968–983. http://onlinelibrary.wiley.com/doi/10.1111/j.1467–789X.2011.00903.x/abstract.

Simmons, S. E., B. K. Saxby, F. P. McGlone, and D. A. Jones. (2008). "The Effect of Passive Heating and Head Cooling on Perception, Cardiovascular Function, and Cognitive Performance in the Heat." *European Journal of Applied Physiology* 104:271–280. doi: 10.1007/s00421-008-0677-y.

Simon, D. (2012). *In Doubt: The Psychology of the Criminal Justice Process*. Cambridge, MA: Harvard University Press.

Simons, D. J., and C. F. Chabris. (2011). "What People Believe about How Memory Works: A Representative Survey of the U.S. Population." *PLoS ONE* 6 (8): e22757. doi: 10.1371/journal.pone.0022757. http://journals.plos.org/plosone/article?id=10.1371/journal.pone.0022757.

Singer, T., B. Seymour, J. O'Doherty, H. Kaube, R. J. Dolan, and C. D. Frith. (2004). "Empathy for Pain Involves the Affective but Not Sensory Components of Pain." *Science* 303:1157–1162. http://www.sciencemag.org/content/303/5661/1157.long.

Skinner, B. F. (1988). *The Selection of Behavior: The Operant Behaviorism of B. F. Skinner: Comments and Consequences* (A. Charles Catania and Stevan Harnad, eds.). Cambridge: Cambridge University Press.

Slater, M., A. Antley, A. Davison, D. Swapp, C. Guger, et al. (2006). "A Virtual Reprise of the Stanley Milgram Obedience Experiments." *PLoS ONE* 1:e39. doi: 10.1371/journal.pone.0000039. http://journals.plos.org/plosone/article?id=10.1371/journal.pone.0000039.

Smith, C. (2001). "Sleep States and Memory Processes in Humans: Procedural versus Declarative Memory Systems." *Sleep Medicine Reviews* 5:491–506.

Solzhenitsyn, A. (1974). *The Gulag Archipelago*. New York: Basic Books.

Soufan, A. (2011). *The Black Banners: The Inside Story of 9/11 and the War against al-Qaeda*. New York: W. W. Norton.

Spence, S. A. (2008). "Playing Devil's Advocate: The Case against fMRI Lie Detection." *Legal and Criminological Psychology* 13:11–26.

Spitznagel, M. B., J. Updegraff, K. Pierce, K. H. Walter, T. Collinsworth, E. Glickman, and J. Gunstad. (2009). "Cognitive Function during Acute Cold Exposure with or without Sleep Deprivation Lasting 53 Hours." *Aviation, Space, and Environmental Medicine* 80:703–708.

SSCI (Senate Select Committee on Intelligence). (2014). *Committee Study of the Central Intelligence Agency's Detention and Interrogation Program*. December. http://www.intelligence.senate.gov/study2014/executive-summary.pdf.

Stephens, R., J. Atkins, and A. Kingston. (2009). "Swearing as a Response to Pain." *NeuroReport* 20:1056–1060. http://thepsychologist.bps.org.uk/volume-26/edition-9/swearing-language-life-and-death/.

Stickgold, R., and M. P. Walker. (2013). "Sleep-Dependent Memory Triage: Evolving Generalization through Selective Processing." *Nature Neuroscience* 16:139–145. doi: 10.1038/nn.3303. http://biomech.media.mit.edu/wp-content/uploads/sites/21/2014/02/Nature-Neuro-Memory-triage-20131.pdf.

Stix, G. (2008). "Can fMRI Really Tell If You're Lying? Will Brain Scans Ever Be Able to Tell If You're Really Being Deceptive?" *Scientific American,* July 21. http://www.scientificamerican.com/article/new-lie-detector/.

Storba, J. A. (1990). *Field Management of Accidental Hypothermia during Diving*. Navy Experimental Diving Unit, Report No. 1-90. http://archive.rubicon-foundation.org/xmlui/bitstream/handle/123456789/4248/ADA219560.pdf?

Structured Clinical Interview for the *Diagnostic and Statistical Manual* (SCID). N.d. "SCID—Frequently Asked Questions." http://www.scid4 .org/faq/scidfaq.html.

Summers, J. (2011). "Rick Santorum: John McCain Wrong on Torture." *Politico,* May 17. http://www.politico.com/news/stories/0511/55140 .html.

Swallow, K. M., J. M. Zacks, and R. A. Abrams. (2009). "Event Boundaries in Perception Affect Memory Encoding and Updating." *Journal of Experimental Psychology: General* 138, 236. doi:10.1037/a0015631.

Swartz, J. R., A. R. Knodt, S. R. Radtke, and A. R. Hariri. (2015). "A Neural Biomarker of Psychological Vulnerability to Future Life Stress." *Neuron* 85:505–511. doi: 10.1016/j.neuron.2014.12.055. http://www.cell.com/neuron/abstract/S0896-6273(14)01164-7.

Talarico, J. M., and D. C. Rubin. (2003). "Confidence, Not Consistency, Characterizes Flashbulb Memories." *Psychological Science* 14:455–461.

Talbot, M. (2007). "Duped: Can Brain Scans Uncover Lies?" *The New Yorker,* July 2. http://www.newyorker.com/magazine/2007/07/02 /duped.

Talwar, V., and K. Lee. (2011). "A Punitive Environment Fosters Children's Dishonesty: A Natural Experiment." *Child Development* 82:1751–1758. doi: 10.1111/j.1467-8624.2011.01663.x. http://www .kangleelab.com/articles/Talwar%20&%20Lee%20%282011%29.

Tamir, D. I., and J. P. Mitchell. (2012). "Disclosing Information about the Self Is Intrinsically Rewarding." *Proceedings of the National Academy of Sciences* 109 (21): 8038–8043. http://www.wjh.harvard .edu/~scanlab/Papers/2012_disclose_PNAS.pdf.

Tassi, P., and A. Muzet. (2000). "Sleep Inertia." *Sleep Medicine Reviews* 4:341–353.

Thomas, M., H. Sing, G. Belenky, H. Holcomb, H. Mayberg, R. Dannals, H. Wagner Jr., D. Thorne, K. Popp, L. Rowland, A. Welsh, S. Balwinski, and D. Redmond. (2000). "Neural Basis of Alertness and Cognitive Performance Impairments during Sleepiness: I. Effects of 24h of Sleep Deprivation on Waking Human Regional Brain Activity." *Journal of Sleep Research* 9:335–352.

Tölle, T. R., T. Kaufmann, T. Siessmeier, S. Lautenbacher, A. Berthele, F. Munz, W. Zieglgänsberger, F. Willoch, M. Schwaiger, B. Conrad, and P. Bartenstein. (1999). "Region-Specific Encoding of Sensory and

Affective Components of Pain in the Human Brain: A Positron Emission Tomography Correlation Analysis." *Annals of Neurology* 45:40–47.

Torelli, F., N. Moscufo, G. Garreffa, F. Placidi, A. Romigi, S. Zannino, M. Bozzali, F. Fasano, G. Giulietti, I. Djonlagic, A. Malhotra, M. G. Marciani, and C. R. Guttmann. (2011). "Cognitive Profile and Brain Morphological Changes in Obstructive Sleep Apnea." *Neuroimage* 15:787–793. doi: 10.1016/j.neuroimage.2010.09.065. http://www .ncbi.nlm.nih.gov/pmc/articles/PMC4169712/#!po=70.6897.

United Nations Convention against Torture and Other Cruel, Inhuman or Degrading Treatment or Punishment. (1984). Entered into Force 1987. http://www.ohchr.org/EN/ProfessionalInterest/Pages/CAT.aspx.

United States Power Squadrons. (2007). "Hypothermia Safety." *Compass* 1 (1). http://www.usps.org/national/ensign/uspscompass /compassarchive/compassv1n1/hypothermia.htm.

Valtin, H. (2002). "'Drink at Least Eight Glasses of Water a Day.' Really? Is There Scientific Evidence for '8 × 8'?" *American Journal of Physiology: Regulatory, Integrative, and Comparative Physiology* 283:R993–1004.

Van Reeth, O. (2000). "Interactions between Stress and Sleep: From Basic Research to Clinical Situations." *Sleep Medicine Reviews* 4 (2): 201–219.

Van Reeth, O., L. Weibel, K. Spiegel, R. Leproult, C. Dugovic, and S. Maccari. (2000). "Interactions between Stress and Sleep: From Basic Research to Clinical Situations." *Sleep Medicine Reviews* 4:201–219.

Vrij, A., P. A. Granhag, and S. Porter. (2010). "Pitfalls and Opportunities in Nonverbal and Verbal Lie Detection." *Psychological Science in the Public Interest* 11:89–121. http://eprints.port.ac.uk/5823/1/PSPI _article_Vrij,_Granhag_and_Porter.pdf.

Wallach, E. (2007). "Waterboarding Used to Be a Crime." *Washington Post,* November 4, http://www.washingtonpost.com/wp-dyn/content /article/2007/11/02/AR2007110201170_pf.html.

Weierstall, R., T. Elbert, and A. Maercker. (2011). "Torture: Psychological Approaches to a Major Humanitarian Issue." *Zeitschrift für Psychologie / Journal of Psychology* 219:129–132. http://dx.doi.org/10.1027 /2151-2604/a000059.

Westen, D. (2007). *The Political Brain: The Role of Emotion in Deciding the Fate of the Nation.* New York: PublicAffairs.

Williamson, A. M., and A. M. Feyer. (2000). "Moderate Sleep Deprivation Produces Impairments in Cognitive and Motor Performance
Equivalent to Legally Prescribed Levels of Alcohol Intoxication."
Occupational and Environmental Medicine 57:649–655. doi:
10.1136/oem.57.10.649.

Yoo, J. (2014). "Yoo: The Feinstein Report Cannot Deny a Clear Record
of Success." *Time,* December 9. http://time.com/3626957/yoo-senate
-torture-report-feinstein/.

Young, A. J., and J. W. Castellani. (2001). "Exertion-Induced Fatigue and
Thermoregulation in the Cold." *Comparative Biochemistry and
Physiology A: Molecular & Integrative Physiology* 128:769–776.
http://www.sciencedirect.com/science/article/pii/S1095643301002823.

Young, A. J., J. W. Castellani, C. O'Brien, R. L. Shippee, P. Tikuisis, L. G.
Meyer, L. A. Blanchard, J. E. Kain, B. S. Cadarette, and M. N. Sawka.
(1998). "Exertional Fatigue, Sleep Loss, and Negative Energy Balance
Increase Susceptibility to Hypothermia." *Journal of Applied Physiology* 85:1210–1217. http://jap.physiology.org/content/85/4/1210.

Zelikow, P. (2012). "Codes of Conduct for a Twilight War." *Houston Law
Review* 49:1–52. http://www.houstonlawreview.org/wp-content
/uploads/2012/05/1-Zelikow.pdf.

Ziemann, A. E., J. E. Allen, N. S. Dahdaleh, I. I. Drebot, M. W. Co-
ryell, A. M. Wunsch, C. M. Lynch, F. M. Faraci, M. A. Howard
III, M. J. Welsh, and J. A. Wemmie. (2009). "The Amygdala Is a
Chemosensor That Detects Carbon Dioxide and Acidosis to Elicit
Fear Behavior." *Cell* 25:1012–1021. doi: 10.1016/j.cell.2009.10.029.
http://www.ncbi.nlm.nih.gov/pmc/articles/PMC2808123/.

Zimbardo, P. (1971). The Stanford Prison Experiment. http://www
.prisonexp.org/.

Further Reading

Brain, Behavior, Neuroscience, and Physiology

In a good many instances, I have not cited specific sources in the course of this book because the material is available in an appropriate undergraduate textbook. I list the latest available editions of the textbooks here.

Excellent high-level treatments of cognition and cognitive processes:

Sternberg, R. J., and K. Sternberg. (2012). *Cognitive Psychology*. 6th ed. Belmont, CA: Wadsworth.

Memory:

Baddeley, A. D. (2007). *Working Memory, Thought and Action*. Oxford: Oxford University Press.
Baddeley, A. D., M. Eysenck, and M. C. Anderson. (2009). *Memory*. Hove, UK: Psychology Press.
Lieberman, D. A. (2012). *Human Learning and Memory*. Cambridge: Cambridge University Press.

Principles discussed in relation to brain, behavior, and neurophysiology:

Kolb, B., and I. Q. Whishaw. (2013). *An Introduction to Brain and Behavior*. 4th ed. New York: Worth.

Brain damage and neuropsychology:

Kolb, B., and I. Q. Whishaw. (2008). *Fundamentals of Human Neuropsychology*. 6th ed. New York: Worth.

Deeper introductions to brain imaging and cognitive processes:

Banich, M. T., and R. J. Compton. (2010). *Cognitive Neuroscience*. 3rd ed. Belmont, CA: Wadsworth.
Gazzaniga, M S., R. B. Ivry, and G. R. Mangun. (2013). *Cognitive Neuroscience: The Biology of the Mind*. 4th ed. New York: W. W. Norton.

There are many excellent introductions to psychopathology and psychiatric disorders. One such is:

Davey, G. C. (2014). *Psychopathology: Research, Assessment and Treatment in Clinical Psychology*. BPS Textbooks in Psychology. New York: Wiley.

There are similarly excellent textbooks on the neurobiology of psychiatric disorders. One excellent and high-level treatment is:

Linden, D. (2011). *The Biology of Psychological Disorders*. New York: Palgrave Macmillan.

There is a vast literature on stress, fear, and anxiety. A great starting point is:

Conrad, C. D. (2011). *The Handbook of Stress: Neuropsychological Effects on the Brain*. Chichester, UK: Wiley-Blackwell.

A specific and important treatment of memory, stress, and trauma:

McNally, R. (2004). *Remembering Trauma*. Cambridge, MA: Harvard University Press.

There are many excellent textbooks of general human physiology. See:

Sherwood, L. (2015). *Human Physiology: From Cells to Systems*. 9th ed. Boston: Cengage Learning.
Silverthorn, D. U. (2015). *Human Physiology: An Integrated Approach*. 7th ed. New York: Pearson Education.

These are good places to start in understanding respiratory, gastric, and thermal physiology and related topics.

Finally, the effects of drugs are mentioned from time to time in the text. An excellent reference is:

> Meyer, J. S., and L. F. Quenzer. (2013). *Psychopharmacology: Drugs, the Brain, and Behavior.* Sunderland, MA: Sinauer Associates.

Other Works on Torture

I am not the first by any means to present a utilitarian argument against torture: in an extremely important article, Jean Maria Arrigo presents just such an argument rooted in thinking derived from criminology, organizational theory, social psychology, the historical record, and her interviews with military professionals:

> Arrigo, J. M. (2004). "A Utilitarian Argument against Torture Interrogation of Terrorists." *Science and Engineering Ethics* 10:543–572. http://www.ethicalpsychology.org/materials/Arrigo-Torture-SEE.pdf.

Arrigo deals with a great many issues in this article, but her argument against the ticking time bomb is especially potent. She presents the standard ticking-time-bomb rationale presented by Alan Dershowitz (for example, 2002) and many others and comments as follows:

> Terrorists selected for such a role can probably stand up to commonplace tortures from untrained and unequipped staff for a long time—like most American POWs in North Vietnam. The use of sophisticated torture techniques by a trained staff entails the problematic institutional arrangements I have laid out: physician assistance; cutting edge, secret biomedical research for torture techniques unknown to the terrorist organization and tailored to the individual captive for swift effect; well trained torturers, quickly accessible at major locations; prearranged permission from the courts because of the urgency; rejection of independent monitoring due to security issues; and so on. These institutional arrangements will have to be in place, with all their unintended and accumulating consequences, however rarely terrorist suspects are tortured. Then the terrorists themselves must be detected while letting pass without torture a thousand other criminal suspects or dissidents, that is, avoiding a dragnet interrogation policy.

The moral error in reasoning from the ticking-bomb scenario arises from weighing the harm to the prospective innocent victims against the harm to the guilty terrorist. Instead—even presuming the doubtful long-term success of torture interrogation—the harm to innocent victims of the terrorist should be weighed against the breakdown of key social institutions and the state-sponsored torture of many innocents. Stated most starkly, the damaging social consequences of a program of torture interrogation evolve from institutional dynamics that are independent of the original moral rationale. (150)

Another especially important philosophical paper is by Henry Shue:

Shue, H. (1978). "Torture." *Philosophy & Public Affairs* 7:124–143. Stable URL: http://www.jstor.org/stable/2264988.

Shue in particular addresses the following argument: "Since killing is worse than torture, and killing is sometimes permitted, especially in war, we ought sometimes to permit torture"(125), an argument often made and recycled in a variety of forms. Shue step-by-step picks apart the casuistic reasoning associated with this position.

I have not cited specifically many of the most important works on the philosophy, ethics, history, morality, legality, or politics of torture as they are not central to the discussion at hand. I apologize to the relevant authors for this decision but emphasize that no insult is intended by the lack of citation.

Important Collections of Articles from a Psychological Perspective

I single out three very important collections of articles:

Bartone, P. T., R. H. Pastel, and M. A. Vaitkus. (2010). *The 71F Advantage: Applying Army Research Psychology for Health and Performance Gains*. Center for Technology and National Security Policy. Washington, DC: National Defense University Press. http://permanent.access.gpo.gov/gpo124/71F-Advantage.pdf.
"Torture Is for Amateurs: A Meeting of Psychologists and Military Interrogators." (2007). Special issue, *Peace and Conflict: Journal of Peace Psychology* 13:391–465. http://www.tandfonline.com/toc /hpcn20/13/4#.VN-6JuasUrV.

"Information Gathering in Law Enforcement and Intelligence Settings: Advancing Theory and Practice." (2014). Special issue, *Applied Cognitive Psychology* 28:815–950. http://onlinelibrary.wiley.com /doi/10.1002/acp.v28.6/issuetoc.

Field and Experimental Studies of Human Brain Functioning under Extremes of Stress

Charles A. Morgan III (Yale University School of Medicine and the National Center for PTSD at the Department of Veteran Affairs; http://www.ptsd.va .gov/about/divisions/clinical-neurosciences/charles_a_morgan_md_ma .asp) and his colleagues have conducted one of the most important series of field and experimental studies of human brain functioning under extremes of stress (such as thermal, dietary, combat and predator, interrogative, and sleep deprivation) in military personnel (for a full listing of Morgan's publications, see http://www.ncbi.nlm.nih.gov/pubmed/?term=morgan+ca+3rd).

Aikins, D. E., D. J. Martin, and C. A. Morgan, III. (2010). "Decreased Respiratory Sinus Arrhythmia in Individuals with Deceptive Intent." *Psychophysiology* 47 (4): 633–636. doi: 10.1111/j.1469-8986.2010.00976.x.

Lieberman, H. R., G. P. Bathalon, C. M. Falco, C. A. Morgan, III, P. J. Niro, and W. J. Tharion. (2005). "The Fog of War: Decrements in Cognitive Performance and Mood Associated with Combat-Like Stress." *Aviation, Space, and Environmental Medicine* 76 (7 Suppl.): C7–C14.

Lieberman, H. R., G. P. Bathalon, C. M. Falco, F. M. Kramer, C. A. Morgan, III, and P. Niro. (2005). "Severe Decrements in Cognition Function and Mood Induced by Sleep Loss, Heat, Dehydration, and Undernutrition during Simulated Combat." *Biological Psychiatry* 57 (4): 422–429.

Morgan, C. A., III, A. Doran, G. Steffian, G. Hazlett, and S. M. Southwick. (2006). "Stress-Induced Deficits in Working Memory and Visuo-Constructive Abilities in Special Operations Soldiers." *Biological Psychiatry* 60 (7): 722–729.

Morgan, C. A., III, G. Hazlett, A. Doran, S. Garrett, G. Hoyt, P. Thomas, M. Baranoski, and S. M. Southwick. (2004). "Accuracy of Eyewitness Memory for Persons Encountered during Exposure to

Highly Intense Stress." *International Journal of Law and Psychiatry* 27 (3): 265–279.

Morgan, C. A., III, G. Hazlett, S. Wang, E. G. Richardson Jr., P. Schnurr, and S. M. Southwick. (2001). "Symptoms of Dissociation in Humans Experiencing Acute, Uncontrollable Stress: A Prospective Investigation." *American Journal of Psychiatry* 158 (8): 1239–1247.

Morgan, C. A., III, A. Rasmusson, R. H. Pietrzak, V. Coric, and S. M. Southwick. (2009). "Relationships among Plasma Dehydroepiandrosterone and Dehydroepiandrosterone Sulfate, Cortisol, Symptoms of Dissociation, and Objective Performance in Humans Exposed to Underwater Navigation Stress." *Biological Psychiatry* 66 (4): 334–340. doi: 10.1016/j.biopsych.2009.04.004.

Morgan, C. A., III, S. Southwick, G. Hazlett, A. Rasmusson, G. Hoyt, Z. Zimolo, and D. Charney. (2004). "Relationships among Plasma Dehydroepiandrosterone Sulfate and Cortisol Levels, Symptoms of Dissociation, and Objective Performance in Humans Exposed to Acute Stress." *Archives of General Psychiatry* 61 (8): 819–825.

Morgan, C. A., III, S. Southwick, G. Steffian, G. A. Hazlett, and E. F. Loftus. (2013). "Misinformation Can Influence Memory for Recently Experienced, Highly Stressful Events." *International Journal of Law and Psychiatry* 36 (1): 11–17. doi: 10.1016/j.ijlp.2012.11.002.

Morgan, C. A., III, S. Wang, J. Mason, S. M. Southwick, P. Fox, G. Hazlett, D. S. Charney, and G. Greenfield. (2000). "Hormone Profiles in Humans Experiencing Military Survival Training." *Biological Psychiatry* 47 (10): 891–901.

Morgan, C. A., III, S. Wang, A. Rasmusson, G. Hazlett, G. Anderson, and D. S. Charney. (2001). "Relationship among Plasma Cortisol, Catecholamines, Neuropeptide Y, and Human Performance during Exposure to Uncontrollable Stress." *Psychosomatic Medicine* 63 (3): 412–422.

Morgan, C. A., III, S. Wang, S. M. Southwick, A. Rasmusson, G. Hazlett, R. L. Hauger, and D. S. Charney. (2000). "Plasma Neuropeptide-Y Concentrations in Humans Exposed to Military Survival Training." *Biological Psychiatry* 47 (10): 902–909.

Taylor, M. K., and C. A. Morgan, III. (2014). "Spontaneous and Deliberate Dissociative States in Military Personnel: Relationships to Objective Performance under Stress." *Military Medicine* 179 (9): 955–958. doi: 10.7205/MILMED-D-14-00081.

Acknowledgments

There are a great many people to thank for their help, assistance, readings, discussions, and willingness to listen to me over the past few years. In particular, I would like to especially thank Ruth Byrne, Charlotte Callaghan, Jennifer Edmond, Ted Lynch, Robert McKenna, Kim Ronnqvist, Jennifer Rouine, Jeremy Skillington, Marian Tsanov, and Katharina Ulrich for reading versions of the manuscript at different points and providing very helpful and detailed comments on it. Susan Cantwell and Katy Cagney provided outstanding secretarial assistance—without them, this book would have taken much longer to emerge. I would also like to thank Richard English, Ian Robertson, Aine Kelly, Vincent Walsh, John Aggleton, Michael Kearns, Stavroula Kousta, Richard Wise, and Kristen Maglieri as well the many members of my research group past and present for helpful conversations and for continued encouragement. Any mistakes, errors, omissions, or other problems with the text are, of course, my fault. I have done my very best to fairly represent the relevant literatures, but any failures in this regard are also mine alone.

The Royal Irish Academy deserves special thanks for holding a special interdisciplinary meeting on torture June 26, 2013, to recognize the United Nations International Day in Support of Victims of Torture. This was a very valuable opportunity for me to air some of the arguments and data presented here. My editor at Harvard University Press, Ian Malcolm, deserves a special mention for his support for this project, as do the anonymous reviewers who provided very helpful critical readings of the text. Trinity College, Dublin, also deserves a special mention: it is a truly great university, providing the space, time, and especially the academic freedom to pursue the writing of this book. I would also like to thank my grant funders—in particular, the Wellcome Trust and Science Foundation Ireland—which have generously supported my research work over the past fifteen years or so. I am very proud of my association with both of these agencies.

Index